ARENA
MASTER '05

→170 A12

The shelf contains labeled binders:

DAVOL LOFT CLIENT (2) 0604

DAVOL LOFT MECHANICAL 0604

DAVOL LOFT CODE / ZONING 0604

COOPER HEWITT ADMINISTRATION 0606

PUBLICATIONS PHOTO PERMISSIONS

CLIFFSIDE PARK ADMINISTRATION 0607

CLIFFSIDE PARK SITE INFO 0607

CLIFFSIDE PARK CLIENT 0607

CLIFFSIDE PARK ASSOCIATE ARCH 0607

CLIFFSIDE PARK STRUCTURAL 0607

CLIFFSIDE PARK SKETCH LOG 0607

CENTER FOR ARCHITECTURE 0608

RISD EXHIBITION ADMINISTRATION 0609

FURNITURE MISC. QUOTES AND ORDERS 06FU

BALZ KITCHEN 060...

LAW FIRM STAIR ADMINISTRATION 0704

122 A.1, 171 A.1, 172 A.1

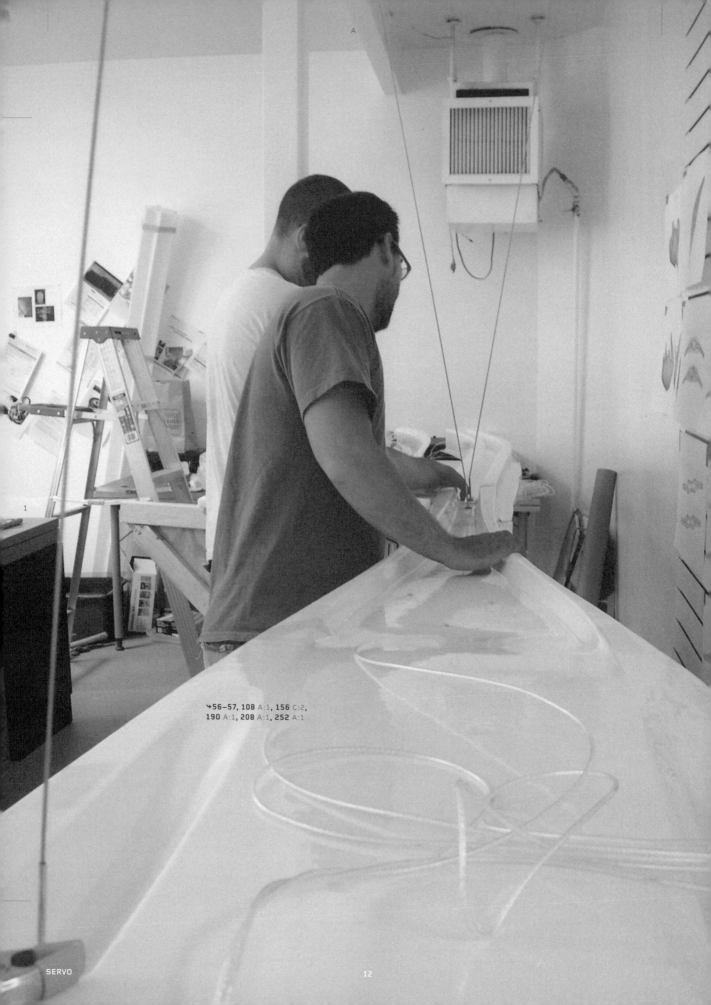

↳56—57, 108 A:1, 156 C:2,
190 A:1, 208 A:1, 252 A:1

Provisional— Emerging Modes of Architectural Practice USA

Edited by Elite Kedan, Jon Dreyfous, and Craig Mutter

Princeton Architectural Press
New York

Organizational Notes
**The structure of the book fore-
grounds the process behind
the featured projects. Output
from practices is presented
in sections categorically determined by use, such that like
documentation falls in the same
section regardless of office or
project. The result is an acute
comparison of the featured
practices' ethodologies across
the following sections:**

Completed Projects
Images of the final product, defined
to include virtual as well as physical
constructions

Diagrams
Explication of projects' origin,
assembly, or performance

Mock-Ups and Renderings
Testing of formal, structural, and
experiential properties of a project,
including the iterative development
of all aspects and scales of a project

Construction Documents
Instruments used to guide, execute,
and implement the building
of projects, including architects'
instructions to builders and
fabricators

Construction/Assembly
Assembly or implementation
of projects

Offices
Snapshots of day-to-day operations
of the offices, dispersed across book

Essays
Practitioners reflect on the field
of architecture

Interviews
Conversations between practitioners.
(Note: in some cases interviews are
compiled from several different
conversations, and in cases where
multiple members of a firm were
interviewed, all are represented
as one voice.)

Linking
Given the categorical divisions,
elements of a single project
are dispersed throughout the
book. A system of links provides
connections between consecutive
occurrences of a project, firm,
or idea. Each link comprises
a page number and coordinates.
For example, **88** B:4 denotes
coordinate B:4 (indicated at
perimeter of page) on page 88.

Contents

A

Introduction

Provisional is a term we have struggled with. It does not refer to an architecture tentative in purpose. Rather, it is a working term for the content and positioning of practices that not so long ago would have been considered on the margins of the profession. The approach of each practice is provisional in its own way. Due to new technologies and attitudes concerning a kind of culture of consultancy, the margin is informing the very core of how architects make work today. The collective body of practice to which we refer emerges as an open-ended and recursive network of permeable and shifting boundaries in which the *edge* is a less useful, even irrelevant, idea.

Provisional, which we might also call *post-edge*, practices do not position themselves against mainstream social, political, or philosophical agendas. Their objectives are more opportunistic, pragmatic, strategic, and optimistic. While such qualities have a stereotypical postwar American flavor, they suit the times because they focus on the performative aspects and efficacy of built work rather than theoretical or conceptual underpinnings. The book you have in your hands profiles nine especially dynamic architectural practices that exemplify this new pragmatic approach to the discipline. While all are based in the United States, much of their client base, and increasingly, much of the manufacturing they rely on, is situated in the rapidly expanding economies of Asia.

A willingness to explore the architectural applications of emerging technologies and means of production is a common thread in each practice. These tools include computational software for visualization, simulation, and fabrication; digitally linked hardware such as CNC (computer numerical controlled) milling machines, laser cutters, three-dimensional scanners and printers; and the various softwares that implement building information modeling (BIM) processes. Equally transformative for the way these firms operate on a day-to-day basis are the internet and related communication

technologies—for it is through them that knowledge bases, gossip, and job opportunities spread.
The result has in many ways given smaller firms
a greater strategic advantage over larger offices
to bid on projects in far-flung locales. Large and
small practices both are able to occupy a broader
range of identities than ever before—they work
in a more interdisciplinary fashion, and their
projects are more complex, from both the standpoint of programming and production.

Beyond technology, there are important
methodological innovations. Provisional practices
collectively are driving a broad reformulation of
the idea of *critical practice*, with the aim of bridging
the too often separate subdisciplines of theory
and building. For example, all nine firms resuscitate
and redefine in various ways the otherwise traditional concept of craft. Through serious material
and fabrication research they've jettisoned the
conventional understanding of software as a tool
for mere representation, while also questioning
the bolder claims of a purely generative, techno-
deterministic architecture.

The practices profiled here engage these
dynamics in various ways. For instance,
nARCHITECTS undertakes sensitive and rigorous

↳225 A:1

investigations of perceptual and experiential
phenomena, which they use to engage the
occupants and users of their projects. Through
their hands-on approach to material exploration
they achieve subtle, ephemeral effects, seam-
lessly turning the analytical into the experiential.
Lewis.Tsurumaki.Lewis (LTL) employs hand- and
↘24 A:1, 129 A:1
computer-generated drawings to develop and
speculate on new relations and organizations of
space. They assemble many of their projects themselves in their shop and on site, and have revised
conventional contractual relationships so as
to maintain comparable levels of material and
fabrication control on larger projects. Craft has also
come to encompass scripting and digital fabrication
methods, as exemplified in the work of Meejin Yoon.
↘177 A:1
Yoon embraces cutting-edge technology in her
kinetic installations and sensor-activated pieces,
which investigate and explore various theoretical
approaches towards material envelopes including
skin, clothing, and architecture.

SHoP is a prime example of a firm that lever-
↘136 A:1
ages emerging technologies to exert control
over their designs. They take on responsibility
traditionally outside the architect's purview, both
in terms of financing (they maintain fiscal interest

in many of the projects they design) and development scope (they often do extensive in-house research before their projects are sent out to bid). Gehry Technologies (GT) is itself a developer of much of this revolutionary technology. They are a software and building consultant that grew from the challenge of translating Frank Gehry's sculptural forms and complex geometries into outputs that could be fabricated and assembled on time and on budget. GT's integration of software and consultancy not only allows for innovation at a building and urban scale, it also empowers small and midsize firms to participate in design and production processes in a more engaged manner, and on a potentially much larger scale than was previously possible.

Greater control has also come about through strategic positioning of firms in relation to conventional notions of clients and practices. George Yu's small firm, for instance, is engaged by, and engages large corporate clients on sometimes massive projects by making architecture that is central to their identity. By convincingly foregrounding the spatial and environmental components of corporate identities, his work demonstrates that architectural innovation can be a central component in branding

↳182 A:1

↳232 A:1

1
5
10
15
20
25

strategy. Front's consultancy, similarly, approaches
↘87 A:1
its highly specialized work through innovative
and collaborative relationships with clients—many
of whom include other architects. By focusing
their energies on conceptually and technologically
sophisticated facades (as well as developing innovative procurement strategies and patenting new
products), they have considerable influence on
high-profile projects—such as the China Central
Television Headquarters (CCTV) in Beijing by Office
of Metropolitan Architecture (OMA)—despite being
a comparatively small office.

In this new climate, overlap and cross-fertiliza-
tion among firms is the norm. It is not uncommon—
even within the few firms profiled here—to see
several studios working in tandem on one project.
For instance, for the New Museum in New York,
Front utilitized GT's software to develop the
facade that Chris Hoxie and his collaborators built
↘28 A:1, 81 A:1
virtually for the Japanese firm Sejima + Nishizawa
Associates (SANAA). This technologically
mediated network is the current site of architectural practice in the United States. It is a landscape
of entangled scales and operations in which
conventional notions of practice are inverted or
redefined. Individuals working alone or in loose

collectives have a major impact on big projects. A single practice, such as Servo, may be split up ↘**190** A:1 geographically in four different cities across the globe while producing conceptually exciting architecture. Established firms such as Skidmore, Owings & Merrill (SOM) explore provisional, or ↘**43** A:1 post-edge, strategies; and post-edge firms like SHoP adopt mainstream tactics. Big offices operate as lean, agile research laboratories, and small ones direct projects thousands of miles away from their offices and their collaborators.

From this unstable network no identifiable style or archetype emerges. Again, what is at issue is far more fundamental and transformative than that. It's the infrastructure supporting architectural practice, the horizontal modes of communication between office members, the reconceptualization of tools, and the strategic positioning of firms vis-à-vis architectural production. In this way, process and output are more fluidly related, with only provisional solutions and definitions at any given point. It's an exciting mess.

Beyond?
by Marc Tsurumaki

The question of *beyond*, in the context of architectural production, inevitably invokes the transgression of limits and boundaries—a superseding of the constraints of routinized practice, rigid institutional territories, outmoded technologies, and anachronistic economic and political models. But is it possible to short circuit this desire for an escape from limits—to reposition the question of beyond? In a global culture, where the recognizably new is no longer shocking but strangely familiar, the most apparently radical architectural forms are incorporated into circuits of publicity and consumption with astonishing ease. Meanwhile, far from the supposed fluidity and dematerialization of global systems, normative forms of architectural practice often plod along in a tangle of conventions that are stubbornly resistant to transformation.

Buildings are inconveniently mired in gravity, materiality, standardized modes of construction, byzantine codes, and bureaucratic procedures. What if one could move beyond this dilemma, beyond the fantasy of escape from the limitations of architectural production on the one hand, and the surrender to the stultifying forces of convention on the other? What if invention could emerge through an opportunistic exploitation of restrictions? Such a methodology entails an imaginative engagement with limits—a renegotiation of the complex network of use values, political imperatives, technological systems, consumer desires, and economic formulas that invariably circumscribe the architectural project. By maneuvering tactically within these operational boundaries, architects can tease out the latencies of normative configurations, generating new social and spatial possibilities from within the logics of the given. In this way, architectural production is recast as a form of restricted play, a pleasurable manipulation of bounds and constraints, an improvisation within the parameters of emergent and pervasive organizational structures.

Such a practice exists beyond either critical resistance or complicity. It assumes agility and cunning on the part of the architect—a willingness to playfully engage the rules, to bend but not break them. It is simultaneously optimistic and pragmatic, surviving through a provisional consent to dominant systems in the service of creative desires.

This approach transforms the architect from visionary into equal parts con artist and alchemist, operating not through the grand gesture but through sleight of hand, the subtle artifice that has the power to transform the commonplace into the extraordinary. Here the architect effects a shift that leads "always from familiar objects into the unfamiliar,"[1] from the known into the possible.

This approach exists beyond the narrow uses of conventional logics. Through the ruthless application of imagination, the rational trajectories of the architectural project are put into play, extrapolated to the point that they render a productive excess—a precipitate of paradoxical effects and surrational possibilities, often at odds with the very imperatives that generated them. In this way, the underlying logics of the project are both amplified and diverted, catalyzing unforeseen couplings of form and program, speculative affiliations of function and inhabitation. Operating opportunistically within the legislations of existing formations, these tactics open up the potential for pleasure, play, and imagination inside the rationalized spaces of contemporary systems.

1. Excerpt from the mission statement of the Museum of Jurassic Technology, Los Angeles, CA, on the museum's website: http://www.mjt.org/intro/genborch.htm.

Essay first published in: Volume *issue 1 (Columbia University GSAPP), 2005. Courtesy LTL Architects. Marc Tsurumaki is Partner of Lewis.Tsurumaki. Lewis Architects in New York City.*

⤳129 A:1

Convergence: Toward a Digital Practice
by Chris Hoxie

To practice digitally within the ever-expanding field
of architecture can mean any number of things today.
The profession has clearly become more interdisciplinary,
with research being done in information design,
building simulation, parametric and computational
form-generation, prototyping, and fabrication, to name
but a few subfields. We are starting to see a simultaneous fracturing of these research strands into their own
bodies of disciplinary knowledge. At the same time there
is an obvious movement toward convergence—i.e. an
attempt to use these bodies of knowledge in a vertically
integrated way toward a sort of meta-digital practice.
Our practice—by which I refer to the work of myself and
of like-minded colleagues with whom I collaborate—
is shaped by autonomous research within various applied
digital technologies, as well as through anticipation

of how these technologies are integrated into a cohesive, disciplinary whole.

We look at the generative capacity of digital media within the entertainment industry to see how it could reframe the cultural production of the built and un-built environment. Specifically for us, this means working at the intersection of film and architecture to see how the techniques of rendering and animation and the simulation of digital content within the entertainment industry can expand the practice of architecture. We are, in essence, borrowing methodologies from the entertainment industry to improve our industry, though we're also interested in expanding what it means to practice architecture by seeking out design opportunities within the entertainment industry. This is a unique niche for an architectural firm, to say the least. We seek to fold in the design, construction, simulation, and presentation of virtual constructs and their environments by recreating various physical phenomena—such as artificial and natural light dynamics, specific qualities of physical materials and landscapes, and the precise behaviors of wind and heat upon a structure and its environment.

This medium is not well understood within the discipline of architecture. It's often thought of as an after-the-fact tool for representation or image-making, overlooking its generative capacity for designing, testing, and substantiating digital form- and space-making. For us, then, the medium

Digital Practice

needs to be understood and codified. It requires a certain suspension of disbelief—that is, in part, what we find so compelling and powerful about it. There is a disconnect between what is understood as real and as unreal. In certain ways a virtual construction has become, as present, and therefore as real an artifact, as material space. It presupposes and frames expectations but manifests itself as completely autonomous and separate. In this sense, it creates a kind of "bridge artifact" that negotiates virtual and material space. It feels real but wholly and markedly unreal at the same time, and we're interested in this tension.

The medium creates a kind of flickering of possible readings that, in turn, creates a perceptual tension between the idealized and the real. To that end, the virtual construct has its own autonomy as a cultural artifact, serving to test and substantiate ideas in the built environment.

Chris Hoxie is an architect with a digital design consultancy based in New York City.

The Digital Design Ecosystem: Toward a Pre-Rational Architecture
by Paul Seletsky

Thirty years since its introduction, the personal computer's impact on visual and industrial design has been ubiquitous. Changes in productivity and form-making have been revolutionized. In that time, however, digital technology has not significantly altered the paper-driven design and documentation process synonymous with architectural practice. Increased productivity, moreover, now threatens architects as primary leaders of that very process. This dichotomy beckons closer examination and discussion.

An Architecture of Our Time
Every generation seeks to create art as a manifestation of its time. Industrialization and the concomitant increased production of goods and services at the turn of the twentieth century, implied that life could no longer be viewed as before. Architecture was certainly not immune. A societal epiphany

lies inexorably at the heart of modernism's advent: Adolf Loos admonished architects to view ornament as crime, while Le Corbusier chastised those with "eyes which do not see."[1] Science offered no room for equivocation, considering that advancements in knowledge led to broader advancements for mankind. Enter the heroic era of modern architecture.

The work and writings of Walter Gropius, Le Corbusier, and Mies van der Rohe sought to instill architectural meaning through a representational embodiment of industrialization, alluding to what might someday be achieved, and portending vast social and political change. Modern architecture's new raison d'être, in particular, was improving public health. The sanitized white surfaces of Alvar Aalto's Paimio Sanatorium, devoid of bacteria-collecting molding, implied that design could expedite recovery from tuberculosis. Frank Lloyd Wright focused on new formal and spatial expressions. He envisioned the human spirit uplifted by architecture, thus instilling a new social order of utopian democracy. Louis Kahn, inspired by the engineering feats of ancient Rome, sought to disseminate that spirit to others, albeit through an implicit metaphorical dialogue with its archeological remains, "I asked the brick what it wanted to be, and it replied, 'An arch!'"[2]

From the mid-twentieth century onward, architects have mined an artistic and social currency posited on a variety of theoretical merits: exposed building functions and structure;

historical references and proportional formulae; ideas from avant-garde film, literature, and alternative social behavior. In the 1990s, the personal computer not only heightened these dialogues but also permitted unheralded experiment-ation with massing (blobitecture) and surface. An elitist cadre deemed certain architects esteemed enough to have their work purveyed as the ultimate art collectible. To the broader public, all the hoopla remained inconsequential. Architecture was an upper-class luxury, understood only by obscure provisions to supply "firmness, commodity, and delight."[3]

Modernism's failure to enact a new social order inevitably reduced its referential aesthetic into surface frontispieces—Venturian billboards. Richard Meier transformed Le Corbusier's utopian visions into white-on-white mannerism; Roy Lichtenstein, newsprint pixilation into romantic imagery; and Andy Warhol, portraiture into pop iconography. Le Corbusier famously proclaimed, "Revolution can be avoided."[4] And it was.

Elitism and Epiphany

Minimalist modernism remains an omnipresent aesthetic favored by many young architects. This may negate critical dismissal but only in so much as dated musical genres can eschew "progressive" or "classic" relabeling. In time, repeated massing and surface interplay descend into a bland familiarity, as does a photogenic retinue of young architects clad in black, fashionably paraded each month in the design journals hawked by image merchants. These young aesthetes care little for social awareness beyond satisfying an urban middle-class's fascination with "cool" (albeit unaffordable) prefab housing, or institutions seeking upscale architectural branding. Architecture as cultural phenomenon may raise public awareness toward a creative genre, but one that's short-lived; surplus retinal stimulation in an already media-saturated society.

Frank Gehry's adaptation of technology, however, should be viewed as a watershed moment for architects: Transforming the computer transformed from a tool to expedite production of the traditional "instruments of service" into the instrument of services itself. Architecture imbued with the formal and structural qualities of art but manifested *exclusively* through computational technology. One may discern a formal shift in Gehry's oeuvre—from predominantly orthogonal to anthropomorphic forms—resulting from this implementation. Gehry's innovation may over time be compared to Brunelleschi's dome in Florence for its historic impact.

Gehry Technologies, the software company spun from his practice, mirrors a similar venture put forth by SOM in the 1980s. Both convey a subliminal message: Embrace technology to reinvigorate and empower architectural practice. Reestablish the creative and technical primacy of architects, dispelling notions that they serve merely as "exterior decorators."

Daniel Willis and Todd Woodward in their insightful essay, "Diminishing Difficulty" (*Harvard Design Magazine*, Fall 2005 / Winter 2006), call for similar technological ascendancy, beckoning architects to think beyond software and toward new areas of expertise. They argue that a longstanding "mystique"—the difficulty laymen have in comprehending drawings—will quickly give rise to the relative ease by which three-dimensional Building Information Models (BIM) can be perceived. Such a scenario does not seem implausible, given the appeal and sophistication of consumer-friendly 3D kitchen modeling software— an appeal that begins to put into question the professional credentials of architects. A particular historical reference— medicine's transformation into modern practice—may serve as an educational paradigm for architecture to follow.

Medicine, Architecture, Science, and Society

Architecture and medicine both evolved sometime prior to the French Enlightenment as disciplines portending to offer new areas of "expertise." French medical practitioners, however, began to embrace science and scientific method to counter a variety of panaceas "prescribed" for curing illnesses, some dating from antiquity. Among them was bloodletting—draining the body's blood supply through selective incisions. The practice became widespread, to the point that a specialized box, the scarificator, was invented to automate cutting through skin. Barbers, with their assortment of razors, however, became sole practitioners—relieving "physicians" of the messy task and helping originate the barbershop pole as a unique street signage.

As medicine began to evolve from such practices into a system of formal education and training, it was accompanied by a new type of collective knowledge system, known as the Encyclopedia. Denis Diderot's pioneering "System of Human Knowledge" was among the first, and facilitated a broader avenue for sharing information and advancing science, mathematics, history, philosophy, art, and poetry. Parochial knowledge became accessible to a wider audience, fostering greater understanding of the human condition. Ideas were now subjected to controlled experimentation, and the results recorded to validate or controvert theories.

Social caricaturists Edme Pigal and Honoré Daumier portrayed a mid-nineteenth-century French public leery of doctors and medicine, and derided architects as equally untrustworthy for their unpredictable methods. The response from the nascent medical community was to organize concerted efforts to engender public trust. Scientific research was published and succeeded in assuaging fears. Doctors surpassed their counterparts at l'École des Beaux-Arts and, two hundred years hence, are regarded as integral to protecting public health, safety, and welfare. Architects never demonstrated such fundamental changes in their services, or publicized any research that might promote an equal necessity, albeit over a much longer period of observation.

Medicine's transformation sealed its position within society. It could demonstrate methodical insight (examination), directly linked to codified interpretation (diagnosis), and produce creative expertise (prescription). Art and science were not subjugated but augmented, defined by clarity of vision and simplicity of purpose. One precept of scientific method, Ockham's Razor, advocated shaving or minimizing assumptions when testing ideas, positing that simple solutions tended to resolve highly complex problems. Modernists' ideas were similar: Picasso sketched bulls with great detail in his youth but at life's end, drew their shapes with a few simple lines.

Interpretive reasoning became a trusted and integral component of modern medicine: One seeks the radiologist's interpretation of x-rays, not the lab technician's; surgeons assess conditions and justify procedures that they, in turn, must perform by leading teams; responsibilities are not consigned; actions imply knowledgeable reactions; and new procedures must be validated under direct supervision of one's colleagues. This foundation—and not solely a series of multiple-choice exams or timed vignettes—lays the groundwork for licensure.

Supercomputing fundamentally underlies the data feedback and monitoring systems, which have advanced medical research. Behavioral conditions can be studied virtually and physically, augmenting research. Medicine's decisive path toward change must now become Architecture's.

Ideology, Authority, and Responsibility

Ideologues have long argued architecture's principal foundation lies in ideas and a differentiation from construction. They promote an intellectual realm marked not by physical manifestation but philosophical critique. This author would argue that architectural practice can incorporate technical, theoretical, and artistic license equally, through a holistic feedback system responsive to the design process *in toto*. This represents an opportunity to dramatically alter all that has previously been considered and accepted in architectural practice.

Architects are taught to investigate the origin and nature of conditions, materials, and objects. The advent of BIM has only heightened this awareness and created an instinctive desire to understand the means of fabrication and the methods of logistics and assembly. Such knowledge has been stymied by an antiquated system of contractual restrictions emanating from mid-nineteenth-century building conditions.

Digital simulation, applied simultaneously within a conceptual framework, could augment architects' ideas and substantiate their expertise over the entire design process. It will not obviate dialogue with consultants, nor supersede their advice, but help elevate them. Authority can only be conferred on those willing to take risks and assume the responsibilities stemming from their actions.

Form Follows Factor: Pre-Rational Design

Architectural morphology is often the culmination of ideas that painstakingly attempt to synthesize meaning from metaphoric or programmatic exploration. Unique methods of introspection often distinguish those considered masters of their realm versus those deemed journeymen. Post-rational physical and virtual analysis tests are typically applied to formalized concepts that are well past any significant revision, and demonstrate endurance to environmental conditions but overlook a potential application toward form finding itself. Immediate procedural needs are met but opportunities for process change lie fallow.

Pre-rational design aims to address this missed opportunity, using supercomputing to impart implicit and explicit conditions into the earliest stages of conceptual exploration. In 2007, this idea led to the

Digital Design Ecosystem (DDE) initiative. Participants from Georgia Tech, Square One Ecotect, Gehry Technologies, and SOM discussed creating a system that could analyze program requirements and subject formal concepts to an array of software tools that, analogous to an automobile dashboard, would provide simultaneous feedback.

The Digital Design Ecosystem

The fundamental concept of the Digital Design Ecosystem is to address a number of design's what-ifs:

— What if multiple design concepts could be produced in considerably less time?

— What if design iterations could be accelerated, enabling them to be compared to one another?

— What if performance factors could be incorporated into the generation of shapes, enabling greater selectivity?

— What if design constraints could "suggest" alternatives, versus having those "value-engineered" from the design?

— What if building information models could mimic and then moderate actual building performance?

— What if consultant expertise could be acquired from anywhere around the world—in real time?

In schematic design, traditional space planning and programming requirements are driven by area calculations and site limitations. The Digital Design Ecosystem would accelerate this process, integrating all spatial and performance requirements, and then applying environmental, financial, material, or other types of analysis into preliminary "block and stack" models. A number of design considerations could then be examined and prioritized further. Design would be transformed from a linear process into an ad hoc arena, displaying bi-directional transfers of information simultaneously across multiple screens— or multiple continents.

Design is thereby transformed from a highly linear process into an elliptical one. A holistic landscape—similar to the gauges on an automobile dashboard, or the display monitoring a hospital patient's vital signs—enables a broader design purview through analysis, simulation, and dynamic 3D models, broadcast simultaneously across multiple screens.

Collaboration, Carbon, and Comprehension

The Digital Design Ecosystem requires modernization of design collaboration: Simultaneous over sequential

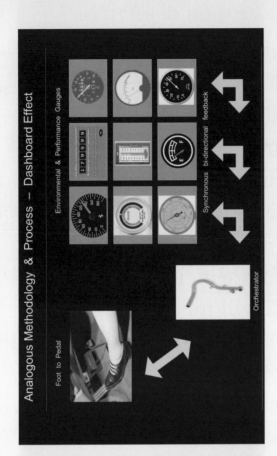

Analogous Methodology & Process – Dashboard Effect

Environmental & Performance Gauges

Synchronous bi-directional feedback

Foot to Pedal

Orchestrator

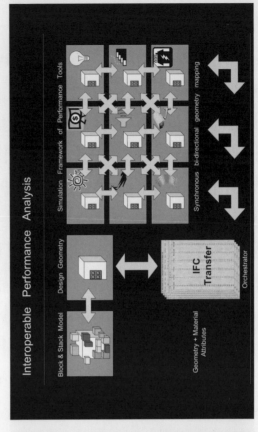

Interoperable Performance Analysis

Simulation Framework of Performance Tools

Synchronous bi-directional geometry mapping

Design Geometry

Block & Stack Model

IFC Transfer

Geometry + Material Attributes

Orchestrator

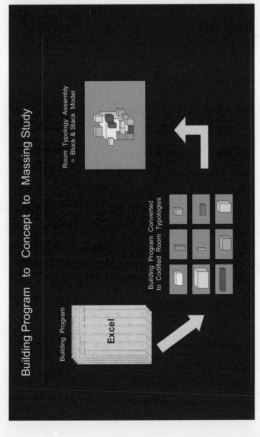

Building Program to Concept to Massing Study

Room Typology Assembly = Block & Stack Model

Building Program

Building Program Converted to Codified Room Typologies

Excel

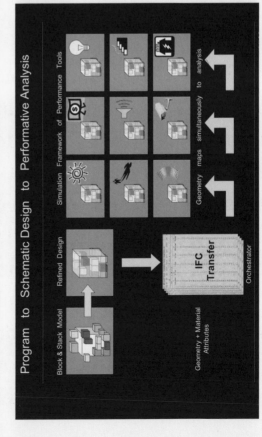

Program to Schematic Design to Performative Analysis

Simulation Framework of Performance Tools

Geometry maps simultaneously to analysis

Block & Stack Model

Refined Design

IFC Transfer

Geometry + Material Attributes

Orchestrator

information delivery; model exchange over file transfer; metadata over specs, consultant involvement at project onset; optimized material cost, availability, and delivery via internet search and tracking; automated code compliance. These changes will impact design and construction on an unprecedented scale—without any compromise to design integrity.

Architects have more to offer their clients and society than they realize. Integrating design morphology, material science, and environmental sustainability will undoubtedly inform everyone what is possible or achievable in the built environment, in a manner not previously seen. A focus on architectural science (distinct from building science) must equal our overwhelming obsession with form. It must become the foundation by which to certify a new architectural expertise—comparable in breadth and scope to medical research. The National Science Foundation should be the logical choice to fund such research but—incredibly—it does not recognize architecture as a science! We must demand that our representative organizations, such as the AIA, lobby to change this.

Today's broad societal concerns—global warming, greenhouse gases, resource depletion—will focus greater public attention than ever before toward architects for answers and innovative solutions. Should they fail, such attention will quickly be redirected elsewhere. The US

Green Building Council, Architecture 2030, and Architecture for Humanity all raised broad public awareness on these issues well before any of the profession's organizations did. This is not a coincidence but a wake-up call. Talking about green design can only go so far. Metrics derived from controlled testing—automobile fuel mileage or appliance energy ratings, for example—enable those with ideas to speak above the fray. Those who now seek government-funded building programs but fail to address the opportunity for digital design process change will have missed the point.

Those who suggest that technology-driven design is an attempt to pre-define or automate solutions are mistaken. Performance feedback will increase the amount of design information available to architects but cannot make the decisions for them. Professional merit should be based on interpretative skills and—as medical students clearly know—one cannot properly analyze results without first knowing how to correctly calibrate the tools being deployed.

Architectural licensure must be governed by substantial hands-on practice extending beyond drafting. Understanding safety codes simulated in physical and virtual environments is a good place to start. The profession's governing licensure body has unfortunately become a source of fear and frustration, with decisions that are seemingly opaque and rules outmoded. Exams measuring comprehension of life-safety are now as predictable as those for college admissions—replete with the very same preparatory enterprises.

A Momentous Opportunity for Change

The primary focus of architectural pedagogy today is to engender aesthetic awareness but cries for augmented digital analysis. Change cannot simply mean acquiring advanced computers or software, nor imply vocation. Architecture programs must jettison antiquated methods and modernize their curricula. Computer science and construction management must not remain insular.

The ascent of BIM in the professional marketplace brings no guarantees to architects. BIM's cost and scheduling advantages may line it squarely within the construction administration camp, delivering fully coordinated bid packages in less time, but also requiring less design input—an approach relegating architects to design "branding"—adding enclosure patterning or unusual massing onto design/build ventures. Daumier's caricatures resonate from two centuries ago and unless architects abandon their worship of form, a pre-ordained future may await them.

The aspirations of the early modernists may have concluded as appliqué but a momentous opportunity awaits architects willing to seize it. Integration of analytical technology into the design process, improved interpretive skills, and revamped internship will begin to establish a codified architectural science without forgoing the forms or aesthetic ideals so beloved. On the contrary, their value will increase as the art and science of architecture coalesce.

Mies van der Rohe's words, uttered a half-century ago at the Illinois Institute of Technology, still ring true and should serve as a clarion call to architects everywhere:

Technology is rooted in the past. It dominates the present and tends into the future. It is a real historical movement—one of the great movements which shape and represent their epoch. It can be compared only with the Classic discovery of man as a person, the Roman will to power, and the religious movement of the Middle Ages. Technology is far more than a method, it is a world in itself. As a method it is superior in almost every respect. But only where it is left to itself, as in gigantic structures of engineering, there technology reveals its true nature. There it is evident that it is not only a useful means, but that it is something, something in itself, something that has a meaning and a powerful form— so powerful in fact, that it is not easy to name it. Is that still technology or is it architecture? And that may be the reason why some people are convinced that archi- tecture will be outmoded and replaced by technology. Such a conviction is not based on clear thinking. The opposite happens. Wherever technology reaches its real fulfillment, it transcends into architecture. It is true that architecture depends on facts, but its real field of activity is in the realm of significance. I hope you will understand that architecture has nothing to do with the inventions of forms. It is not a playground for children, young or old. Architecture is the real battleground of the spirit. Architecture wrote the history of the epochs and gave them their names. Architecture depends on its time. It is the crystallization of its inner structure, the slow unfolding of its form. That is the reason why technology and architecture are so closely related. Our real hope is that they will grow together, that some day the one will be the expression of the other. Only then will we have an architecture worthy of its name: architecture as a true symbol of our time.[5]

1. Adolf Loos, "Ornament and Crime," 1908; Le Corbusier, *Towards a New Architecture*, 1923.

2. Louis Kahn, "Lecture at Pratt Institute (1973)," in *Louis Kahn: Essential Texts*, ed. Robert C. Twombly (New York: W. W. Norton & Co., 2003), 271.

3. Quote attributed to Vitruvius.

4. Le Corbusier, *Towards a New Architecture*.

5. Excerpt from 1950 address to IIT given by Ludwig Mies van der Rohe. From Ulrich Conrads, *Programs and Manifestos on 20th-Century Architecture* (Cambridge, MA: MIT Press, 1975), 154.

Paul Selestsky is Senior Manager of Digital Design for Skidmore, Owings & Merrill in New York, and was Chair of the Technology Committee of the American Institute of Architects New York (AIANY) from 2002–2008.

→97 A:1, 145 A:1, 179 A:3, 193 B:1

3 Degrees of Felt, Aztec Empire Exhibition
Guggenheim Museum
MY Studio/Meejin Yoon
with Enrique Norten/TEN Arquitectos
New York, New York
2004

→83, 99 A:2, 147 A:3, 242–243

Avra Verde Residence
MARCH/Chris Hoxie Consultant
Architect: Rick Joy Architects
Saguaro National Park West;
Tucson, Arizona
2008

↘100 A:2, 150 C:2, 194 A:1

Bornhuetter Hall
The College of Wooster
Lewis.Tsurumaki.Lewis
Wooster, Ohio
2004

Camera Obscura
SHoP
Greenport, NY
2005

↘101 A:1, 142 B:32, 152 A:3, 197 A:1, 198 A:1

Camera Obscura
SHoP

**Canopy: MoMA/P.S.1 Young
Architects Program
P.S.1 Contemporary Art Center
nARCHITECTS**
Queens, New York
2004

Canopy: MoMA/P.S.1 Young
Architects Program
P.S.1 Contemporary Arts Center
nARCHITECTS

Dark Places
Servo
Santa Monica, California
2006

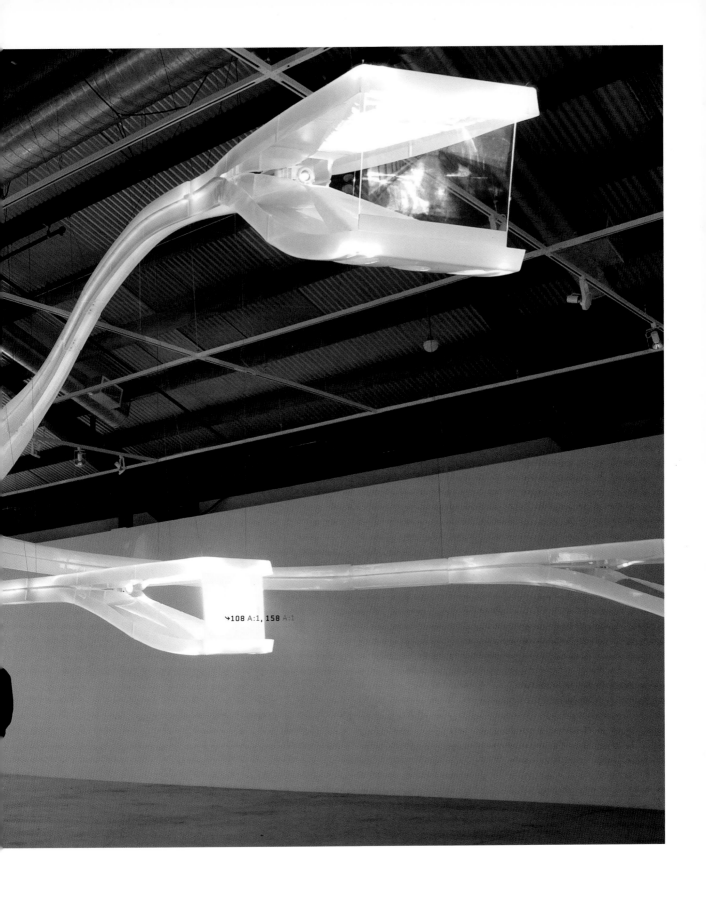

→108 A:1, 158 A:1

Dark Places
Servo

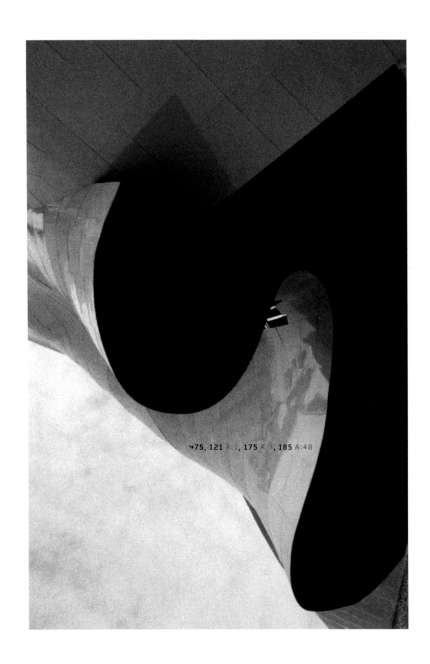

➔75, 121 A:1, 175 A:3, 185 A:48

Experience Music Project
Gehry Partners
Seattle, Washington
2000

Within the image:
→110 A:1, 160 A:3, 254 A:1
→255 A:2

Fluff Bakery
Lewis.Tsurumaki.Lewis
New York, New York
2004

FutureGen Power Plant
United States Department of Energy
MARCH/Chris Hoxie
Prototype plant, multiple locations
2008

111 A:1

FutureGen Power Plant
United States Department of Energy
MARCH/Chris Hoxie

IBM Center for e-Business Innovation
George Yu Architects
Chicago, Illinois
2001

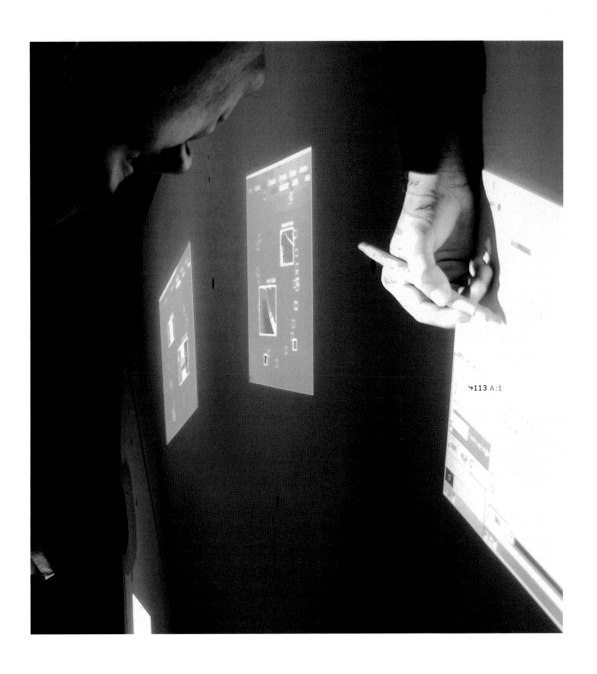

IBM Center for e-Business Innovation
George Yu Architects

↘114 A:1, 165 B:1, 180 A:41, 260–261

LoRezHiFi
MY Studio/Meejin Yoon
Washington DC
2006

MaxStudio.com
George Yu Architects
various locations throughout the
United States
2001

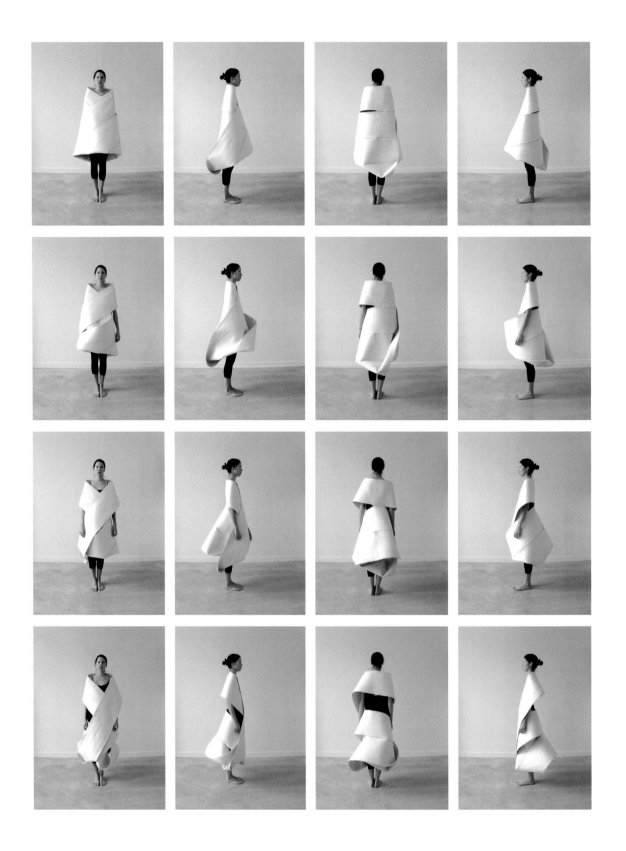

↗120 A:1, 166 A:1, 178 B:28

Möbius Dress
MY Studio/Meejin Yoon
2004

Olympic Sculpture Park
Seattle Art Museum
MARCH/Chris Hoxie consultant
Architect: Weiss/Manfredi
Seattle, Washington
2007

One Island East
Gehry Technologies consultant
Architect: Wong & Ouyang (HK) Ltd.
Hong Kong, China
2008

Seattle Central Public Library
Front consultant
Architect: OMA/LMN joint venture
Seattle, Washington
2005

↳124 A:1, 175 B:1, 266 A:1

Shop Lift: Rethinking Retail, Transcending Type
Installation in the US Pavilion at the 2004 Venice Biennale
George Yu Architects
Venice, Italy
2004

Sony Design Center
George Yu Architects
Santa Monica, California
2004

Weatherhead School of Management
Case Western Reserve University
Gehry Partners
Cleveland, Ohio
2002

White Noise/White Light
Interactive Sound and Light Installation
MY Studio/Meejin Yoon
Athens, Greece
2004

↳126 A:1, 176 A:1, 179 B:3, 224 A:1, 268

↘127 A:1, 226 A:30, 269–272

Windshape
nARCHITECTS
Lacoste, France
2006

Windshape
nARCHITECTS

Xing Restaurant
Lewis.Tsurumaki.Lewis
New York, New York
2005

Chris Hoxie

So Chris, what is the nature of your company, what do you do? Well, actually, our company is more of a loose collaborative, kind of the Broken Social Scene (Canadian indie rock collective) of architecture, working as both collectives and individuals. Sometimes I work as an individual consultant, but most of my projects have been done in collaboration with Brandon Hicks and Kevin Cimini. Those collaborations are an outgrowth of our working together at KDLAB, an experimental digital design company that was exploring the relationship between emerging technologies and architecture. KDLAB was a think tank for the three of us along with the founding partners Dean DiSimone and Joseph Kosinski, and the five of us have all collaborated in some form or another over the past four years. Kevin collaborated with both Joe and Dean, Brandon and I worked exclusively together, Brandon and Kevin and I worked together, and most recently Brandon and Kevin have worked on a project with Dean. So it really has been a series of discrete entities that sometimes collaborate. There is a common thread there, but all five of us have started to refine our respective areas of interest. Dean has since formed a branding, graphic design, and interactive media firm called Tender Creative. Joe has gone on to broadcast, video, and film, landing a director role for two upcoming feature films. Brandon and Kevin are about to launch their new design firm MARCH, and I went out on my own in 2007, although I continue to work regularly with both of them. Regardless, the common thread behind all the work has been exploring the relationship between new media and the constructed environment, whether it's through the filter of film, information design, or parametric design technologies.

Do you think there's something substantive to be learned from the use of digital media? Do you think digital forms of representation contribute substantively to the end design? Or are they only a means to an end? Design thinking has always had a symbiotic relationship with technique and ideation. Technique is instrumental to thinking. Especially when a nascent technology is developing, technique influences the way we think. We have been in a 15-year gestation period now—between the emergence of new digital technologies—in which technique has been seen as a priori to ideation. But now we have a more mature technology that's going to fundamentally alter the way we think about and produce architecture.

What's the difference between rendering and visualization for you? We define rendering as an art form coming out of entertainment-industry software, not as visualization or something that's just pictorial or representational.

What we're trying to do is appropriate tools that have emerged from the entertainment world (software such as Maya and 3D Studio). We hope to explore how that medium—in dealing with the comprehensive simulation of things—can reframe architecture. I'd say what we do is analogous to what (Frank) Gehry did with tools from the aerospace industry. In a similar way, we're trying to prove to the broader architectural community that these tools are a valid way to create and explore form. **It's interesting because, let's say, a hundred years ago rendering was a Beaux-Arts craft, and drawing or watercolor** was seen as a kind of testing ground for the idea, in that it allowed for meditation not just on that single idea but on a whole discipline, i.e. the practice of projecting space, etc. But there seems to be a difference between that tradition and newer forms of digital representation. The digital environment is more fluid and interactive, there's no fixed idea or point of origin. Rather, the idea is moving and changing all the time. Well, analog methodologies have always relied on the idea of representation for both technical and design drawings. Today classical representation (in the form of perspectives, for example) is a byproduct of working three dimensionally—the byproduct may still be pictorial but now it is a snapshot of a much more complex, ambitious, and fluid process.

You have an engineering background, but you also went to art school and then architecture school, which brings technology and art together. You had a mentor along the way that helped you think about visualization or interactive representation. Maybe you could talk about your story? Ironically, I was studying petroleum engineering, but I found the subject too narrow and prescriptive and wanted a more liberal arts education. What excited you about engineering? Studying the mechanics of the physical world, I enjoyed calculus and physics and rock lab. But I also enjoyed literature, history, and economics. I went to a liberal arts school in Ohio, but it was a very conservative school. So I transferred to Bennington College in 1989 to study architecture and painting. Bennington had an abstract expressionist legacy in painting, and my only training, if you could call it training, was in figurative art. I didn't even know what abstract expressionism was, so there was a lot of hostility toward my painting teachers [laughter]. Did you conform? Well, sure. I started painting my night-mares [laughter]. But I still had contempt for it, and I didn't understand it. Certainly I do now. And now, I think, if I'd been an enlightened 18-year old I would've embraced it. But at the time I turned to sculpture and started building. Of course it came from an abstract expressionist trajectory, from David Smith and Anthony Caro and all the heroic modernists of the Bay Area School in San Francisco. So I started working very large with steel, plaster, concrete… I learned how to weld and so forth, and that's really what got me into architecture, that's what really consolidated my interest in architecture. What were some of the things you were focusing on? Were there specific architectural issues or ways of thinking that you drew from? Sculpture provided a great outlet for a sort of unmediated, three-dimensional testing ground for ideas

within architecture. And when I finally went to Harvard (Graduate School of Design, GSD), my inclination was to continue with that. I was planning on getting into a sculpture studio, but the facilities were really bad for working in the way I needed. I didn't understand how I was supposed to get a two-ton dump truck full of steel up the ramp of the Carpenter Center. Sculpture came off the pedestal a long time ago, and the Carpenter Center was not up to the task. So how did you move into this fascination with digital media? Virtual space became the next best thing to working one-to-one. I was self-righteous about working in analog media but fortuitously I bought a secondhand computer that was loaded to the gills with software. I called up Alistair Standing, who had been doing digital design for Zaha Hadid in the early '90s, and asked if he had ever heard of 3D Studio, and that was pretty much it. It's amazing how ideas can be so viral.

How did you teach yourself? Did you sit there with a manual? I just got in and started doing stuff, looking at the help menu, online tutorials, and whatever. By the time I entered the GSD, I was pretty skillful, and that became my substitution for sculpture, in that here was a medium where technique was transparent to design, at least theoretically, in the sense that you could get in there and carve out space and look at it and manipulate it in an immersive environment.

So where did you go from there? How did you use those skills when you actually started at the GSD? I remember my first studio. I'd started designing in 3D Studio, until my machine was forcibly removed from the premises. That was in 1993, when Columbia University started their paperless studios. I remember staring at my desk mate, who had to move his site plan over a half an inch… He transferred every single point to a piece of paper via needle, erased the entire drawing, retransferred the points via needle, and redrew it. That represented a rigorous analog methodology and intellectually I had enormous respect for it, but it was still absurd to be implementing it in production.

Finally, in my fourth semester, I had a studio with (Preston) Scott Cohen, and I was absolutely frightened of him. He was very active in the school and his studios were the center of attention. Harvard was very different from the AA (Architectural Association School of Architecture in London). The AA, as I indirectly experienced it through my teacher at Bennington, was about letting the student find his own voice, it had a pluralistic ideology. Whereas at Harvard, you knew your studio instructor was there because they each had a very specific ideology. You were to try it on, you were to define yourself by aligning yourself with or

→50, 99 A:2, 147 A:3, 242 A:1

against it. Scott had a very strong ideology, and he would usually pick one or two students and entrust them with his agenda to explore things. His studios were a feeding ground for new talent, so he would take on people and they would inevitably become involved in his professional work.

I was unfamiliar with Scott's work when I entered his studio. I knew nothing of stereotomy, or the way Scott was using projective geometry. For our very first studio review I showed up with this object based on anamorphic projection. It was something that I was working on in painting and sculpture, because I was always fascinated with flatness and depth and the conflation of the two. So I did a little conceptual model of an anamorphic projection of a piece of architectural threshold that had projected itself out and created a volumetric form. When you moved around it, it would collapse and expand based on your point of view. So he saw that, and he was like, what the hell is this? And that was the beginning of ten years of working with Scott Cohen. **So how did you work with him?** Well, originally we started using the computer, because we were designing systems and forms based on projective geometry, and solid modeling applications were inherently good at projective geometry. We were always trying to evaluate the forms and make design decisions but the medium was inherently poor for that, so I started researching radiosity-based systems that could accurately simulate depth perception via light propagation. That was a watershed moment, when we could actually perceive depth and react to the designs in a much tighter feedback loop. **What exactly are solid modeling applications?** There are many different modeling paradigms and platforms. Solid modeling comes out of the manufacturing industry— including everything from the high-end of aerospace and automobile production to the lower end of mechanical CAD (computer-aided design). In our case we started using a solid modeling kernel called ACIS that has been around for about 20 years. It's a very robust solid modeler. Scott and I were using it for the creation of all of our forms. Naturally, those investigations led to the question of how to replicate those forms three-dimensionally, and that, in turn, launched an exploration into prototyping and the use of laser cutting and 3D printing. The latter was a proprietary technology at MIT (Massachusetts Institute of Technology), and they were farming it out to over five different industries, including medical, architectural, military… We started hounding the GSD to get a 3D printer, which they did. It was the first 3D printer at Harvard.

Let's jump ahead a little bit. When people talk about developments in digital design, they usually break them up into a number of strands: for example, one is CNC (computer numerical control) manufacturing capabilities… Yes, digital design can be thought of as a meta-enterprise or a series of smaller strands within a larger, more comprehensive field. The past 15 years have borne witness to a number of variants of research, any one of which could represent their own discipline. Several of these strands—taken to their inevitable conclusion— could have catapulted people out of the discipline as it is currently defined. This is both exciting and also slightly cautionary—cautionary in the sense that you are always striving to find that balance, not going down any one strand too far. **Another development of digital design is building information modeling or BIM, which consists of a more holistic approach to the design process, where every system and way of producing a building is thought about from the beginning.** Yes, it has gone through many names and false starts, but there is no question that it will fundamentally reorganize the way we think of and produce architecture. **And yet another series of strands are what is called generative design, or algorithmic design, or performative architecture. Can you describe what those are?** Well, again, there are numerous strands and substrands driving digital design. Generative architecture generally refers to work that's generated by scripts, mathematical equations. It's a kind of formalism, a more extreme version of what (Peter) Eisenman was doing. Algorithmic design is related, but tries to merge computational complexity with more human, creative use of computers, partly by integrating rule-based logic inherent in such things as architectural programs, typologies, building codes, etc., to go beyond direct programming. And performative architecture is generally a privileging of the performance aspects of the building envelope over its form, with more innovative research conflating form with those performance aspects. Both within algorithmic architecture and performative architecture, there's a kind of new digital formalism where a skin can be subject to constraints, so that, for example, wind patterns in the fall versus wind patterns in the spring might have a certain impact on the landscape and the building skin can deflect and conform to those forces.

Perhaps it's more useful, if slightly reductive, to understand the two larger trajectories or trends that have emerged within digital architecture. On the one hand you have the construction-based strand coming out of the techniques and processes of the manufacturing industry. This, for example, is the Gehry paradigm, and the ultimate trajectory of his work over the past ten years is what's currently called BIM. It comes out of advances in manufacturing and it's a top-down paradigm where a singular object is managed from predesign all the way through construction documents, postconstruction and so on. On the other end, you have a design-based strand, emerging from software based on the entertainment industry such as Maya, 3D Studio, animation techniques. This is the trajectory of what's called performative architecture, algorithmic design, generative design. Generally, the people who are exploring this kind of architecture are using free-form NURBS (non-uniform rational b-spline) modeling software, and particle dynamics coming out of Maya.

Right now, there's still a rift between these broad strands of construction-based and design-based research. But the idea is that they begin to converge and a model develops that starts to blend the two. Offices like SHOP are heading in that direction. **It's interesting that you approach the issue by recounting the history of software rather than the history of architecture. Or that there's a current history of architecture that you can see through the lens of software development...** Well, I think it's a development in the history of architecture that concerns the right tools. And the tools happen to be digital. But it's going to take some time before these two larger trajectories converge. For instance, on the manufacturing end, the use of the technology is still conservative in how it shapes methodology and form-making. It is to some extent affecting construction methodology, and that flows back to design. But the medium is so amazing for its potential as a design tool and a whole lot of people are still using sketches and built models and only later translating that onto the computer. This contrasts starkly with the people using software in the entertainment industry, where this technology is front-heavy as opposed to back-heavy, and it's not about construction per se but generative form. It's about what the computer can do.

Maybe even more important is to understand the importance of parametric architecture/modeling. Parametric architecture—another of these strands— refers to a constraint-based system in which components are "parameterized." Consistent relationships are set up between objects embedded with parameters (such as height, depth, weight, material information), and these objects can respond to different circumstances. It's set up to allow changes in a single element to propagate changes throughout the system. For instance, weeks might be spent designing the parameters behind an object, so that when this propagating object hits a corner or an opening or a parapet, it adapts itself to each of those conditions. But then there's no need to draw or design a hundred unique conditions that occur within a building. And this parametric model is applicable both to the construction side of the discipline— which is about smart objects propagating themselves to facilitate construction—and the design side, where the

objectives of those parametric operations are more about design desire than construction desire. But it still scares me a bit. **What scares you about it?** It's clearly the future of architecture, but it necessitates completely new and different skill sets toward building architecture. For instance, now you need people trained at scripting. So on the one hand, designers are supposedly re-empowered through digital technology, in how it changes the relationship of architects to building and broadens the level of control that becomes available to describe and produce things. But on the other hand, you've got a shift in what it means to practice as an architect, in how these totally new skill sets are developing, and the unique specialties and subspecialties that come out of that which could create a Tower of Babel effect.

What are some digital design projects that have been made or fabricated that you find especially inspirational? Zaha Hadid's office has made great leaps on the design side of digital media, whereas Gehry has made amazing progress on the construction side. What will become interesting is the conflation of both design and construction paradigms. And frankly, you're seeing the industry scrambling now, post-Gehry and post-Columbia, to stake a claim in these two trajectories of construction and media.

Do you still believe there's an avant-garde? Well, that's not the term... **Personally, I think if there is an avant-garde, then it's no longer about pushing the boundaries of architecture as an abstract discipline. It's about assimilating new technologies and working with new materials in ways that inform architectural practice.** Well, in that sense I very much think that there's still the perception of avant-garde and what that represents. I mean Columbia has transformed architecture schools around the world. To be able to get Columbia disciples into an organization is analogous to what, at the time, it meant to recruit disciples of the Bauhaus. **What does Columbia mean in terms of setting a paradigm of architecture, or architectural representation that's coming out of this exploration with software?** Well, there are a number of things being produced today that have amazing virtuosity and have amazing suggestive qualities, but I don't see it currently as part of an architectural practice per se. I think it's still a form of research. With any new emerging technology in any industry, you have to incubate it in isolation and look at all its possibilities. It requires research. **What are you working on currently?** Well, again, we are always striving to find the balance between our own design work and our research and consulting. We have been working with architects as technology consultants on everything from building information modeling, to digital assets management, to prototyping, direct manufacturing, and media design; so the projects themselves and the nature of those projects are quite varied. Most of the projects we work on last for months and years in parallel with the design process. **And how does the process unfold?** We manage all the digital assets of a particular project and see a project through from schematic design through design development, and then guide a number of specific types of outputs from the digital database. This can be anything from one-to-one full-scale CNC mockups, to SLS (selective laser sintering— a rapid prototyping process) studies of the model, to intensive material and detail studies through renderings, to managing control geometry for the construction document set, to imaging and animation.

What is the medium you are working in and what tools are you using? Well the medium is just ubiquity of virtual space. And the software… Honestly we use so much software, dozens of different types, that we need a spreadsheet to manage all of it. Every time we start a new project we introduce new techniques and new software. We have two tracks: software that is tried and true and folded into production; and software being evaluated for research and development. For BIM software, for example, Brandon is evaluating Revit while I'm in turn evaluating Gehry Technologies' Digital Project. In trying to find a rendering engine to fold into production we literally developed projects in almost every software before settling on V-Ray. In that instance it was a slightly obsessive search for the right tool. Luckily Kevin had been doing freelance work with some Hollywood production companies who had great success with V-Ray. But that could all change tomorrow. It's quite fluid and you just need to continuously keep up with new developments. Also it's a tricky balance juggling technique and design. We are designers first and foremost, so it's difficult finding the right balance between all this experimentation and design. **The learning curve is the only limitation with software?** Well, there's still a holy grail kind of aspect to the level of proficiency needed before you can really use it. But we're verging on the moment where you're not constantly trying to overcome technique. Instead it just becomes a background operation like drawing or building a model, in that you can actually start to think plastically, in real time, through the medium.

If I can jump off the rails for a second, when Scott and I started working together we were great at representing exteriors because we'd build fabulous models. But the main medium outside of exhibitions was design publications, and you couldn't do so much with a model in a magazine. This was theoretical architecture, so it was formally challenging.

We had to inhabit it somehow and render the inside. The Prado competition, which we were working on in 1995, precipitated this exploration into rendering interiors and inhabitation, and we had a team of people working for us who built this beautiful virtual model. At the same time, a program called Radiance had come out of Lawrence Berkeley Laboratory. It was an algorithm-based software used in the military industry for the detection of heat. I'd previously been experimenting with this program, fleshing out three-dimensional virtual models with light so you could accurately perceive depth and so forth. But when we tried using it to render our model for the Prado competition, the interior renderings were just horrible. **Why?** With these computer graphics, it all comes down to the perception of depth. And it all comes down to light. If you can't have realistic light, there's no way to perceive, and the renderings just collapse. So I desperately drove over to MIT and found Wade Hokoda, who was also teaching at GSD at the time. He brought me into a lab with a bunch of UNIX machines and sat me down with Lightscape (the rendering software available at the time). I think it was the summer of 1995 and I basically spent that entire time with 24 UNIX machines in a poorly ventilated lab. The result was an amazing series of interior renderings for the Prado. And the discovery was that it was really about a true perception of depth in the digital representation which was needed to make these incredible, immersive, photographic spaces.

A lot of people use these technologies, but it seems very few are bringing it together the way you are. Do you think you use the technology differently? Or is there something you bring to the table personally that's different? Well, I know at least that Brandon, Kevin, and I live and breathe this stuff; so yes, there is something about our personalities that is conducive to this way of thinking. But the endgame for us is to have all this technology be transparent to design thinking, so that we can be more productive and creative as designers.

Interview with Chris Hoxie was conducted in New York City in 2005 by Jon Dreyfous. It was continued by email and telephone in 2008 with Elite Kedan.

↳28 A:1

Bruce Nichol of Front

Dennis Shelden of Gehry Technologies (GT) told us he thought Front was a good example of a young firm using cutting-edge technology to solve problems. What technology do you use and how has it affected your practice? Well, one of the pieces of software we use is Gehry Technologies' adaptation of CATIA (computer-aided three-dimensional interactive application). We invested in it because we very much believe in the ethos described by Shelden. Architectural fabrication is definitely heading in that direction, since it short circuits a lot of paperwork and makes communication centrally based. On the other hand, we're also committed to a roll-up-your-sleeves, hands-on approach to design, especially with making system mock-ups.

In project coordination, you can readily see how that technology creates a different way of working—everybody's linked in and communicating in a different way. But how is it different from the point of view of design? I don't think this software is primarily a design tool. Like any CAD (computer-aided design) program, it shouldn't be, though it is pretty seductive. You can get drawn into using it as a design tool, but I don't think that's its best utilization. It allows you to test designs and see how they'll work very quickly, but it doesn't replace sketches and models and so forth, as I think Gehry's work shows. It's more of a test bed. We were working with Gehry Partners on a couple of projects and so got to see the way they were using it. At the time, we were collaborating with them on a winery in Toronto, focusing on the glazed components, which were geometrically very complex. We were converting 3D drawings into 2D AutoCAD for our input, so we considered

CATIA for a while and finally decided to jump in. **Why did they come to you?** The complexity of their facades tends to be geometrical, but the construction is often straight-forward, rain screen cladding applications mostly. Architects may collaborate with contractors to execute design-build services, but when it comes to glazing systems, they don't necessarily have the in-house knowledge to deal with all thermal, waterproofing, and glass engineering issues in this context. Before we came on board, there was an existing contract between DMP (Dewhurst MacFarlane Partners) and Gehry Partners for facade consultation. My partners were working at DMP at the time. When we formed Front, some clients requested continuity with the same team of people.

I was formerly with RPBW (Renzo Piano Building Workshop) in Paris and after two years there I came back to New York to found Front. I've known my partners since the early 1990s. We'd talked about setting up a firm, but it was never clear exactly what it would be, or when the opportunity would arise. In the summer of 2000, the stars aligned and we said okay, this is it. **And then you moved to Rotterdam?** Yes, pretty much straight away. That was kind of a sucker punch, because up until that time I was with Renzo Piano in Paris. I'd never been happier and was loath to leave. But the others were in New York, so we decided that's where we'd set up our office. And then as soon as I got to New York, we got our first project with Rem Koolhaas.

How did you get the job consulting for Office for Metropolitan Architecture (OMA)? Well, Joshua Ramus (of OMA at the time, currently of REX) was partly responsible for that. He'd worked very closely with Marc (Simmons) on

the Seattle (Central Public) Library project, which was
a success, so he wanted to continue that relationship.
He lobbied for us to be given a chance, and we literally
walked across Varick Street to OMA's New York office and
interviewed with Rem. When we walked in, he was busy
as always and there were journalists and a photographer
waiting for him. He said okay, sit down, I've got a few
minutes. **Were you nervous?** Yes, we'd never met before.
He and Marc had, but still he wasn't familiar with us,
and he was blunt about it. The project—China Central
Television Headquarters (CCTV) and the Television Cultural
Centre (TVCC) in Beijing's Central Business District—
was the biggest construction project in the world at that
time. It's vast, covering 20 hectares. OMA already had other
facade consultancies engaged on several of their projects.
Why should they give us this job over the others? So
we gave him our pitch and sincerely believed we could do
a good job. He said he'd need somebody from our firm
in the OMA Rotterdam office at all times, "to work as a part
of my team, essentially as my architects." **He was counting
on you being young and hungry?** That's right, exactly.
Whilst other consultant's offices are located in London and
they can cross the Channel easily, OMA preferred consultants
full time in Rotterdam. Of course we said we'd parachute
in and stay there, and Rem said he'd consider it. And that
was that. We left thinking it was basically a coin toss. Two
weeks later we got a phone call saying we'd got the contract
and they needed someone in Rotterdam right away.

**What role did Front play in the Seattle Public Library
project?** That's really a question that should be directed
to Marc, because it predates my involvement. However,
it was an incredibly involved process concerning the development of aluminum mesh glass. I believe Josh and Marc
designed that together, and it came out of the building's
structural framework. At that time, the structure was a
diagrid of steel profiles. Because of the faceted geometry of
the different planes, it wasn't clear how one could strengthen
the building in certain areas to allow for massive spans
over some of those big halls and inclined and overhanging
planes. And that turned out to become a structural map
of sorts. The steelwork was doubled up where it needed to
be strengthened and then just truncated at the edge of
the zone. The facade was originally an orthogonal pattern,
laid on top of the diagrid, so there was a mismatch. And
Marc and Josh came up with the idea to rotate the facade
onto that diagrid, to collapse the skin together and to
insert a brise-soleil layer within the glass. ↘71, 174 A:1, 264 A:2

**In a lot of OMA's earlier work, there seemed to be
a link to Koolhaas's analysis of highrises in *Delirious***

New York, **where he comments on the disconnect
between the facades of those buildings and what
goes on inside. So in some of his early works the
section of the building is the facade. Then I
remember seeing the submission for the Seattle
Library project and thinking that there was a distinct
move away from that in the office. But maybe it's
just an evolution of the original thesis, where you
have these programmatic pieces that are now
wrapped in a skin, and it's done in such a way that
the skin can pull away to create spaces between
programmatic boxes. It's a different approach,
a different kind of facade. The mesh provided that,
I think—it became structural and spatial...** The forms
of Seattle Library and Casa da Música in Porto appear
largely generated by their program. But in-between spaces
are allowed as mixing zones between the programmatic
parts and the skin of the building. I think this is one of OMA's
theses in development. My reading of Seattle Library, in
particular, is of a very intelligent organization of program,
and collapsing the skin allowed it to wrap whatever shape
the architecture generated. It allowed them to build the
unusual forms that you can see in their work since then.
**I would call it not a curtain wall, but a curtain space,
because now it really pulls away from some of the
programmatic chunks...** OMA has departed from the
conventional curtain wall idea. It's certainly not something
Rem was interested in for CCTV. He wants to allow a reading
of the building in the facade imbued with integrity in that
it's not a stacked series of volumes wrapped in the dumbest
way but a more honest and provocative articulation. That's
what's common to the Seattle Library and the CCTV
Headquarters. The structure is expressed on the outside
↘105 A:1, 154 A:1
of the building; the facade is a contour map of the stresses
and forces in the structure. That's both interesting and
unique. **There seems to be a fixation on looping
in all these projects.** Do you mean the circulation or
the arrangement of spaces? **Both. It starts to be a
critique against the highrise as a kind of optimized,
late-capitalist structure, looping together rather
than segregating and controlling. Is OMA maybe
attempting to make explicit something that's
normally suppressed or hidden? That planning
strategy, it seems to me, makes a volume out of
circulation. The building's use generates the form
in a volumetric way. Definitely in Porto, that's
the case.** That's evident in some of the models OMA has
produced—beautiful diagrammatic design models where
they just express the pedestrian circulation within the
building, in a bright orange color, and then wrap that in
a clear skin so that you can see how the spaces are

organized and how people move through the building. Because CCTV is a series of studios and production suites in combination with a planned tour through the building—the public goes up one tower, across the top floors and then down the other tower—circulation is one generator of the building's form.

How was Rotterdam? What was it like working there? It was different from our experience with other clients, though for me personally it was pretty straight-forward. I'd just come from RPBW in Paris, where activity was very much about testing the design and details through models. The model shop enjoys a street frontage and the architects sit behind it, out of sight. I was used to working closely with model-makers at every stage of the design process, but at RPBW none of the architects are allowed to work on the models directly, because the Workshop is an industrial environment with professional craftsmen. Also, Paris is one of those cities with a tradition of skilled tradesmen. You must be a *maquetiste* to use any of the tools. If you push the *maquetistes* too hard, they'll go on strike [laughter], so we sometimes needed someone to mediate between them and the architects.

I was an architect on the team responsible for the facades of the New York Times Building. Facade work was a default specialization in my career. At Polshek Partnership, where I had been just prior to working at RPBW, I had always worked on facades, including the renovation of Smith College in Massachusetts. There we designed a curtain wall with brises-soleil; a series of horizontal tubes held out on armatures to provide solar-shading for perimeter art studios. RPBW's New York Times Building was for me an evolution of that idea.

The facade was always a part of the building that interested me. When you are particularly experienced in one aspect of architecture you become more useful to an office and so I was seen as a "facade guy." After Gehry declined the New York Times Building and RPBW was awarded the commission, a colleague at Polshek who had previously worked with Renzo was asked to go back to join that project team. RPBW needed another person with facade experience, so they interviewed me here in New York and invited me. I went right away. It was an easy transition, returning to Europe, and because the facade concept was a double skin similar to that of Smith College—except that it was over 52 stories instead 4.

How would you describe the difference between that system and the one on CCTV in Beijing? Well, it's comparable, but more articulated—and our strategy was a bit more direct. **But the relationship of the wall to the rest of the building is very different, isn't it? Piano's facades indicate a narrative about how the thing was constructed, a kind of didactic exhibition of the curtain wall, whereas the CCTV project seems almost to be a spatial cloak that responds directly to program, pulling away and laminating onto program. Spatially, it's very different, isn't it?** Spatially it's quite different, the collapsing of the system in CCTV has more to do with the way that the structure is expressed, and I would say that CCTV is didactic with respect to its structural engineering rather than the facade. So those two things become integrated ostensibly, even though the process wasn't as straightforward as that.

As someone who has worked in both Piano's and Koolhaas's offices, do you think there is a political difference in their respective approaches to architecture? Clearly there is quite a difference politically. For instance, with the New York Times Building Renzo was concerned with undermining the typical concept of the highrise curtain wall, which renders the building anonymous, as if it were wearing dark sunglasses. So he rejected the idea of a tinted glass curtain wall like those you see throughout New York City. He wanted a clear skin, so that the activity within the building was open and transparent to the public. It's not cynical architecture. **Transparency equals honesty?** I don't want to over-simplify, but it's a kind of socialism. Honesty, lightness… He wanted his architecture to engender joy. Looking around New York, by contrast, and seeing the modern highrises that are going up, they can seem quite sinister. **What about them seems ominous to you?** Well, they're opaque and closed. They reflect only their surroundings. **Isn't that partly the architectural legacy of (Rudy) Giuliani–era New York? Economically efficient, developer-driven buildings with big tax breaks?** That's true, but I think it has much more to do with the bottom line, developer approach. It involves the way facade technology has evolved to solve certain problems for the least amount of money. Tinted glass and various treatments applied to curtain walls are the direct manifestation of that technology as it has evolved in North America. Now, it's developed in different ways in Europe. It would be nice to think that was because there's a more inherent socialism and that the people are more open, but of course it's not. It's also that the design is governed less by capital cost. There's stricter government regulation, and you have a certain energy-saving conscious-ness that encourages clearer facades and so forth. Those kinds of rules are in some form or another finally being implemented in North America too. It's just taken longer. One reason is that energy has always been more expensive

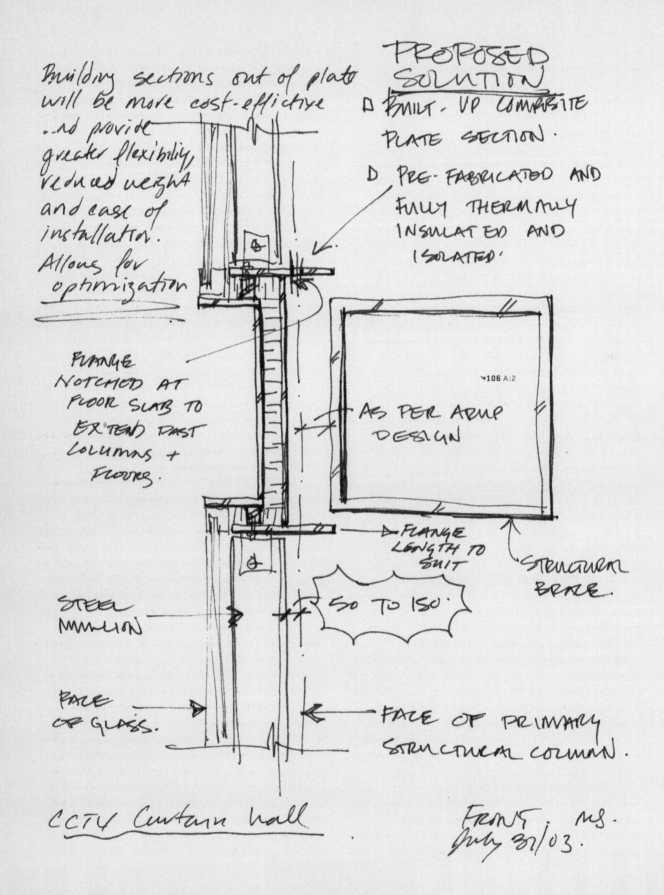

Building sections out of plate will be more cost-effective and provide greater flexibility, reduced weight and ease of installation. Allows for optimization

FLANGE NOTCHED AT FLOOR SLAB TO EXTEND PAST COLUMNS + FLOORS.

PROPOSED SOLUTION

▷ BUILT-UP COMPOSITE PLATE SECTION.

▷ PRE-FABRICATED AND FULLY THERMALLY INSULATED AND ISOLATED.

↘106 A:2

AS PER ARUP DESIGN

▷ FLANGE LENGTH TO SUIT

STRUCTURAL BRACE.

STEEL MULLION

50 TO 150.

FACE OF GLASS.

FACE OF PRIMARY STRUCTURAL COLUMN.

CCTV Curtain Wall

FRONT. MS.
July 31/03.

in Europe. Until the price of energy reaches untenable levels here too, there will always be a certain amount of reluctance. People won't care enough about the quality of workspace until they can't afford to pay for the oil.

A more critical reading of Piano's work could be that it's an extension of a machine-age fascination with componentry and the heroics of technology. What do you think? It loops very neatly back to the work of Jean Prouvé. Renzo comes from that generation; his father and grandfather were builders. He has a life-long concern with how things are put together, with finding the most efficient way to construct, perhaps to prefabricate and bring building elements to site, about pragmatics.

One of the most interesting things about how he treated the Times Building was the way RPBW zeroed in on essential details. Particular characteristics of the design were really precious to them. One was visibility through the facade, and the way that would express structure. Another concerned the placement of the building core. Since exterior fire-escape stairs are such a strong and interesting part of the vernacular architecture of New York City, RPBW wanted to express the stairs and pull the core to the perimeter of the floor plan. For reasons of efficiency we couldn't retain an asymmetrical core, but we did position staircases at the corners. Another element was terracotta. He fought very hard for this material. We had to convince the client that New York is traditionally a terra-cotta city. In fact, we had to go back to first principles and really prove why terracotta was a suitable exterior facade material. Traditionally, it was used as fireproofing for cast-iron buildings, (some of which were prefabricated and sold through catalogs), so we went back and did a little research to show where and how it was historically used in places like SoHo. **How did you prove it?** We talked to brick manufacturers, people who'd been in the industry for decades. Through research we had to find a suitable terracotta material and found several good European ter-racotta facade system fabricators. **The terracotta industry is almost extinct in the United States as an artisanal practice.** That's right, and that's a good description. We didn't want to make a facade that was too slick and precisely fabricated, as a modular unitized system with which to clad the structure. It wasn't about that. It had to be something people worked on by hand. It needed to be a tactile material that wasn't too perfect. So we researched different terracotta manufacturers all over the world, comparing the way they made their products and the differences between the materials. These tubes or brises-soleil became known in the office as baguettes, which is something that happens a lot in Renzo's office—calling materials and components by food names.

Terracotta literally means "fired earth," so brick is a basic terracotta building component. But the way you make them varies depending on the way they're fired and glazed. Also, the clay used can be a very fine aggregate, or it can be quite rough and therefore exhibit different structural qualities. We had developed a five-foot-long module with an inch and a half diameter for the rods, spaced to give 50 percent opacity. We started by alternating a one-inch rod and a one-inch space. That spacing was increased to allow for eye-level vision zones, and it became more sophisticated with subtle variation as work progressed. But by and large this became the modular grid, so we had to find a fabricator who could achieve the span with a sufficiently strong product. Eventually we discovered something off the shelf: a kind of terracotta used as rollers in kilns that have a six-foot-wide mouth, and which already happened to be an inch and a half in diameter. We found a fabricator of those units and used that as the benchmark against which companies were invited to tender.

Do you think hands-on, artisanal crafts are relevant in architecture now? Yes, I think so. After all, we're still human, and we respond to our built environment in the same basic ways. **But how can it be made more relevant in a day-to-day way, or in a non-exalted architecture?** Well, I think the Times Building is an example. **But the New York Times is a rarefied client, and that was a very high-end project. Most projects aren't going to have the budget for that level of commitment to craft.** Well, it is and it isn't. It's high-end in that it's the headquarters for a major corporation and its end-user is an elite professional group. But the importance of the craft was also aimed at a wider audience. Again, there is something of an Italian tradition there. What is inspiring to me about some Italian cities is that when times are good, those cities invest heavily in their urban fabric and infrastructure. There is a sense of public munificence. Perhaps the same could be said about Guiliani-era New York. It was a good time economically for the city, and perhaps when times are bad, there will still be a residual benefit for everyone.

That sensibility is something that Renzo is clearly cognizant of. His projects are often about public spaces, about giving people routes through the architecture and allowing them to enjoy the buildings from the outside, even if they're not a part of the elite that get to use them. The Times Building has a lowrise podium, which serves as a plinth for public use. It has a courtyard that you can see from the street, which is a place to stop and dwell and enjoy. It's a passage from one street to another that's articulated through the architecture, and I think the crafts-based approach speaks to that.

How is this consideration for the way things are made brought out in OMA's work? Or is it? Very much so. More and more we see that. It has to do with OMA's recent experience in North America and, following that, in Asia. **By North America do you mean Seattle?** Following the stalled Los Angeles County Museum of Art (LACMA) project and the now-shelved Whitney Museum project, OMA re-centered its energies on Asia and the Middle East. Disillusioned perhaps with North America, they turned their focus on China, and there the industry is a lot more crafts-based and less risk averse. China is gaining ground quickly in terms of industrial sophistication, but there is still an emphasis on crafts in construction. One project we collaborated on with OMA is the Beijing Books Building (since discontinued), a very large building that's part renovation and part new construction. It occupies a city block and is eight stories high. It has three tenants: one is a steel company, one a bank, and the other is a book retailer. OMA gained the commission through an invited competition, and their winning entry shows the whole of the new building clad in glass blocks of a huge scale—one meter wide by half a meter tall by a half a meter deep. That's a product that doesn't exist yet. It has to be cast, which is very labor intensive. As with many projects in China there's a condition that components be made domestically. In our work we look globally to source materials and build on our own knowledge base. **Reverse engineering?** What we do is develop our knowledge base considering what is the best practice in each project locale. We engage with industry either through a joint venture or directly with domestic fabricators, and collaborate in design engineering. **Outsourcing?** It's actually in-sourcing, but yes, that's what we've done.

We were speaking earlier about starting a practice. Front's start, it seems, is pretty unique, in part because of the scale of work you do. Most young firms start with kitchen renovation and gradually work their way up to residences and then hopefully to winning competitions. But you guys entered the fray through consultancy. Was that a conscious strategy? Yes, it was. It was necessary for us to position ourselves in a highly competitive environment, and although we're a young firm, we're not that young ourselves. Most architects set up new firms with one or two partners and a lot of younger people who form a sort of pyramidal hierarchy, but we came together as five partners, hiring and training individuals. Everybody told us that an inverted pyramid would never work. But it was important to us. Not everyone can position themselves in the way we did—a small team with extensive collective experience. So in taking on a variety of projects, we had flexibility in representation.

Each project team had a strong knowledge base because we weren't delegating work to other people, we were carrying it out ourselves. **It's oddly both efficient and inefficient.** Yes. **It's efficient in the sense that not everybody has to go to every meeting, whereas if you have two partners, often both attend meetings and both negotiate. But it's inefficient in the sense that all those billable hours can't be relegated to more junior people. All of those hours that the partners take on should be premium billable hours in a traditional office, but obviously with you they're not.** You're right, and over the past three years we've begun to change the structure of the firm through natural growth. As the work has developed and as we've strengthened the structural engineering side of our operation, we have hired staff. We started with the 5 of us, but we've followed a consistent growth curve to become an office of 35 people, including technical and administrative staff.

Each of the three partners now has a studio that executes its own projects within the firm. Through this managed growth, the partners are able both to pursue projects that comprise their desired portfolio, and to delegate activities within teams. For instance, Marc and Mike (Ra) have each established separate entities related to the development of procurement enterprises.

How many hours a week do you work, typically? Probably eight to ten hours a day, seven days a week. We each work our own hours, according to our own rhythms, but right now everybody works seven straight days. We try to pace ourselves so we're not staying up all night and then spending two days recovering. But a lot of the time, we're traveling; if you're on the road it doesn't matter what day of the week it is or which time zone you're in.

Has Front's role as consultant changed or expanded since you started? By recognizing opportunities to add value to projects we continue to develop our skills and offer a comprehensive and complementary range of services that are tailored to our client's needs. Along with a broad minded approach to hiring and training staff and our belief in innovation, our role has evolved as a protean, creative member of the collective design team. But I think we're also maturing into a known and hopefully respected entity, so that—through the development of our website, public speaking engagements, and publications—we've become less of an enigma and more of a participant in shaping contemporary architectural practice.

How have the day-to-day operations of the office been affected? Naturally, there is a substantial amount of traveling and multiple meetings within our now much larger space. More of the administrative work is done by dedicated business management and financial staff. Technical training and professional development takes the form of in-house classes and presentations that ensure the dissemination of valuable knowledge and experience, and raises our collective IQ. We're interested in establishing a laboratory environment that engages the smartest people, technology, and appropriate tools with which we hope to generate projects from the bottom up.

And this ties into how you'd like to see Front evolve? It does. We intend to take on more project scope in the future. We're all qualified engineers and architects, so we would like to generate building designs and participate more in the development and construction phases. The work we do and the way we work broadens our skill set and level of involvement in design and construction processes; and it allows us to provide a seamless delivery of services. Ultimately, through participation in shaping the way buildings will be made in the future, we hope to instigate projects of our own authorship and ownership.

One way we're developing currently involves formalizing the work we already do, such as developing custom building components through industry collaboration and seeing systems fabricated and installed on projects. We'd like to develop components that are, to use the cliché, "mass-customized" engineered products for which there is evident demand. We can enable procurement through sourcing and fabrication and intelligent cost control to satisfy the needs of the client, whether they be developer, architect, whomever…

Whether it was (Rudolph) Schindler's light framing details or (Walter) Gropius and (Marcel) Breuer's prefab experiments, a lot of the modernist masters were interested in creating systems or components that would be mass-producible and made available to a mass-market. But none of them really worked out. What do you think you could offer that is different from their attempts, and ultimately their failure, to bring to market a lot of these experiments? Why do you think you could do it successfully? Well, we're not trying to reinvent the wheel. Finally we're seeing the advent of good quality, modern prefab housing, at least 80 years after the Werkbund advocated this kind of thinking. The products we develop owe more to innovation than invention. We work in a lineage of alternate technologies, transfer technologies, or technologies that are already used in the building industry but aren't manifest in products

that architects can specify. That may be due in part to geographical circumstance.

As you know there are certain products available elsewhere, for instance in the European market, that aren't sold here. Frequently architects ask us for a particular product or system they've seen, perhaps on a building overseas, that they'd really like to have here. The majority of our projects have tight budgets; nevertheless there is a growing demand for this kind of thing. How do you facilitate that in a smart way? Well, you must understand the characteristics of each product. How to put it together in an affordable way, how to improve on it—this may be where innovation comes in: how do you engineer it in a slightly different way and perhaps make it from another material or with another production technique? How do you grade it thermally if isn't already? How do you increase the span or put a different coating on it? How do you make it curved instead of straight? After you improve it, you have to fabricate it and deliver it to architects, owners, and contractors.

How has the work developed? Gradually we are establishing a collective track record of built work and refining our role accordingly. As the domestic and international construction markets fluctuate, we focus on project types and locations that suit our aspirations. Most projects result from referrals, and several clients and collaborators return to invite further proposals for new projects.

How many active jobs do you have? How many are in the United States? We have, let's say 25 active jobs at the moment, and 20 of them are in the States. We are trying to do more and more work in the US, because we're trying to travel less. Obviously, we have some key projects in Asia. You mentioned outsourcing before, and it factors in our work. We look to Asian fabricators, because they offer comparable products to those made in the West, but often considerably cheaper. Glass engineering and fabrication in Asia now is on par with Europe. It's become highly sophisticated. Chinese companies set up manufacturing plants and equip them with machinery from Italy and Spain, which is state of the art. They hire factory managers and engineers from the best international companies to gain the necessary expertise. Then by training local people and shipping globally they're able to compete.

Can we talk about your background? You told us before you're from Newcastle. Have you always known you wanted to be an architect? Newcastle is an old shipbuilding city and a coal mining area in the UK. The environment I grew up in was one of manufacturing industry. That was my background. I went to a comprehensive school, an academic and vocational secondary school in Britain. It had metal shop, wood shop, technical drawing, all of which I was terrible at. In fact, I never managed to make anything successfully in any of the shops, and when I sat my final examination for technical drawing I wouldn't use the instruments, I did everything freehand and the faculty didn't give me a grade. I was always interested in art. That was really what lead me to architecture; the desire to work in art and design. I managed to get into college with a decent portfolio; I had studied art and art history and could draw, photograph, make prints, and paint, but I decided that architectural design was a good profession. **Did you think it was a "responsible art"?**…A compelling combination of making and improving the environment. So I went to Oxford Polytechnic, which had a school of architecture offering a multifaceted, practical education. I spent my postgraduate thesis year at Virginia Tech, just outside of Washington DC, where I studied with others on overseas scholarships and worked in DC practices. After masters graduation and gaining licensure, Britain was entering (Margaret) Thatcher's fourth term of government, so I left the country.

Speaking of politics, CCTV, the media building in Beijing, is part of a very different kind of political machine, one that creates opinion in a very slanted way, some would say. Is that something your firm talked about before taking on the job? Can you justify it by saying that you're trying to bring about change from within? Well, I would not delude myself and say we're here to effect change from within, because we're too small and inconsequential for that. Not that I abdicate responsibility for what we do. We strive to be responsible to those who hire us. So long as we feel we were hired for the right reasons, we will effect change in a modest way on each particular project. And often that has to do with procurement, assisting in providing work to people who can do it well for the best price in a global market place. **Are you saying that being a good consumer is a key part of this?** I think it's important as a contemporary practitioner of design, yes.

What are the prospects for US production and fabrication? US construction manufacturing has to pull itself up by the bootstraps. It's industry-specific. The focus of US production is on the military and scientific sectors because that currently attracts the most investment. Until architecture and engineering come to grips with industrial fabrication, as exemplified by automotive and aerospace manufacturing, it will continue to fall behind Europe, and

in a short space of time Asia as well. So it's incumbent upon us, within our own industry, to try to effect change. **Which firms are doing that now, if any?** Many, including Gehry Partners, Kieran Timberlake, and a number of other practices, and several very smart contractors and fabricators. **By being essentially a lean architecture and engineering firm, are you attempting to make things more directly connected to leaner production?** Front is not a corporate multidisciplinary firm offering structural, mechanical, fire, and transport engineering. It's a completely different entity. We are able to offer a seamless process from concept design through project completion in which an idea evolves into a digital model that becomes the data from which components are directly manufactured, assembled, and constructed.

What's the ideal office size for Front? It's vital that we remain a studio environment without opaque layers of management. We want to maintain transparency and openness in the office, from a management perspective, and yet still be able to execute sizable projects. When we're working with multiple consultants on large projects we often find inefficiencies in scope delineation. Controlling liability is such an imperative in this industry, and it results in paranoia when the primary concern is limitation of risk rather than optimal design. There's just no benefit for an engineer in the United States to experiment unless that's the owner's desire, which is relatively rare.

Is Front one of those firms willing to take a chance? We are. We're enthusiastic about innovation without exposing anyone to risk. By employing the best methods, tools, and practices we believe we can reduce risk and simultaneously streamline the design-to-construction experience. And good working relationships are also a part of that. The problem is that the industry in this country is mired in litigation or else in fear of being so. And we've got to move away from that, because it creates a defensive position and lack of trust. In fact, a lot of people enter into contracts thinking they can exploit that situation—for example, through change orders, delays, and so on. And that's a horrible way to enter into a relationship. By taking on more risk responsibly, we're able to facilitate more productive working relationships from the start. We've been fortunate to develop strong relationships with industry partners, resulting in improved communication and a streamlined exchange of ideas.

It's amazing how the idea of America as a powerhouse-of-making has changed. Europe has always been known for turning cutting-edge materials into

quality product. **And as you say, Asia is becoming more and more respected for doing so. Is there any way to put a positive spin on what's happening in the United States?** It's inappropriate for the United States to revert to a European or Asian model. What I mean is there's a design-build environment in those places where a certain kind of enlightened collusion is possible. There's less of a defensive stance taken by designers, engineers, consultants, and contractors. What America can do is improve the means and methods of its fabrication and construction. They just have to short circuit the process. If everyone were to give their input at the correct stage of the design process, it would limit the double or triple handling. Our practice is to get the necessary parties involved earlier in the process and work together. It's kind of a design-build framework, but it's not only directed at problem solving. Sometimes we focus on quite abstract or experimental aspects of the design.

Paul Seletsky of SOM (Skidmore, Owings & Merrill) talks about how a new way of working on building projects is evolving, and it's something owners and architects are going to have to live with. Do you think architects are gaining more power over the building process from the computer? Can they? I think architects have gradually forfeited control because we were scared of such responsibility. I agree with the premise of regaining certain controls through the use of smart tools and processes. It has to do with taking on a project as a cohesive, seamless sequence, and computers can facilitate this with the collaboration of the entire project team. It's a reinterpretation of a modernist tenet.

↳32 A:1

How would you define master builder? Or is the term irrelevant now? I'd say it's the considered understanding of all aspects of how design, manufacturing, and construction together inform a building. It requires a clear lens of the implications of what you design and the ability to bring those designs to fruition in a deliberate and informed way. **But shouldn't we also call it *master navigator*? We find that a lot of our work is about navigating through all the hoops and problems particular projects present. It's an architecture of execution, and above all persistence. The amount of work that goes into shepherding a project is at least as much as designing it.** That's where the relevance of the word *master* comes from. It describes a central figure that has an overview, skill, and wisdom. **But specialization pays more, and you're able to manage that workload with a fairly small staff. Are your tasks as a partner more limited, do you have fewer tasks to do the way you've set up the office?** Specialization does not pay

more, but it does allow involvement in a greater number of projects. In a small firm one has more tasks to do, including all aspects of consultancy, which must be delegated. Everything from putting together proposals and contract negotiation, through to running Xeroxes and delivering reports. We're basically hands-on at each stage. As you mentioned, it's not ideal in some ways since it does not optimize billable hours and so forth, but we don't have sufficient staff yet to delegate. We tend to charrette on projects. Usually, two partners are involved on each job to provide peer review, but we're also chasing down invoices, booking flights, talking to clients. It enables a clearer overview of the process, and to increase our knowledge of all aspects of the project such as structural engineering, material research, fabrication... I'd like to have more time to visit factories, to spend more time on site and in the model shop, doing all the things that I think are integral to our job.

Being on site is the acid test. It's where you most clearly appreciate everyone else's input. You gain a valuable appreciation of what it takes to construct a building well. If you return years later and you see that the occupants have made alterations, you have to look hard at what you did and assess whether or not you failed. What really puts me off is the pornography of architectural publications, where buildings are depicted as perfect products. That kind of imagery is the work of the master art director... It's dishonest and boring and such rubbish.

What are some of your biggest failings? Not doing enough of what I just described. Not being diverse enough in developing a broader range of skills, and getting too focused on certain things to the exclusion of others. I left the UK without traveling in Europe as much as I should have. There is a fantastic wealth of architecture in the cities of Europe and this is the point of departure in an architectural education. One omission that I would still like to address that I've never physically made a building. I've worked on site a little, assisting contractors, but I would like to construct a building. I don't have any carpentry or metal-working skills and I think a better understanding of those trades would be invaluable. During architectural education in the UK, one does a three-year undergraduate degree, one year in industry, and a three-year postgraduate degree (plus a minimum of one year to become licensed). I think instead of spending the entire fourth year in an architectural office, I should have also worked on a construction site and gained pragmatic construction experience.

It seems that the idea of going back to the source and to how things are made is a relatively recent development in architectural practice. Or rather, new

technology has facilitated reconnection with an idea that's very old, at the foundation of architecture. It's the origin of the subject, and that's where the term *master builder* comes from. The architect is master builder because the first architects that came to the site were stonemasons; they were the individuals skilled in the craft of fitting stone structures together.

Even after the emergence of architecture as a profession, the architect made a limited number of drawings, a limited number of details, and handed them over to the builders and craftsmen. There was a tacit understanding between the architect and people that built it... It is sad that that tradition has gone. I don't think it will entirely come back. There's a very different way of working now between so-called professionals and the people who make things... However, we can try to regain that understanding in new and better ways.

Interview with Bruce Nichol of Front was conducted in New York City in 2005 by Jon Dreyfous, Elite Kedan, and Craig Mutter and was continued by email in late 2008.

3 Degrees of Felt
Aztec Empire Exhibition
Guggenheim Museum
MY Studio/Meejin Yoon
with Enrique Norten/
TEN Arquitectos

We were asked to collaborate on the
exhibition design by Enrique Norten
of TEN Arquitectos, who was commissioned to design the exhibition
for artifacts from the Aztec Empire.
The desire was to create a singular
but non-uniform experience through
a material intervention that could
mediate between the artifact,
viewer, and space. Since there were
over 450 objects from the Aztec
Empire the challenge was twofold:
first, how to accommodate over
450 objects of varying scales and
requirements, and second, how to
operate within Frank Lloyd Wright's
unique architectural proposition.
In studying the collection of artifacts
and the space of the museum, we
learned that the all the objects
would not fit along the circumference
of the ramp space in the rotunda. In
order to accommodate the enormous
quantity of artifacts, we began to
undulate the wall, folding in and
out of the bays to expand the linear
square footage of the display by
approximately 1.5.

This ribbon wall was then
slit at various heights bending and
peeling away to create the display
for the museum artifacts. Creating
a continuous experience along the
ramp and focusing on the experience
of the perimeter and periphery, as
opposed to the center, the project
creates a smooth non-uniform display
system that organizes the artifacts
at their appropriate scales. (over)

1

2

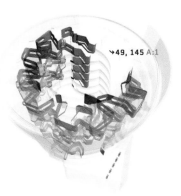

→49, 145 A:1

3 Degrees of Felt
MY Studio/Meejin Yoon
with Enrique Norten/
TEN Arquitectos

We began by defining a series
of "pocket parameters" by which
information assigned to each object
would generate the ins and outs
of the walls. A series of plug-ins and
scripts were written by Stylianos
Dritsas, from MIT, to test a low-tech
parametric generative design process
without using high-end parametric
software. Each of the objects was
modeled in Rhino and linked
to a definition that contained the
information on how to build its
pocket. Once the definitions are
assigned, a script generates the
continuous walls in space to accommodate the objects. As objects are
rearranged, deleted, swapped out,
and redefined, the script allows it
to continuously regenerate itself into
a variable smooth surface.

↳49, 145 A:1, 179 A:3, 193 B:1

```
pocket=middle,a=3500,b=3900,c=1200
pocket=single,a=1400,b=5000,c=1800,d=-1.2
pocket=middle,a=600,b=3200,c=800,d=1,e=0
pocket=single,a=2200,b=5600,c=2200,d=-.5
pocket=single,a=2200,b=2600,c=2200,d=0
pocket=single,a=3000,b=5400,c=5500,d=-0.55
pocket=double,a=2600,b=2400,c=3
pocket=middle,a=600,b=2400,c=600
pocket=middle,a=1000,b=4200,c=-800
pocket=middle,a=800,b=3700,c=-800
pocket=middle,a=800,b=3200,c=-800
pocket=middle,a=800,b=4500,c=1200
pocket=single,a=1600,b=2500,c=1600,d=0
pocket=single,a=2000,b=3000,c=2200,d=-.4
pocket=single,a=1500,b=7400,c=3100,d=-.4
pocket=single,a=1500,b=4400,c=1600,d=-.4
pocket=middle,a=900,b=2200,c=600
pocket=middle,a=4800,b=2200,c=1200
pocket=single,a=2600,b=3600,c=2200,d=-.1
pocket=middle,a=4200,b=1800,c=600
pocket=single,a=1200,b=4000,c=1200,d=-.1
pocket=double,a=900,b=900,c=2200,d=-.1
pocket=middle,a=400,b=6200,c=800
pocket=double,a=2000,b=600,c=2200,d=-.1
pocket=single,a=900,b=1500,c=800,d=-.1
```

1

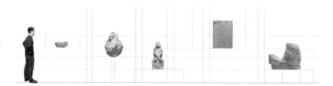

2

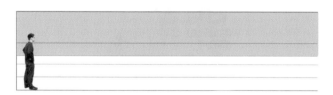

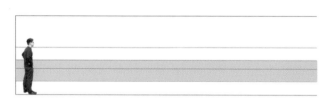

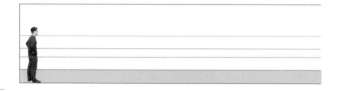

Arthouse at the Jones Center
Lewis.Tsurumaki.Lewis

Located in the heart of downtown Austin, this project is a renovation and expansion of an existing contemporary art space. We were commissioned to design 14,000 square feet of new program within the building envelope. The existing building is an idiosyncratic hybrid of a 1920s theater and a 1950s department store.

We sought to intensify this peculiar accumulation of history by conceiving of the design as a series of integrated tactical additions and adjustments (described in the exploded axonometric at right). These supplements revive and augment existing features—such as the 1920s trusses, concrete frame, and ornamental painting, as well as the 1950s awning, storefront, and upper-level display window. The design will also open the second floor and roof through new vertical circulation and, most importantly, efficiently add program spaces and objects.

The elevation is perforated by 162 laminated glass blocks. Aggregated where light is needed on the interior, these apertures unify the building and form a logical yet unconventional facade appropriate for an experimental art venue.

Avra Verde Residence
MARCH/Chris Hoxie consultant
Architect: Rick Joy Architects

Avra Verde is a speculative development of eight houses in the desert. We were brought in by Joy's office to virtually prototype the architecture in its natural setting. We used a special photographic technique called high dynamic range imaging (HDRI) that allows us to digitally simulate the site's particular light phenomena, including time of day, directionality, intensity, and color temperature.

Part of this process involves programming the camera to shoot a series of multiple-exposure light-probe images with a filter that cuts the intensity of the sun by a factor of one thousand, so that we can capture the dynamic range of the sun and sky.

This is the conversion algorithm that was used to unroll the spherical fisheye images into equirectangular, or landscape format, images so that the HDRI light probes can be viewed more conventionally.
↳50, 83, 147 A:1, 242–243

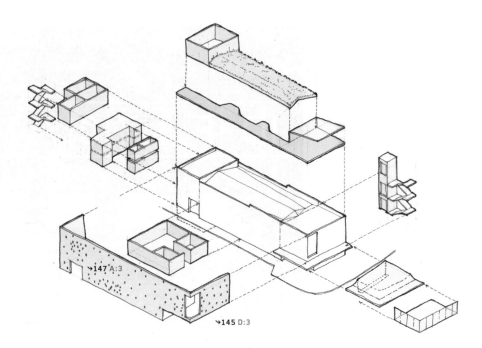

147 A:3

145 D:3

$$r = \frac{\sin\left(\frac{1}{2} \arccos(-D_z)\right)}{2\sqrt{D_x^2 + D_y^2}}$$

$$(u,v) = \left(\tfrac{1}{2} + rD_x, \tfrac{1}{2} - rD_y\right)$$

$$(u,v) = \left(1 + \tfrac{1}{\pi} \operatorname{atan2}(D_x, -D_z), \tfrac{1}{\pi} \arccos D_y\right)$$

1

2

Beijing National Stadium
Gehry Technologies consultant
Architect: Herzog & de Meuron

The most striking and complex feature of Herzog & de Meuron's stadium design is a double-curved roof "woven" of steel box girders in an elaborate truss arrangement. Understanding the geometric and constructional complexity of this system was fundamental to the project's success.

The project team built a parametric model in Gehry Technologies' Digital Project of the stadium roof, beginning from wireframe roof geometry, and subsequently building the box girder and connector element assemblies. Different methods for curving the steel geometry in 3D space were compared and evaluated in detail. The 3D model was reused to simplify the roof structure and reduce steel quantities. It enabled basic redesign in weeks and completion of the stadium on time.

Construction was facilitated by various classification systems which organized, at various scales, the many systems and components of this complex project.

↘150 A:1, 244–245

Bornhuetter Hall
The College of Wooster
Lewis.Tsurumaki.Lewis

This residence hall was configured by research performed on many levels. This spatial diagram is the product of resolving conflicting pressures. The college requested a single building not to exceed four floors. This required each floor to hold 46 students, yet we found the ideal hall unit should be limited to 25–30 students. To solve this dilemma, the building was split into two parts connected by an exterior courtyard. The existing site features—a parking lot and a pine grove—determined the different lengths of each portion of the building. Because the brick and glass skins of the building extend around the courtyard, the two residence halls appear to be a single building.

A collective outdoor courtyard is created by this split, and this exterior room functions as the public center of the building. It is an unusual space, containing both social and private spaces simultaneously, at the heart of the building and at the ends of each wing. It provides a sequence of entry into the building and a passage from the campus to the park beyond. ↘51, 131 A:33, 150 C:2

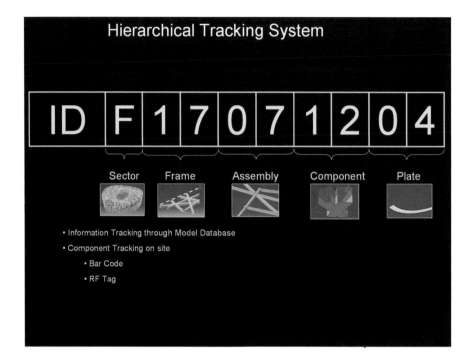

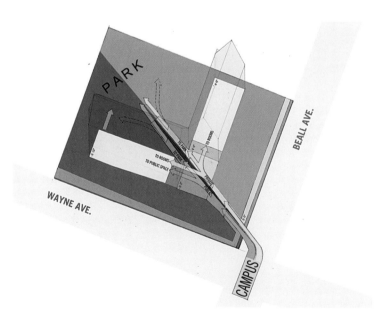

Camera Obscura
SHoP

Camera Obscura (Latin, "dark room") is one of four buildings designed for a waterfront park for the Village of Greenport on Long Island, NY. Through an optical lens and a mirror, a live image of the Camera's surroundings is projected down onto a flat, circular table that is raised or lowered to adjust focal depth.

The Camera Obscura was conceived as a research and development project that is small in size but not in scope. The goal was to construct a building entirely from digitally fabricated components. In the past, SHoP had utilized digital fabrication for individual trades, such as laser-cut metal panels or CNC (computer numerical control) millwork. For the first time, we brought together multiple processes, to test tolerance and coordination issues. Designed entirely as a 3D computer model, the construction of the Camera was communicated as a kit of custom parts accompanied by a set of instructions for assembling the components.

↪152 A:3, 198 A:1, 241

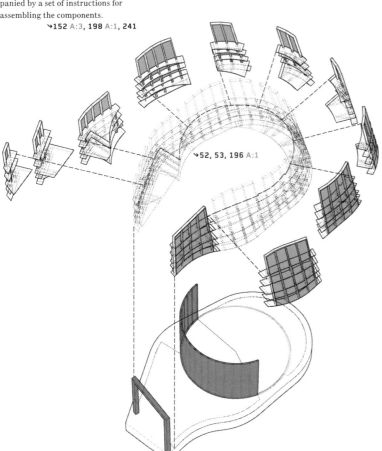

↪52, 53, 196 A:1

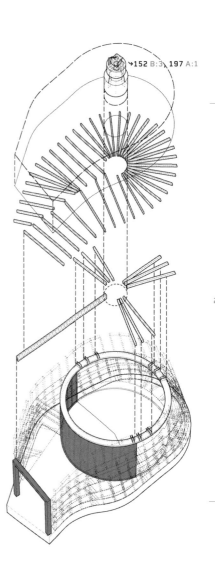

↪152 B:3, 197 A:1

1

2

Camera Obscura
SHoP

Construction matrix explaining
the assembly sequence of
components to fabricators and
contractors ↘198 A:1

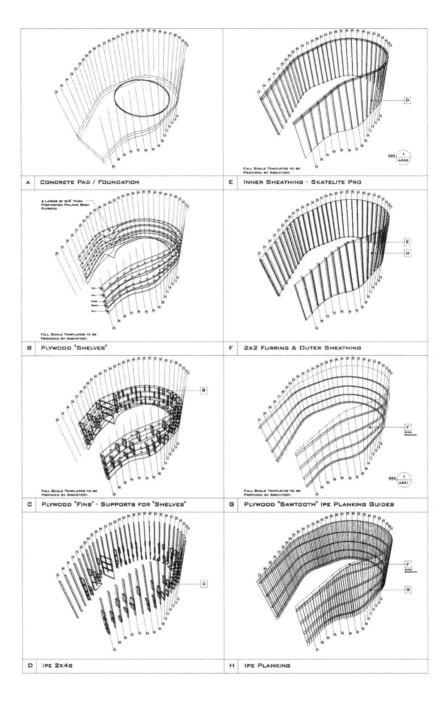

A CONCRETE PAD / FOUNDATION	E INNER SHEATHING - SKATELITE PRO
B PLYWOOD "SHELVES"	F 2X2 FURRING & OUTER SHEATHING
C PLYWOOD "FINS" - SUPPORTS FOR "SHELVES"	G PLYWOOD "SAWTOOTH" IPE PLANKING GUIDES
D IPE 2X4S	H IPE PLANKING

I	FLITCH BEAM	M	COMPRESSION RING
J	MOMENT FRAME	N	TENSION RING
K	2x6 IPE ROOF JOISTS	O	3x6 IPE COMPRESSION CHORDS
L	ZINC COPING, ROOF, SIDING + PIVOT DOOR	P	ROTATING METAL WALL

Canopy
MoMA/P.S.1 Contemporary
Art Center
nARCHITECTS

Canopy was a temporary structure built with green bamboo in the courtyard of P.S.1, a contemporary art and music venue whose weekly Warm Up music parties attract eight thousand revelers every Saturday in the summer. The weekday and Sunday audience is quieter: students, and families with children. Overall, Canopy was host to more than one hundred thousand visitors during its five-month existence, during which it underwent a transformation as the freshly cut bamboo turned from green to tan. This rapid trans-formation emphasized Canopy's brevity, allowing visitors to experience the effects of time in a direct and tactile way.

Our challenge resided in the physical construction of a geometrically precise structure, using a natural material with inherently variable characteristics. Every arc in Canopy was digitally modeled in 3D, then exported as a 2D elevation drawing, indicating length and points of intersection. The type, general shape, and critical radius of the arc dictated the pole selection, orientation, and splicing method. We and our team of students and recent graduates then spent six weeks on site testing each arc type to determine maximum span, minimum bending radii, and overlap dimensions, before building the structure over a period of seven weeks. The project utilized 9,400 meters of freshly cut *Phyllostachys aurea* bamboo from Georgia, spliced and bound together with 11,300 meters of stainless-steel wire.

A phasing sequence was devised to optimize the structural capabilities of bamboo and minimize break-ages. Starting with small areas of the canopy, the team erected structural spanning arcs first and non-supporting arcs second, repeating the sequence until the final shape developed.

At the end of the summer, nARCHITECTS sold the bamboo to the studio of the artist Matthew Barney, for the construction of scaffolding on a film set. Everyone assumed that the bamboo would have lost its elasticity after being molded into shape for so long; it was a surprise when it immedi-ately sprang back as soon as it was cut down.

ARC PROFILES

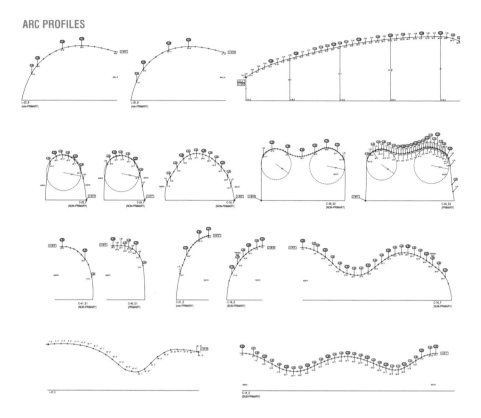

ERECTION SEQUENCE

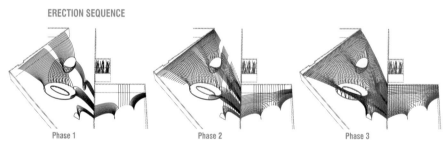

Phase 1   Phase 2   Phase 3

↗54–55, 153 A:3, 200–203

China Central Television
Headquarters (CCTV)
Front consultant
Architect: Office for Metropolitan
Architecture (OMA)

This project is meant to challenge
the notion of what a tall building can
be. Instead of competing in the
hopeless race for ultimate height—
dominance of the skyline can only
be achieved for a short period of
time, and soon another, even taller
building will emerge—the CCTV
project proposes an iconographic
constellation of a high-rise structure
that actively engages the city space.

CCTV combines administration
and offices, news and broadcasting,
program production, and services—
the entire process of TV-making—
in a loop of interconnected activities.
Two structures rise from a common
production platform that is partly
underground. Each has a different
character: one is dedicated to
broadcasting, the second to services,
research, and education; they join
at the top to create a cantilevered
penthouse for the management.
A new icon is formed—not the
predictable two-dimensional tower
"soaring" skyward, but a truly
three-dimensional experience,
a canopy that symbolically embraces
the entire population. The consol-
idation of the TV program in a single
building allows each worker to be
permanently aware of the nature of
the work of his coworkers—a chain
of interdependence that promotes
solidarity rather than isolation,
collaboration instead of opposition.
The building itself contributes
to the coherence of the organization.

The series of diagrams at right
tell a number of stories about
the behavior of the building's skin.
The top set of diagrams represents
the solar radiation performance
of the facade, while the middle
diagram represents the annual
cumulative solar gain performance
of the facade. The diagram at
bottom is the facade of the tower
unfolded. (over) ↘88 B:33, 154 A:1, 248

Summer Solstice
March 15th
最长日照时间

Mid-Solar Year
June 21st
平均日照时间

Winter Equinox
December 21st
最短日照时间

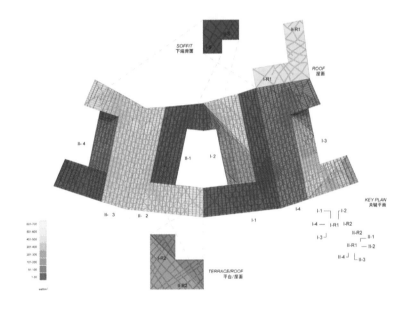

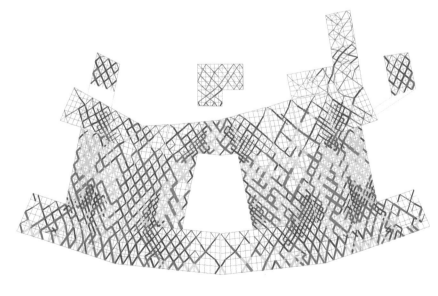

A

CCTV
Front consultant
Architect: OMA

While CCTV is a secured building for staff and technology, public visitors will be admitted to the "loop," a dedicated path circulating through the building and connecting to all elements of the program and offering spectacular views across the multiple facades toward the CBD (Central Business District), Beijing, and the Forbidden City."

1

The diagram to the right is a section through a portion of the facade's curtain wall system. The drawing below is a detail of the facade's diagrid cladding, referencing the drawing above.

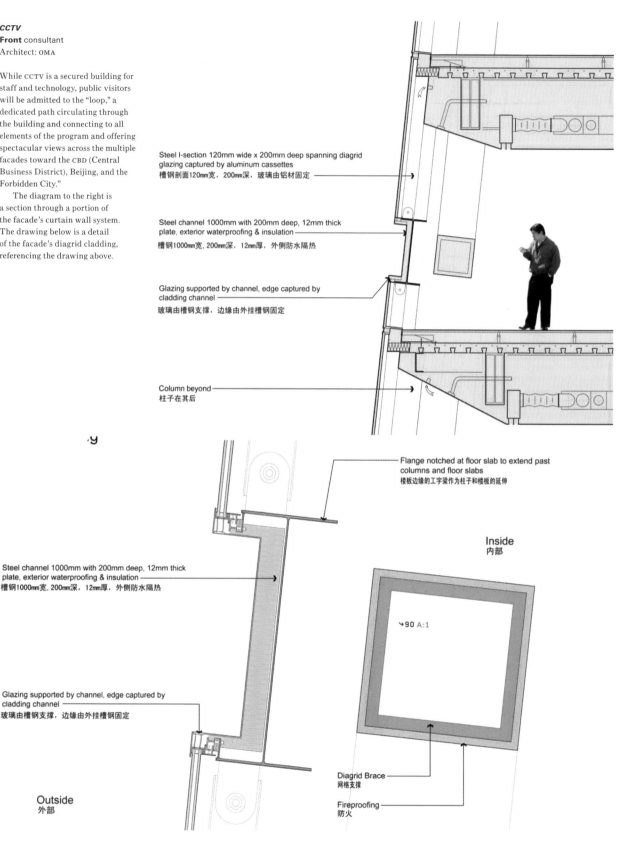

Steel I-section 120mm wide x 200mm deep spanning diagrid
glazing captured by aluminum cassettes
槽钢剖面120mm宽，200mm深，玻璃由铝材固定

Steel channel 1000mm with 200mm deep, 12mm thick
plate, exterior waterproofing & insulation
槽钢1000mm宽，200mm深，12mm厚，外侧防水隔热

Glazing supported by channel, edge captured by
cladding channel
玻璃由槽钢支撑，边缘由外挂槽钢固定

Column beyond
柱子在其后

Flange notched at floor slab to extend past
columns and floor slabs
楼板边缘的工字梁作为柱子和楼板的延伸

Inside
内部

Steel channel 1000mm with 200mm deep, 12mm thick
plate, exterior waterproofing & insulation
槽钢1000mm宽，200mm深，12mm厚，外侧防水隔热

→90 A:1

2

Glazing supported by channel, edge captured by
cladding channel
玻璃由槽钢支撑，边缘由外挂槽钢固定

Diagrid Brace
网格支撑

Fireproofing
防火

Outside
外部

D Gallery
Front consultant
Architect: Point B Design

Working initially as facade consultants to the architect, Front developed the design of the glazing system and steel portal frames with Point B using advanced parametric modeling tools to fully understand and control the sloped geometries of the roof and walls. After sourcing viable material suppliers and a capable custom fabricator, Front continued to collaborate in the design process as part of the contractor team, providing in-depth design engineering analysis (as in image below right) and detailed shop drawings to complete the steel frame–and-glass system design.

During fabrication and construction Front was active in coordination efforts between the architect and the fabricators, and made frequent factory visits for quality review. To demonstrate successful project coordination and to check the results of the design model-to-fabrication drawing process, Front arranged for a test assembly of the finished steel portal frames and glazing. The finished pieces were erected in a warehouse in China to show the US installers how the elements would fit together correctly, before they were carefully disassembled and shipped to the site.

Tools such as CATIA (computer-aided three-dimensional interactive application) were used (above) to visualize the dimensional constraints for the primary steel portal frames. The portal frames are governed by a consistent logic and are parametrically linked to the glazing system, allowing the CATIA model to automatically generate fabrication drawings.

↘155 A:2, 204 A:1, 249 A:1

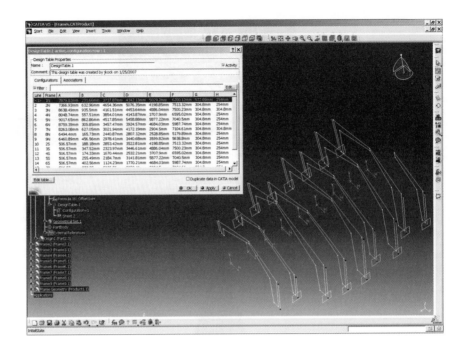

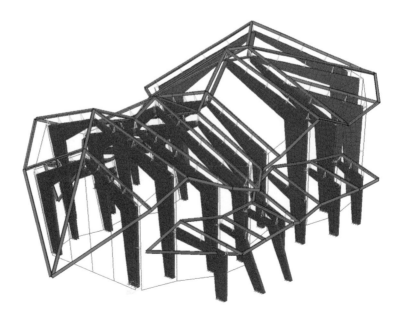

Dark Places
Exhibition at the Santa Monica Museum of Art
Servo

Our proposal for the Dark Places exhibition, curated by Joshua Decter and exhibited January 2006– May 2006, distributes 76 selected artworks through four woven together plastic strands, each containing different types of projections. There are a total of three environments formed as each strand torques into alignment with its neighbor. A large-format front projection "peels" off the outer perimeter of the gallery space; a collection of floating "cinematic objects," rear projected at head height, are grouped into two clusters in the space; and all biographical information about the artists is contained in four touch screens, rooted in the ground, shooting upward into the strands, where visitors (when investigating the artists' backgrounds) activate the system and stimulate lighting effects that span the space at large.

Components of this project included a vacuum-formed plastic infrastructure with a plastic-and-aluminum endoskeleton; twelve digitally formatted collections of artwork distributed through four touch screens, eight projectors and eight stereo systems; four rear projection units with a custom fabricated acrylic projection surface; as well as a fiber optic system linked to GUI (graphical user interface) touch screens via custom designed interaction software and hardware.

↘158 A:1, 208 A:1

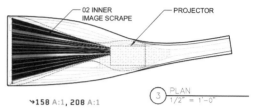

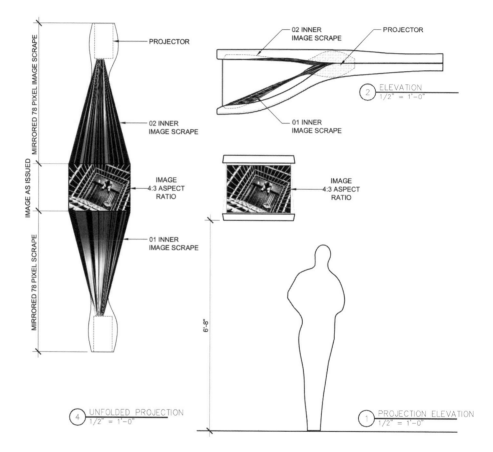

Dee and Charles Wyly Theater
Front consultant
Architect: REX/OMA

Imagining a new home for the
Dallas Theater Center posed
the challenge of creating a new
building that maintained the
provisional, flexible quality of an
innovative theater company with
a limited budget. The architects'
response was to reposition
traditional front-of-house and
back-of-house functions below-house
and above-house. This maneuver
redefines the traditional theater by
liberating the perimeter of the
theater's chamber to directly engage
the city around it. It also turns the
building into one large fly tower,
a "superfly" or "theater machine"
that eliminates the traditional distinction between stage and
auditorium. The resulting project
is a 575-seat multi-form theater with
the ability to take on proscenium,
thrust, traverse, arena, flat floor, and
black box configurations.

Clad in a facade composed
of six different aluminum
extrusions (at right), arranged in
different combinations this series
of varying shapes gives the facade
dimensional depth. With a series of
secondary components, the facade
allows for selected views from the
interior to the exterior, maintenance
access, and integrated signage
without detracting from this parti.
↳159 A:1, 214 A:1

TUBE EXTRUSION CAPS

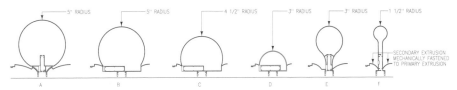

TUBE EXTRUSIONS

East River Waterfront
Master Plan
SHoP
with Richard Rogers Partnership
and Ken Smith Landscape Architect

Commissioned by the City of
New York to submit designs for
the revitalization of the East
River waterfront, this master plan
transforms a neglected, inaccessible
stretch of land into a renewed area
that will draw the city fabric to
the East River. The approach
is planning by evolutionary rather
than revolutionary measures. By
adding the new among the old, and
smaller public interventions into the
larger waterfront context, positive
change is in place to bring new
programs and uses for neighborhood
and citywide benefit.

This diagram shows the site
(indicated with dashed line) and its
connection to a continuous greenbelt
around the perimeter of Manhattan.
↳139, 140, 141 B:43, 159 A:3

Fluff Bakery
Lewis.Tsurumaki.Lewis

LTL's design for this 800-square-foot
bakery and coffee shop fuses a
highly efficient plan with an
expressive surface that cloaks the
walls and the ceiling. The plan
provides the required space for the
bakery and bathroom, maximizes
the number of seats by locating
booths in the storefront, and directs
take-away traffic to the center. The
storefront was recessed two feet
from the property line to allow the
entry to appear to extend into the
sidewalk. The attention of patrons
is drawn immediately to the walls
and ceiling, a robust surface made
from layers of common materials.
Almost 18,500 feet (more than
three miles) of ¾-by-¾-inch strips
of felt and stained plywood
were individually positioned and
anchored into place. The surface
performs in multiple ways:
as banquette back, as padding,
as acoustic damper, and as visual
seduction. The striking linear
pattern of the strips induces
a horizontal vertigo, which, when
seen through the glass storefront,
serves as a visual attractor
to pedestrians on the street. The
vitality of this architectural surface
becomes the shop's advertisement.

As a counterpoint to the exces-
sive linearity of the strips, a
custom stainless-steel chandelier,
composed of 42 dimmable linear
incandescent lights, branches across
the ceiling. The drawing at right
describes the ceiling layout of
the chandelier and maps out its
components. More akin to a gallery
installation, the interior surface
and the chandelier were built and
installed by LTL's staff.

↘60, 160 A:3, 254–255

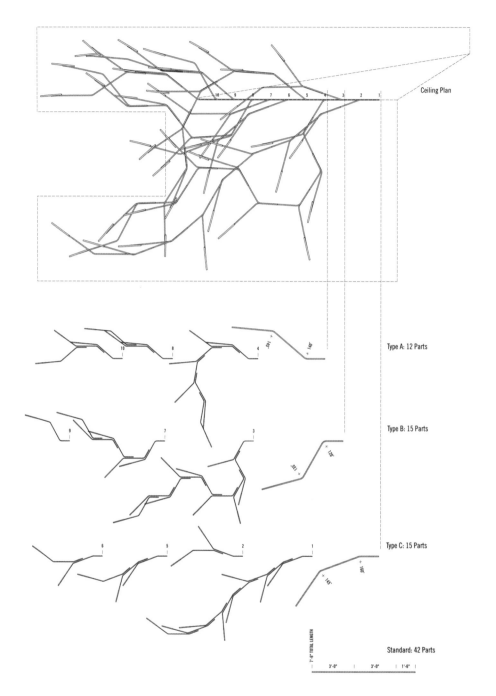

Ceiling Plan

Type A: 12 Parts

Type B: 15 Parts

Type C: 15 Parts

Standard: 42 Parts

FutureGen
Power Plant Prototypes
U.S. Department of Energy
MARCH/Chris Hoxie

We worked with the US DOE
to develop a new syntax for both
the architecture and equipment
layouts of future zero-emission
power plant prototypes. Both the
equipment technologies and the
corresponding architecture modules
were conceived as swappable
nodes that could be reconfigured
based on fuel source type and the
location of the power plant.
The architectural strategy for
these prototypes was threefold:
to develop an architectonic
language that can accommodate
a variety of power-generating
technologies; to have the architecture function in an analogous
modular fashion to the equipment
components; and to reconfigure
and rebrand the image of the
typology as a site-sensitive, envi-
ronmentally friendly infrastructure.
   This diagram is one of a series
of studies performed for each fuel
source technology, evaluating
various equipment specifications
and layout requirements. ↘61–63

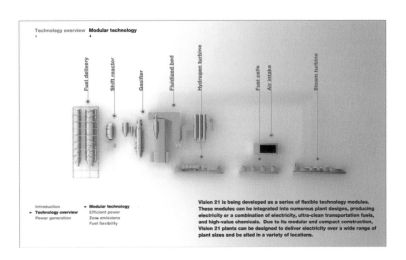

High Line 23
Front consultant
Architect: Neil M. Denari Architects
↘276 A:25

High Line 23 is a 14-floor condominium tower that responds to a
unique and challenging site directly
adjacent to the High Line at 23rd
Street in New York's West Chelsea
district. Partially impacted by the
elevated tracks that make up the
High Line superstructure, the site is
40 feet by 99 feet at the ground floor.
The client's concern was how to
expand the possible built floor area
of a restricted zoning envelope. The
site exacted a special geometry to
allow a larger building to stand in
very close proximity to the elevated
park of the High Line. Together, the
demands produced a building with
one unit per floor and three distinct
yet coherent facades.
   A pair of small fold-up coordination models (right) was produced by
Neil M. Denari Architects with a
digital Rhino model, but its purpose
was to provide an accessible version
of the building for consultants
not using 3D software. It played a
particularly useful role in conveying
the complexities of the building
to various consultants and potential
facade access contractors.

Honda Advanced Design Center
George Yu Architects

For Honda Research &
Development, we designed a new
Advanced Design Center in
Pasadena. A 6,000-square-foot
retail space on the ground floor of
a historic building in the Old Town
area was transformed into design
studios and conference rooms.
Honda's goal was to create a work
environment that would support
the team of ten concept car designers
in the middle of a vital urban
context, removed from its suburban
corporate headquarters. The most
innovative aspect of our solution
is the cocoon, a wall system custom
designed and fabricated for this
project using the same digital
rapid prototyping tools that the car
designers use in their work in the
studio. This molded acrylic panel
wall provides visual separation from
the street and confidentiality while
allowing daylight to enter the studio.

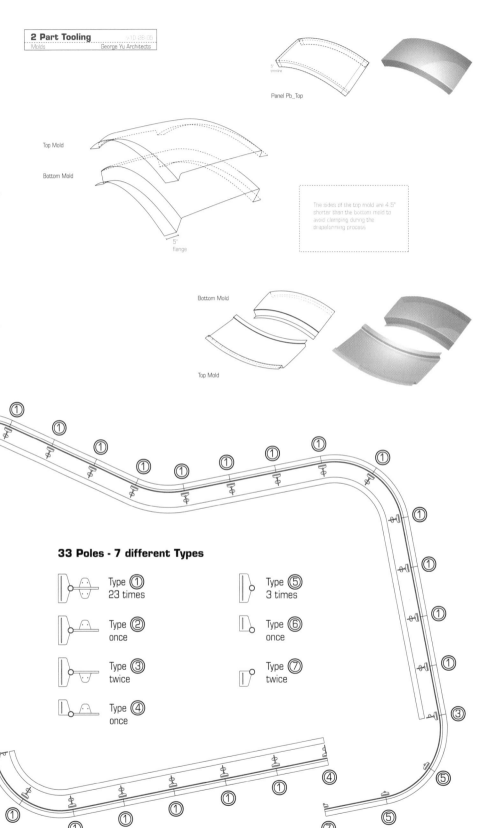

2 Part Tooling
Molds   George Yu Architects

Panel Pb_Top

Top Mold

Bottom Mold

The sides of the top mold are 4.5"
shorter than the bottom mold to
avoid clamping during the
drapeforming process

Bottom Mold

Top Mold

33 Poles · 7 different Types

Type ① 23 times
Type ② once
Type ③ twice
Type ④ once
Type ⑤ 3 times
Type ⑥ once
Type ⑦ twice

➥163 A:3

IBM Center for
e-Business Innovation
George Yu Architects

Collaborating with Imaginary
Forces we created a multidimensional
and more human brand environment
for IBM to sell Fortune 500 clients
their range of e-business capabilities.

A significant portion of our
research addressed IBM's existing
conference room structure and the
interaction, or lack thereof, that
it engendered. The interactive table
was a response to reconfiguring the
spatial dynamic between IBM and
their clients, using technology to
facilitate the delivery of information
and promote engagement.
⤷64, 238 A:31, 256

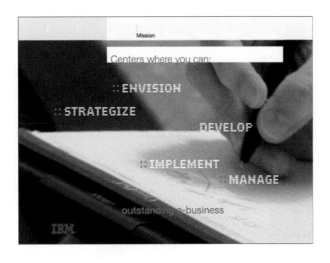

1

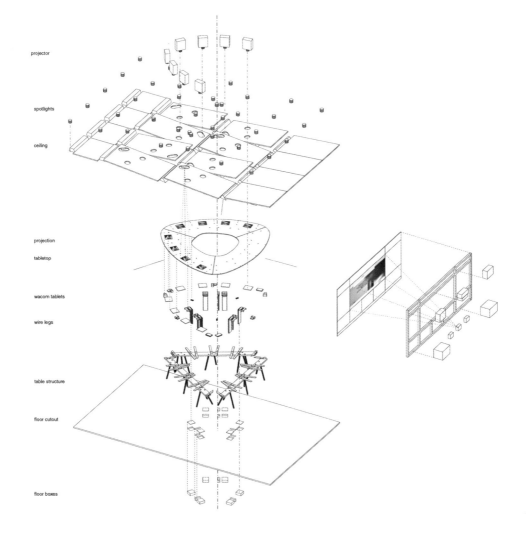

projector

spotlights

ceiling

projection

tabletop

wacom tablets

wire legs

table structure

floor cutout

floor boxes

2

LoRezHiFi
MY Studio/Meejin Yoon

LoRezHiFi engages the public by transforming light and sound into an interactive medium. The project consists of two parts, the Sound Grove and the Light Stream. The Sound Grove is a grove of touch-sensitive stainless-steel poles that are 12 feet high and three inches in diameter. It was conceived of as an urban instrument. The poles are arranged in a four-foot-by-five-foot grid, and each pole is divided into four segments divided by a Lexan diffuser. When touched, each segment triggers a sound, and when released, the sound fades away.

We worked with sound composer Erik Carlson of Area C to compose each of the sound segments. The idea was that each segment was made of essentially a sound and a rest that repeated, but that each segment would have a slightly varied sound and a varied rest, such that the gaps of space between each sound were regular within each segment but always slightly different for other segments. Thus, there would never be any repetition. The other element in this project that is different from White Noise/White Light is that the poles are networked together, so each pole knows if another pole is activated. We worked with Carlson to create a kind of family of networked sounds so that when you let go of one sound segment, another segment on a pole in the distance would be triggered, play, then fade and trigger another one—like an echo moving in space.

We had to develop an interface to study and test the sounds in time and space. Lisa Smith from our office developed an interactive Flash site where we could upload sounds to specific segments of the poles and test them with each other in various configurations and sequences. This site was also used by Carlson in the design process.

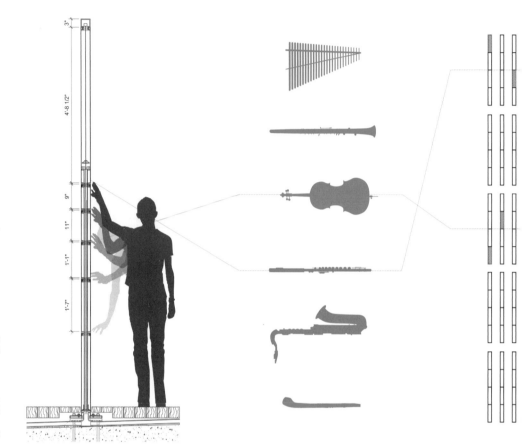

CONFIGURABLE SOUND GROVE

soundfiles

A1	flute1a.mp3	reset	B1		reset	C1		reset	D1		reset
A2	flute1b.mp3	reset	B2		reset	C2		reset	D2		reset
A3	flute1c.mp3	reset	B3		reset	C3		reset	D3		reset
A4	flute1d.mp3	reset	B4		reset	C4		reset	D4		reset

E1		reset	F1		reset	G1	clarinet1a.mp3	reset	H1		reset
E2		reset	F2		reset	G2	clarinet1b.mp3	reset	H2		reset
E3		reset	F3		reset	G3	clarinetc.mp3	reset	H3		reset
E4		reset	F4		reset	G4	clarinet1d.mp3	reset	H4		reset

I1		reset	J1	cello1a.mp3	reset	K1		reset	L1		reset
I2		reset	J2	cello1b.mp3	reset	K2		reset	L2		reset
I3		reset	J3	cello1c.mp3	reset	K3		reset	L3		reset
I4		reset	J4	cello1d.mp3	reset	K4		reset	L4		reset

M1		reset	N1		reset	O1		reset	P1	sax1a.mp3	reset
M2		reset	N2		reset	O2		reset	P2	sax1b.mp3	reset
M3		reset	N3		reset	O3		reset	P3	sax1c.mp3	reset
M4		reset	N4		reset	O4		reset	P4	sax1d.mp3	reset

Q1		reset	R1		reset	S1		reset	T1		reset
Q2		reset	R2		reset	S2		reset	T2		reset
Q3		reset	R3		reset	S3		reset	T3		reset
Q4		reset	R4		reset	S4		reset	T4		reset

1

2

LoRezHiFi

MY Studio/Meejin Yoon
↳66, 114 A:1, 165 B:1, 180 A:27, 220 A:1, 259 A:1

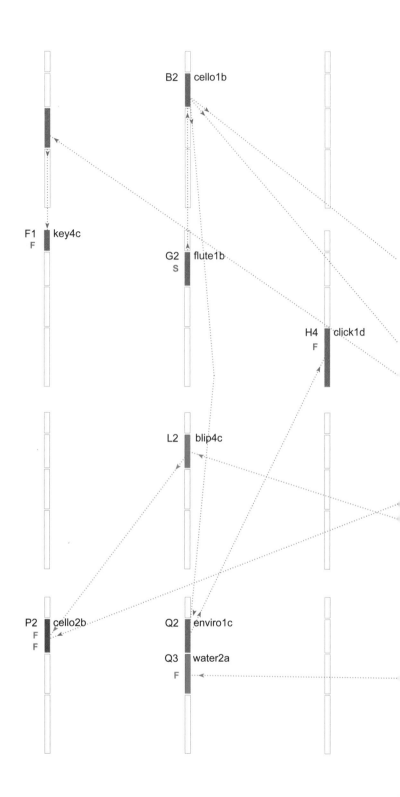

B2 cello1b

F1 key4c
F

G2 flute1b
S

H4 click1d
F

L2 blip4c

P2 cello2b
F
F

Q2 enviro1c

Q3 water2a
F

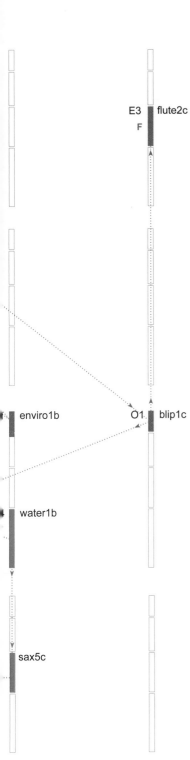

E3 · flute2c
F

enviro1b O1 · blip1c

water1b

sax5c

LONG SEQUENCE

These network sequences link long-duration sounds from different families together into a multi-branched composition.

See attached diagrams for sequence mapping.

The sequence can only be initiated from the start point, marked with an "S" in the diagram, and continues until its multiple finish points, marked with "F."

When the grove has been inactive for a given period of time, one or both of these sequences should self-activate.

PROPOSED IMPLEMENTATION:

Each segment stores information about loop numbers and the IDs of the following segment. Segments participating in the sequence are preprogrammed with an instruction set:

1. Listen for announcement of own ID.

2. Run through pre-programmed protocol, involving how many loops to cycle through, when and which IDs to send out, and whether or not to fade down.

For typical sequence N4>L2>P2:
v
S3>Q3

N4 is touched + released	N4 plays 2 loops, then fades. At end of 1st loop, announces "L2." At the end of 2nd loop, announces "S3."
L2 hears announcement	L2 plays 3 loops and fades. At end of 2nd loop, announces "P2."
S3 hears announcement	S3 plays 2 loops and does not fade. At end of 2nd loop, announces "Q3."
P2 hears announcement	P2 plays 1 loop and fades.
Q3 hears announcement	Q3 plays 1 loop and fades.
No announcement made	Sequence ends.

SOUND GROVE NETWORK CONFIGURATION DIAGRAMS: 03.28.06

MaxStudio.com
George Yu Architects

Our task was to design a comprehensive brand identity for a woman's clothing retailer for a variety of projects: retail stores, showrooms, tradeshow booths, outlet stores, and an e-commerce kiosk. The challenge was to distinguish the brand from its competitors through environmental design.

Our response had to balance the generic and specific nature of shopping center tenant spaces. Prototypes must confront the absence of "traditional" site characteristics that typically shape an environment and be adaptable to the specifics of each site. Beginning in 1998, 2,000- to 3,000-square-foot stores have been designed and built in over 50 locations.

We configured a formal system where the walls are contiguous with parts of the ceiling and floor and read as the primary diagram of the space—a tube or wrapper lit from beyond. By making an explicit distinction between the inserted wrapper of each store and the implied, luminous shell of the given spaces, we emphasized the generic nature of the site of the project.

↳67, 165 A:3, 235 A:43

1

2

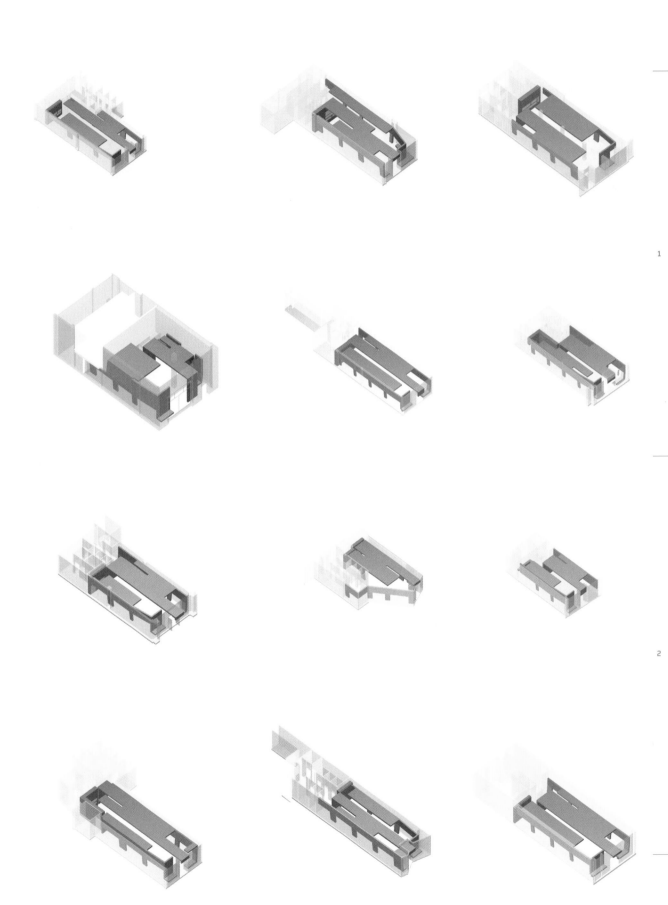

1

2

Möbius Dress
MY Studio/Meejin Yoon

The Möbius Dress uses the mathematical principle of the Möbius
strip, a two-dimensional compact
manifold with a single boundary
component, to re-examine surface
as a seamless transformative
condition between interior and
exterior. The project uses the
topological principles of this one-
sided, one-edged, non-orientable
surface (a loop with a half twist),
as both envelope and spatial device.

   Exploring and exploiting the
continuity of this twisted single-
sided surface, the Möbius Dress
uses the generative logic of splitting
to knot a series of occupiable
spatial loops. The Möbius Dress
is non-directional in terms of form
and materiality. By varying the
parametric relationships between
the measures of the body, splitting
edge, and surface area, the internal
logic and external logic are intertwined to exact elegance. The act
of splitting the Möbius strip reveals
the simple rules and complex
inter-relationships between surface
and space. We used felt, because it is
a seamless material created through
friction as opposed to weaving.

   Structured only by the body,
it twists and turns, forming a
continuously evolving surface as
it unravels. Applied to the body, the
spatial loop creates the appearance
of two intertwining bands of fabric
that meet at points around the
hips and torso. The dress is merely
one continuous loop designed to turn
inside out as it unravels. The Möbius
Dress project challenges clothing's
absolute adherence to conventions
of interiority and exteriority. The
Möbius dress proposes an inherently
inside-out and outside-in garment—
a dress that is worn to be unworn.
   ↳68, 166 A:1

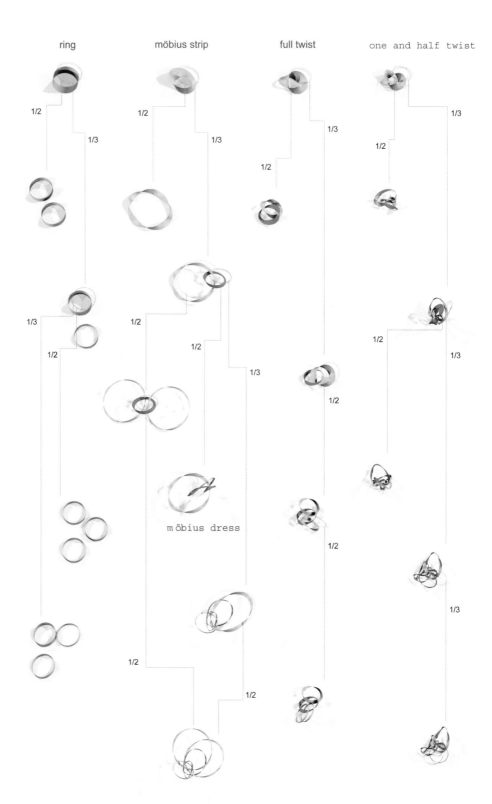

ring   möbius strip   full twist   one and half twist

1/2   1/2   1/3

       1/3   1/3   1/3

                                  1/2   1/2

1/3   1/2

       1/2   1/2   1/2

                          1/3   1/3

                                         1/2

                                         1/2

m öbius dress

                                         1/2

1/2   1/2   1/3

       1/2   1/2

Museum of Tolerance
Gehry Partners

This diagram shows the generating geometry for the "translation surface" approach to the modeling of the Museum of Tolerance atrium roof. The generating geometry creates a swept surface that can be rendered into an assemblage of flat, closed quadrilaterals.
↘**59, 75, 175** A:3, **185** A:48

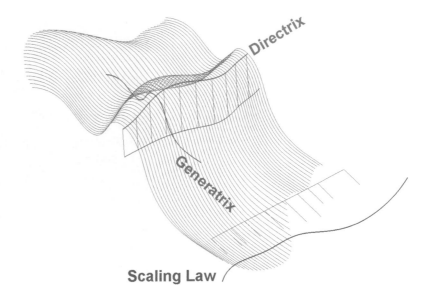

One Island East
Gehry Technologies consultant
Architect: Wong & Ouyang (HK) Ltd.

The owner of One Island East, a 70-story commercial office tower in Hong Kong, drove the use of building information modeling (BIM) and building lifecycle management (BLM) on this project to reduce cost and construction time, increase efficiency, and reduce waste.

One Island East is one of the most substantial implementations of virtual 3D BLM ever undertaken. This owner-driven process combined the entire traditional design and construction information into one 3D building model. As BIM consultants to the owner, Gehry Technologies enabled and facilitated a high degree of information integration and exchange between members of the design and construction teams and the client. The result saved money and time by optimizing construction sequencing through integrated 3D modeling tools.

This image (right) is a portion of the building model, showing the detail and the complexity of coordination in the systems. ↘**70, 170** A:1

P.S.1: LOOP
MoMA/P.S.1 Contemporary
Art Center
Competition Entry
MY Studio/Meejin Yoon

Our proposal, LOOP, creates an immersive condition as a scaffold for activities. Rather than a discrete architectural object positioned as a feature within the courtyard, LOOP presents a "loose fill" of architectural form, allowing simultaneously for complete porosity and total coverage. The geometry is generated through an analysis of cellular aggregates, suggesting an uninterrupted lattice of form that outlines connections between spaces. There is no enclosure and no exposure, but a suggestion of continuous spatial division. In packing the single continuous space of the courtyard with a network of smaller spaces, LOOP both encourages and defines the formation of discreet activity groupings that occur spontaneously during the Warm Up event. The closely packed geometries house the closely packed activities, forming an infrastructure for recreation. ↘171 A:1

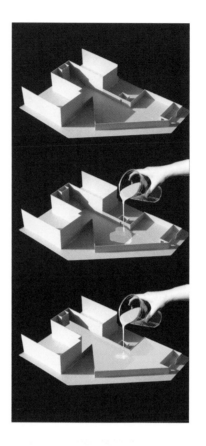

Seattle Central Public Library
Front consultant
Architect: OMA/LMN joint venture

The best drawing on the project was an unfolded elevation with the roof plane represented as a white square, and then all of the surfaces folding out from there. Because of this drawing, everybody on the team—contractors, designers, etc.—were cutting out the form and folding it into reference models and then marking them up. This particular model belonged to the guys in the Seele site office in Seattle. It was used to reference the name of each surface, as well as the dominant directionality of the facade—as every facade surface in fact has a constructionally specific direction that is a very important reference. ↘71, 88 B:19, 174 A:1, 264–265

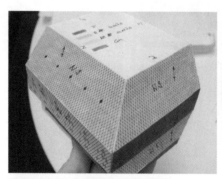
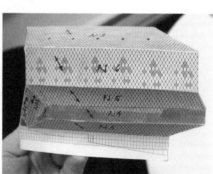
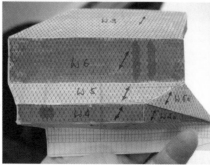
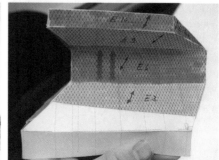

Sensorium
George Yu Architects

Our task was to envision a new work style that grows from the configuration and integration of both the space of work and the physical and electronic tools of work. The client, a large Japanese consumer electronics company, stipulated that this new way to work—the result of a precise relationship of work styles, work space, and work tools—be a patentable product.

The company intended to deploy this prototype initially in a new building to be designed within a 100-cubic-meter (100m × 100m × 100m) volume, on a site in the Shibaura district of Tokyo to serve as the new company world headquarters. This solution is a prototype for the development of similar property into office building developments around the world. Our primary organizational idea for this office building, the Sensorium, is that of the workfield module. For optimal workplace socialization, the most effective group work size was set at 25–30 people, a size that corresponds to a 500-square-meter spatial module. The module is the basic unit of the building, and its 20-by-25-meter dimension orders the building and creates diversity through its systematic, rather than compositional, organization.

In addition to the module, there are a series of middle-ground elements between infrastructure and furniture and software that allow for alternative ways to make boundaries while customizing each space. Making the basic premise manifest in a 140,000-square-meter, 100-cubic-meter volume demanded the integration of several larger-scale spatial and organizational elements.

The primary element for controlling light and air, and for providing a referential space that functions like a sky lobby is the Agora—an enormous void at the center of the building. Dividing the building further into "neighborhoods" are Sector Centers with adjacent atria. They allow one to concentrate typical amenities around the nodes of the building. The Sector Centers serve several floors, with check-in, reception, and a number of shared work amenities adjacent to a green space. ↘172 C:2, 239 A:38

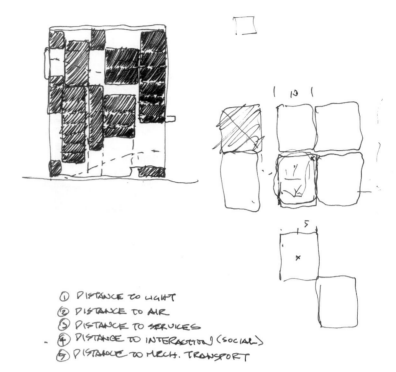

1

① DISTANCE TO LIGHT
② DISTANCE TO AIR
③ DISTANCE TO SERVICES
④ DISTANCE TO INTERACTION (SOCIAL)
⑤ DISTANCE TO MECH. TRANSPORT

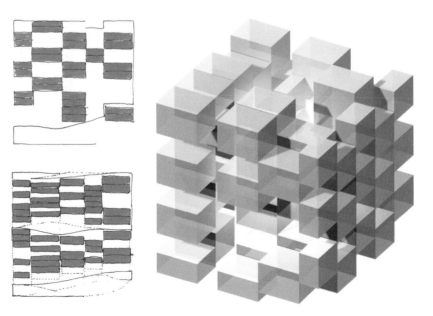

2

Shop Lift: Rethinking Retail, Transcending Type
George Yu Architects

At once a shopping, residential, and recreational complex, Shop Lift envisions a hybrid consumer environment that is strategically integrated with open public spaces and private dwelling units. The resulting architectural typology is analogous, in formal and operational terms, to the term *plex*, which means to plait (interlace), or interweave. A plexus is a complex body, collection, or set of things: a web, network, or any very intertwined or interwoven mass. As with a human or animal structure consisting of closely bundled and intercommunicating tubes, nerves, and vessels, the model presented here compresses a number of known and distinct programs into a dense and highly functioning system. At opportune moments, this combinative strategy relies on the doubling up of, or mutation of, necessary elements.

The continuous column grid equally accommodates the spatial demands and circulation logics of a multilevel parking structure or shed-like big-box outlet at the base. It then supports a deep waffle structure knotted with smaller boutiques that are experienced sectionally from both below and above. Above, this thick layer becomes a giant carpet, with the weft and warp of the structure modulating to allow a new topography to unroll across the site. This landscape is programmed with public amenities and is perforated with voids and courtyards to allow vertical access and light to penetrate below. Residential units organized in floating bars constitute the final layer in the integrated system.

The integrated nature of Shop Lift proposes a maximization of land use and an economy of building stemming from shared infrastructures and structural components. The combination of programs fuse the urban with the suburban. However, just as shopping and habitation remain distinct activities, Shop Lift is an integrated scheme that is careful not to compromise the essential function of each incorporated program. It is a versatile prototype that seeks to expand previous notions of what a shopping center can and could be.

↳72–73, 175 B:1, 266–267

1

2

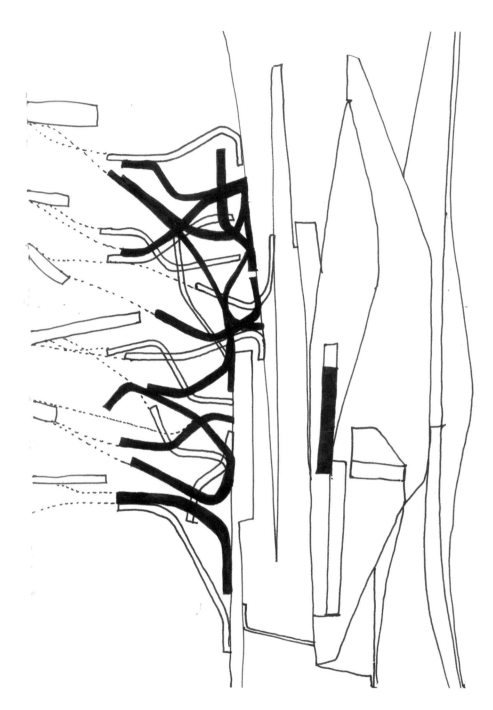

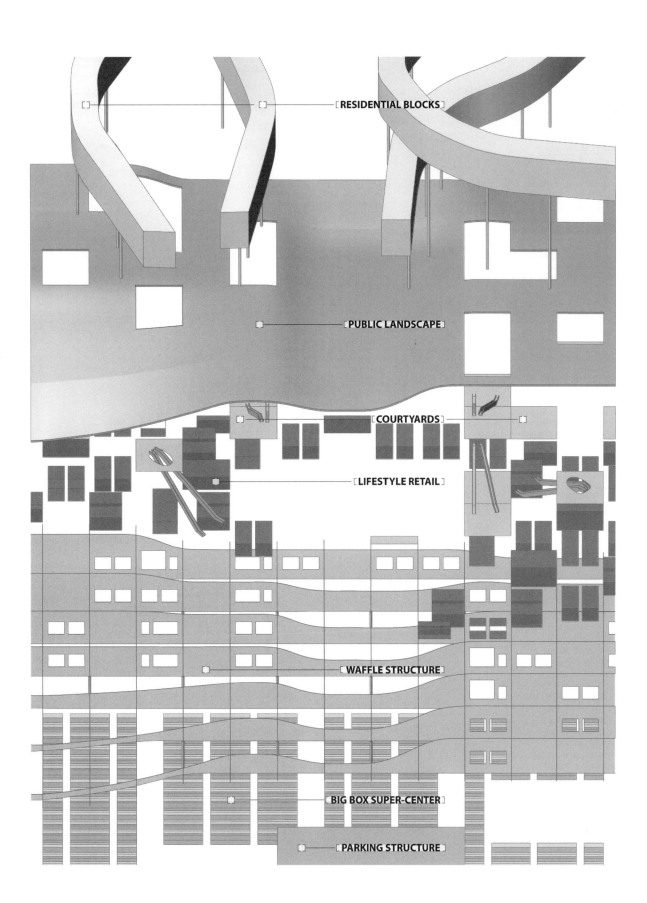

RESIDENTIAL BLOCKS

PUBLIC LANDSCAPE

COURTYARDS

LIFESTYLE RETAIL

WAFFLE STRUCTURE

BIG BOX SUPER-CENTER

PARKING STRUCTURE

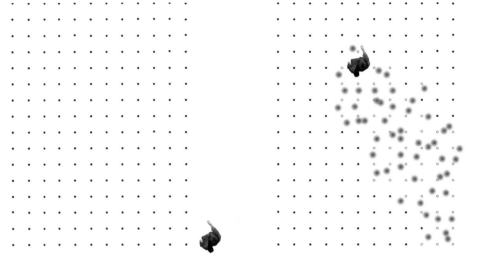

White Noise/White Light
Interactive Sound and Light
Installation
MY Studio/Meejin Yoon

White Noise/White Light was
one of nine interactive installations
commissioned for the Athens
2004 Olympics. The design brief
requested that installations along
a programmed "Listen to Athens"
route record and play back the
sounds of the city to its visitors. In
response to the brief, WN/WL proposed the idea of collecting all the
sounds of the city in such a way that
the accumulation would create a
kind of absence of sound, essentially
a field of white noise—white light
being a full spectrum of color, and
white noise being the full spectrum
of frequencies within the range of
human hearing in equal amounts.

Through adding many frequencies, you could create a condition
whereby all of them and none of
them were measurable. The project
consists of approximately 400
semi-flexible fiber-optic strands.
Treated like a kind of artificial
nature, this non-material material
is arranged in a grid, and the fiber
optics respond one-to-one with
the movement of people through the
field. Activated by the passersby,
the fiber optics transmit light from
white LEDs (light-emitting diodes)
while the speakers emit white noise.
The volume of white noise and the
intensity of white light are controlled
by means of a custom microprocessor
designed by electronics engineer
Matt Reynolds.

In this way the field was
conceived as a sort of measuring
device, recording the movements
of people through the field. But what
was more interesting was that it not
only was able to measure behavior,
but it began to induce behavior.
The field invited a kind of open play.
People would run on it, stomp on it,
wave their arms, and twirl. The field
became an unpredictable aggregation of movement, light, and sound,
creating a kind of saturated
inhabitation, and rendering the
concept of white.

→76–77, 176 A:1, 179 B:3, 224 A:1, 268

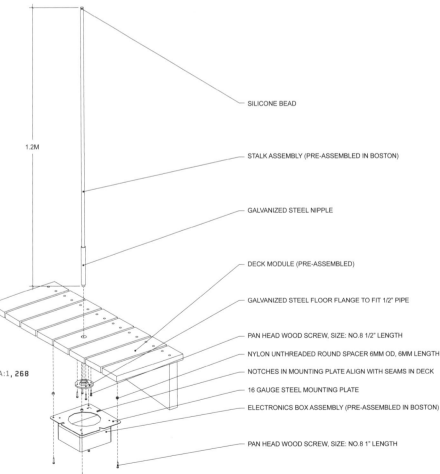

1.2M

SILICONE BEAD

STALK ASSEMBLY (PRE-ASSEMBLED IN BOSTON)

GALVANIZED STEEL NIPPLE

DECK MODULE (PRE-ASSEMBLED)

GALVANIZED STEEL FLOOR FLANGE TO FIT 1/2" PIPE

PAN HEAD WOOD SCREW, SIZE: NO.8 1/2" LENGTH

NYLON UNTHREADED ROUND SPACER 6MM OD, 6MM LENGTH

NOTCHES IN MOUNTING PLATE ALIGN WITH SEAMS IN DECK

16 GAUGE STEEL MOUNTING PLATE

ELECTRONICS BOX ASSEMBLY (PRE-ASSEMBLED IN BOSTON)

PAN HEAD WOOD SCREW, SIZE: NO.8 1" LENGTH

Windshape
nARCHITECTS

Windshape was conceived as two eight-meter-high pavilions that dynamically changed with the Provençale wind. A vinelike structural network of white plastic pipes, joined together and stretched apart by aluminum collars, emerged from the limestone walls and terraces of the hillside of Lacoste, France. Fifty kilometers of white polypropylene string was threaded through the lattice to create swaying enclosures. The string was woven into dense regions and surfaces and pinched to define doorways, windows, and spaces for seating.

Windshape was constructed by nARCHITECTS and a team of students from the Savannah College of Art & Design (SCAD) over a period of five weeks. We developed a construction sequence that optimized the use of measured and non-measured fabrication methods. The basic components of string, plastic pipes, and aluminum collars were all digitally modeled and translated into a set of 2D drawings and data. To achieve the project's complex, interwoven geometries, the pavilions were built as a series of stacked and staggered tripods. Made of groups of three pipes inserted into an aluminum collar, the tripods were preassembled, woven with string on the ground, and hoisted into place. Interstitial string surfaces were then woven in-between the tripods in the air.

We exploited the different properties of two weak and supple materials to create a strong yet elastic structural network. Similar to an archer's bow, the pipes were placed in a bending postition and the string in tension to achieve structural integrity as well as a desired range of movement in the wind. The interdependent structural system of string, pipes, and collars required a flexible fabrication method. An initial stitching of string through the pipes allowed for improvisation in weaving strategies to provide enclosure, openings, or stability. In this way, Windshape's indeterminate structure relied equally on precise translations from digital models as well as in situ building tactics.

The project was a laboratory that allowed us to test the idea of a building that can respond to natural stimuli. (over) ↘78–79, 269–272

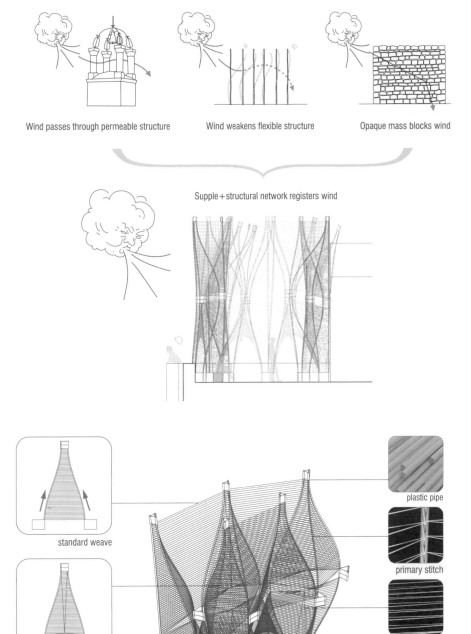

Wind passes through permeable structure

Wind weakens flexible structure

Opaque mass blocks wind

Supple + structural network registers wind

1

2

standard weave

pinch weave

parabolic weave

plastic pipe

primary stitch

secondary weave

alum. base collar + light fixture

alum. base collar + seating

WEAVING STRATEGIES

COMPONENTS

Windshape
nARCHITECTS

Our site was a hilltop overlooking
agricultural fields. You can see those
fields moving in the wind. The wind
is known as the mistral, and when
it approaches, it's a very potent
thing. And also in contrast to the
massiveness of this hewn limestone
town was the idea of creating an
ephemeral double to this medieval
construction that would assume
some of the dynamic properties
of the fields surrounding the town.
There was a search for a spatial logic
that might unite the landscape and
the architecture of the region.

1

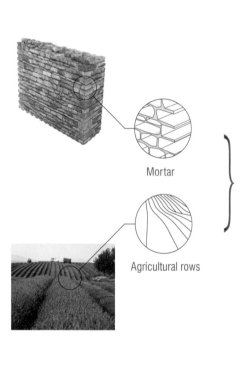

Mortar

Agricultural rows

2

Remix of hard and soft landscapes

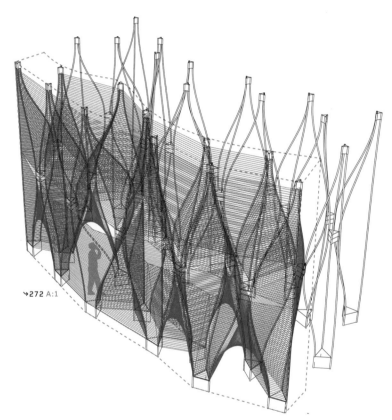

↳272 A:1

David Lewis, Paul Lewis, and Marc Tsurumaki of Lewis.Tsurumaki.Lewis

**The first paragraph in your short text "Beyond"
touches on dissatisfaction with conventional modes
of architectural practice, and also talks about
decoding rules and using constraint to find spaces
for reinvention. With that in mind we wanted to start
with what led you to develop the practice the way you
have. Perhaps, you could talk about how the three
of you decided to work together.** Well, Paul and David
met a long time ago, actually [laughter] (they're twins),
but Paul and I met initially in graduate school at Princeton.
I finished a year in advance of Paul, came to New York City,
and started working for a former professor, Joel Sanders,
while also working on smaller projects, installations, and
competitions independently. When Paul graduated, he
also came to New York and we began working together
shortly thereafter.

**When you were in school, did you recognize that
you had some shared interests? Was it already clear
that you were going to work together?** No. A fellow
named Peter Pelsinski was in my class. When we graduated,
Peter and I came to New York and we were collaborating.
We won the Young Architects Award (sponsored by the
Architectural League of New York) the year we arrived here.
We all knew each other pretty well by the time we graduated, but Peter acted as the hinge. When Paul graduated, the
three of us ended up collaborating, and then a couple of years
later, when David passed through Princeton, after taking
a degree in architectural history at Cornell, he joined us as
well. At that point Peter was starting an independent
practice with Karen Stonely.

But I think, in a way, we really started by attempting
to use the very little free time we had—given that we were
working for fairly demanding offices with long hours—
to do independent work of some kind. This initially involved
a lot of competition-related work, and eventually a series of
installations and exhibitions, principally at the Storefront for
Art and Architecture. Paul was working for Diller + Scofidio,
who were affiliated with Storefront. They were asked to
advise or assist on installations and suggested us as possible
designers. So we gladly committed to taking on that work.

It allowed us the opportunity to get some more
exposure, but it also meant we had to build things ourselves.
Storefront was really the initial catalyst for this do-it-yourself
form of architecture. When there's almost no budget, how
do you get it done? We had a sufficient knowledge of building
things, primarily from making large-scale models in the late
1980s and early '90s in school. We wouldn't just make
a model, we would make a model hanging off a garage door
opener and ridiculous things like that. So that led to a certain
facility with making things, which made it possible to do
two or three exhibitions at Storefront with virtually no
budget, such as Slip Space and Pull of Beauty. For us, these
experiences established the roll-up-your-sleeves ethos that
we've now implemented as a form of alternative practice.

So you can see, the whole position of generative
constraints—how these extremely restrictive parameters
can actually be advantageous—was originally a very, very
high-minded theoretical position [laughter]. It did become
much more proactive and focused when we made a proposal
to Storefront for an exhibition based on a series of projects
we presented as already executed in drawn form. In fact,

they only existed as a couple of sketches and diagrams. We were given a show in January 1997 that ultimately became Testing 1…2…3… that was to open over the summer. **It must have been cold inside Storefront in January.** Well, that show was beastly hot (the show didn't open until the summer). It was either brutally hot or brutally cold when we were fabricating the installations. But in this case, we made a proposition that attempted to clarify our collective interest in looking at conventions of practice. In particular, we wanted to see if we could challenge those rules and conventions through the process of looking at New York in and through drawings. This work was important for us because we shared this productive experience despite the fact that none of us followed the expected professional educational path for an architect. **Meaning?** Meaning we didn't go to big firms where we were mentored by project architects with traditionally established protocols or working methods. In our work, we were put in the position of: here's the challenge, you figure out a way to do it as best as possible within these limits. It was kind of on the fly. We had to find ways, by whatever means necessary, to get the project realized with the ambition we set up in advance. That means we also didn't assume it was our role to find somebody else to do it. We built it ourselves. We didn't assume our role was to research and specify materials produced by others, but actually it was to invent, fabricate, and install the work ourselves. So in a way, because we were never trained to know exactly what we should be doing, we were able to step back and examine conventions of architectural practice. **Does that stem also from the way you were trained in school? We've always felt that there was something missing in our architectural education— at least in terms of technical knowledge—that we always assumed we'd get on the job. Were you ever afraid there would be black holes of knowledge in the work you do?** Oh definitely. But I think what has worked for us is we went from a stage of large-scale models to small-scale installations to these early interior projects where we essentially were the contractor and built everything as well as designed it. We developed a body of knowledge about how to build things and about the problems associated with how things went together. It meant we weren't just following industry standards, and, as our projects grew in size, it allowed us to frame the way we work with contractors.

For instance, if you work in large firms you actually learn through drawing details and often through revising pre-existing conventional details. So oftentimes the work is an extension of translating and adapting work completed by others. There is undoubtedly an economy to this way of working, but we learned to do it differently. We tend to draw details that come from thinking through how we would want to build the thing. It's akin to a kind of shop context or installation context. But it sometimes leads to its own difficulties, because there's a translation there as well. We have to translate the way we would want to build it into the way the contractor wants to build it. It's always an interesting moment, where we have to figure out exactly how to make that translation.

If you ask students or people familiar with your work to consider the image of your work, your drawings would probably come to mind. So it's interesting to hear about this nuts-and-bolts self-education parallel to the projective practice of your drawings. The drawings stem much more from an examination of the conventional modes of architectural representation, such as the conventions of section or axonometric drawings. We can be quite obsessively precise regarding the conventions of drawing, but we never completely accept these norms at face value. We're interested in how you can begin to operate within conventions to produce unconventional effects.

How do the drawings get made between the three of you? Well, it's not one particular medium or one particular method. In other words, we don't have a puritanical stance on either digital technology or hand drawing, which limits the approach. We search for—through the act of drawing—an approach that is more opportunistic, using one system precisely because it is not necessarily essential to the process, in order to get at something else. Ultimately, this impulse is framed by a certain conceptual understanding, where it is clear that different types of representations position the subject. The three of us were trained at a transitional point in architectural education. A pedagogy emphasizing hand drawing, manual methods of drafting, conventional notational systems, still held sway. **We were too. And we miss that.** But at the same time, we were still present at that moment of transition between hand drawing and digital forms of representation. We were still able to engage in both. It's impossible for us to ignore or to push aside the commingling of media, or to have an overly nostalgic view about hand-drawn methods. We have a tendency to hybridize or cross-pollinate those methods. We're reluctant to assume that digital methods of representation constitute in themselves a complete paradigm shift. We're more interested in an opportunistic approach to a translational condition. In other words, in a digital rendering, one is still dealing in many ways in classical perspective, section, and so on. This happens in a more fluid way in a digital environment. Understanding the emerging distance between those languages can actually be advantageous.

You've mentioned the word *play* in your writings. Isn't that a loaded term? It seems to us that some of the past interest in drawing and the oscillation between imagined work and built work is, in fact, our attempt to see one through the lens of the other, or to restrict one against the other, to ask, can you actually build a drawing? It's a curious question how one does that, through establishing datum lines, dimension systems, or ways that you start to think about the building of an inhabited section. This is changing very quickly in new building modeling techniques. In a way, we've always been less interested in the virtuosity of digital representation than in the ability to look at the kinds of conflict or the incompatibilities between digital representation and hand drawing. That's why we've always tried to go between the two, because there's a certain friction that we find beneficial, as opposed to the excesses of one in isolation, or the conservative nature of one in isolation.

Your drawings are inhabitable, and not only by the eye. You've done installations where there is a relationship between the body and the surface of the drawing that seems to come from the physical experience of the act of drawing itself. But now that you are doing large-scale projects, it seems that you've got to contend with this larger gap that emerges—between design and construction—where many things in the process are going to be out of your hands. Yes, it's a little daunting, moving into these larger-scale projects. We went through it to a certain degree on the Bornhuetter Hall in Wooster, Ohio, where we were always recognizing that the dormitory had certain constraints. It had certain built-in limits, not the least of which was that it was our first large-scale building. There were certain desires on our part to make sure that some aspects related to budget, client, service did not trip us up. Our performance as architects had to play out in a much more predictable way than it did on other projects. But we sought out areas where there was still some wiggle room. **Did you find wiggle room?** I think so, but in ways that almost had to operate on two different levels. For example, we had to find ways that we could produce spaces in a building type (dormitory) that actually has almost no excess to it. This is a typology that usually calls for the most efficient planning. Given a limited budget and a desire on the part of the client to maximize the quantity of rooms—maximize in every quantitative aspect, really— we attempted to find ways to produce social spaces that wouldn't be within the footprint of the building but were

in the building's proximity and context. Incorporating exterior spaces became the real way to do that. This led us to think about a building that really developed a logical skin as well as a counter idea about the de-lamination of those skins. It also addressed issues related to the client's desire to work with traditional cladding materials, like brick. We had to intensify the limits that were given to us and turn them into something that was consciously invented as opposed to simply applied. So it was very much a question of taking all the issues that were given to us and accepting them rather than fighting them. The pitched roofs are another good example. We fought the pitched roof for a while with no success. We recognized that actually we could use it as a sectional organizer, which demanded careful consideration of its end facades. It was very clear that one of their program, or formal, expectations was that there be a pitched roof, no question. It stemmed from a literal idea of what being contextual means.

But going back to your earlier question about this gap between design and fabrication: are you pointing to the way in which many architects believe that digital fabrication or digital project delivery tools can somehow circumvent this gap? This is one of the promises of new technologies, but it also misses some of the knowledge that others have in the construction trade. Too often there is a belief in the return to a medieval mastering of building through digital technology—and a return to the stonemason's hands-on role through wielding a much more complex tool. There are aspects of that worth exploring, but it can be mistaken for a holy grail. It misses some of the productive friction that can happen on the job site. In the end, someone's going to install it, someone's going to put it together, and there are going to be tolerances that have to be discussed and worked through. I think it's something we're hoping to be able to bring into the process, because we have experienced many of these issues first hand. **But isn't there a shift now between the idea of being inventive with catalog or mass-produced elements and a more direct, customized way of making architecture that is enabled by these new, more robust modes of production?** It's a question we're still pursuing. But I doubt it'll be a "this will kill that" kind of thing. The ability to do digital fabrication may allow a smooth transition from doing one-to-one fabrication to doing larger projects, but it's not as if all of a sudden you have a fully automated process. I think inevitably there's going to be a whole series of other tools and ways of working. The effectiveness of digital tools will be more at the conceptual level, by which I mean it will affect the way we approach a project. It will allow us to question the givens—understood as both constraints and opportunities—in a new, perhaps more inventive and creative way.

It gets back to that issue of play you brought up earlier. Play requires rules. Restrictions that circumscribe any kind of architectural problem in any format leave us with the question: where is that play? Sometimes play exists at the level of material invention, sometimes it may allow for the kind of forms of digital translation that we were referring to earlier, or sometimes it may be prohibitive or simply not part of the palette. One of the things we are describing about the Bornhuetter project concerns identifying where there is room to maneuver, where there is the possibility of appropriating or misappropriating space within the project. Where are there excesses within the efficiencies? Or in what ways can efficiencies generate productive collisions? **Did the idea of amplification or internalization of all the energy of the outdoor space grow out of your restaurant projects? Perhaps coming from the relationship between the sidewalk and the restaurant interiors?** I think the big difference is that with the restaurant projects there's a development of what you would call the *best plan*. There's a real split personality in the restaurant projects, because there is this excess of efficiency related to plan. It has to work really well. So many times there's clearly a better place to locate the door or place the tables. There's specific space planning that just has to work. You can do it really well or you can do it less well. The invention is almost limited to—not spatial complexity— but surface complexity. How can you be inventive with surfaces? The dormitory project was different. It opens up more complex relationships between program, space, excess, interior, exterior, and that's a much richer palette to work in.

The kind of energy that is deployed over the scope of a larger project—dealing with issues of program, economy, budget, structure—in the case of the restaurant gets compressed into this six-inch zone against the wall. You really do concentrate all your efforts into a kind of membrane. That can lead to some really productive effects, which, in fact, may get redeployed in larger, more complex spatial contexts. There is, in these projects, a pathological obsessiveness, a compulsive nature, because a lot of that energy is being concentrated into a skin. Maybe it came out of an initial frustration, as architects, with the capacity of those typical projects to generate so few spatial possibilities. The envelope and program are predetermined. Clients and owners are rightfully determined to maximize a seating area as well as make their kitchens function properly. The territory over which the architect holds sway becomes increasingly less. It does really become a context of working within these veneers. It was also extremely frustrating for us if we were left with only picking materials. In our restaurant installations, we actively got involved in the making

of things, in experimentation, and actually building what was necessary for us to build. It was a productive blurring and rethinking of the relationship between the contractor and our role as architects and fabricators. We literally rewrote standard contracts to allow that to happen. But in some ways you can only do that at a relatively small scale. It's a do-it-yourself ethos we wholly embrace, but there's also a point at which you start to become the victim of your own success. So we really are pleased about the opportunity to shift to a different, larger scale.

You mentioned contracts. Were you ever getting to the point where you were building in fees for fabrication? Yes, and it produced a split in the drawing technique, where we could produce the base drawing that a contractor could do fairly quickly because he's not detailing, and then we would be building the details, which was where the shop drawings came from. There are benefits to this kind of process. We didn't have to represent the detail information to anyone else but ourselves. It cut out the middle man. I would call it a productive naïveté. You just dive in. A lack of knowledge sometimes helps one define solutions that may not be so rote and might be more experimental by nature. **How do the three of you actually work together?** Typically, all three partners work on the design aspects of all projects. It doesn't necessarily always get realized in that way. For purely logistical and pragmatic purposes, there's a partner who takes the lead in terms of client communication, day-to-day operations, and the running of the project with the project team and project managers. One of the reasons we work as a collaborative office is because we value dialogue as an ideas incubator. We try to bring to the table a "best idea wins" kind of attitude. It prevents each one of us from becoming overly proprietary or precious about designs. It opens it up to a continuous interface with our staff.

As we shift the scale of our work, hopefully, the thought process that goes into any size project will be maintained, in terms of how we take on the constraints that are given to us. I think it goes back to what ties the earlier work such as the Storefront projects to the larger projects. Our particular role as architects may change, but the attitude with which we confront a problem does not. This is why digital fabrication has real potential for us, because it situates the practitioner in a way that is not passive in relation to what is produced. It enables the work to be much more speculative.

Do you feel you're pushing the boundaries and conventions of working with drawings in your design process? We do all our working drawings in digital format.

Our hand drawings tend to be exploratory design drawings and presentation drawings related to the speculative work. The hand drawings usually exist in some kind of relation to digital production.

All three of you do the projective, or research drawings. Do you actually work on the same drawings?
We do on more complicated drawings, but typically one person does a drawing. It also depends on the nature of the construction drawing, and there I think the greatest inventions come at the level of clarifying what we want to do versus what's typical or necessary to meet filing status. And those tend to be two very different types of roles. But what we're looking toward are drawings that incorporate three-dimensional studies where you can begin to work out what would otherwise be understood as a sketch. Here the drawing is actually used to tell someone how a system is brought together, and the means of construction. With the newer forms of representation, I think it's possible to provide precision and dimensional accuracy to contractors who often cannot or will not read plans, sections, and graphic materials.

Something we are keenly interested in asking is how you position theory in your practice, how did it make an impact in your education, if at all? The role of theory is something that has been kind of disparaged in the last several years. It made a huge impact on our education. We approached it with an optimistic curiosity about what might happen as opposed to a cynical negation about what has occurred. We learned to strive to reveal the hidden attributes of a project. It seems to us—and I think this is where critical theory has been helpful—that finding ways of asking critical questions opens up potential territories for projective thinking. I don't think the idea of the theoretical-critical practitioner versus the projective-curious practitioner should always be seen as oppositional. It seems like there's a lot of potential in their overlapping. We've always argued that our projects are implicitly critical in their active pursuit of what happens, but it has to be grounded in a critique or some form of engagement in what is going on. For me, the most insightful curiosity that came out of my theoretical practices was precisely the curiosity about what is invisible.

What kind of thinking really made an impact on you?
One was looking at familiar things and realizing that those things are constructed, whether it was the coffee cup or the building typology. We look at and play with the character of the uncanny, particularly as written about by Anthony Vidler, with whom we had the privilege to study. To be able to look behind that which is now accepted

as normal and that was at one point constructed to be normal is an important skill to have. After all, that which you assume to be the case was not necessarily the case previously; and even more importantly, that which you assume to be the case now doesn't necessarily have to be the case in the future. So theory gives you the skills to not only think critically, engaging things that are currently existing, but also to speculate on something that might come from without. This relates to a double bind that we have identified, and that has to do with the critical distance necessary to maintain an objective approach to the world. On the one hand, there is the cynical position of someone who describes to the world how screwed up it is, but at the same time remains outside of it; and on the other is the position of one who is totally embedded in the world and cannot help but propagate a system precisely because he or she is embedded within capitalist procedures. Instead of just concluding that there is a double bind and that you're damned either way, you've got to find a way to operate productively in between. **But when you hear some architects speak about being Deleuzian (Gilles Deleuze), say, it's not opening up questions; it's actually trying to normalize or rationalize decisions that were probably already made.** There is that tendency, which is a sort of perennial intellectual tourism that architecture seems to indulge in—and has for the past 40, 50 years. We're not part of this particular brand of thinking, but one of the positive residues of the kind of academic experience we've had was the desire to look more within the practice of architecture as well as what's extrinsic to it. The sort of mania for everything outside of architecture, the desire that architecture has to be informed by all these things, is not unproductive, per se. But I think we became much more interested in a route that emerged by working through existing channels and by operating through the transformation of the kind of conventions and systems that are already embedded within architecture, rather than somehow importing ideological material or theoretical positions or models onto architecture. And on some level it's a slippery line between those two things.

Distorting and pushing beyond the so-called conventional or normative is done through a close interrogation of what the normative and conventional is, rather than assuming it's immediately irrelevant or that it's simply a matter of contradicting convention. To contradict convention meaningfully you have to have a very deep understanding of the conventional and the kind of conditions that are embedded in it, for example. We're not interested in articulating the kind of negative critique that's only about stepping outside of systems. We prefer to investigate critically by working within those systems. We understand that criticism needs to evolve from knowledge of how and why those conventions came about. **Maybe you were looking within because you were on the margin looking within. Maybe we're at a fortunate moment where we really don't have to make a choice between theory and practice. But there's still a real tension between those who dismiss theory wholesale and those who say maybe it's already embedded in our thinking.** I think there's currently a tendency to classify theory in a very pejorative manner. Or to dismiss theory as a way of justifying bad practice. We're more interested in having a dialogue about what constitutes architectural practice, whether in our teaching or in our practice. I think in particular the writers we've read—everything from Salvador Dalí's method of working rationally to produce irrational things to Robin Evans's close inspection of things that are taken for granted, such as the corridor—overlap with our interests. We're more interested in using these ideas as a kind of operation, rather than being in the position where the design has to be justified by some parallel formal strategy.

Is it a fair summation of your view to say that you need to know the rules in order to break the rules, or to find room for invention within the rules? It has a lot to do with whether you're attempting to apply what you've learned from those things. One wants to avoid engaging in a kind of perpetual failure. Most of the moments that allow us to simultaneously reconcile opposites or produce paradoxes that are productive have to do with an ability to not see a linear transition from one thing to another. Instead, the goal is to operate at a level where we are trying to negotiate many different aspects of a project. It also goes back to the proposition that the more we know about a project from the standpoint of constraints the easier it is to design. This is an issue of play. The best players are the ones that are always bending the rules without breaking the rules. Most traditional practices set up rules, and then those rules guide and dictate everything about that practice. We see the rules as what you construct just to play the game. **Isn't it less efficient if you talk about a large practice?** One could see it that way, but if you look at efficiency, it's a set of rules about the maximization of something and the minimization of something else. This is usually driven by economies, such as maximization of profit, minimization of cost. But if you can shift the terms away from simply a question of money into other conditions that are controlled by a maximization-minimization ratio, then that system of efficiency, which is really a type of game, can become much more productive in terms of becoming an intentional attribute of a project or process. **Is this a part of your**

conversation with students? The difficulty is that it is much harder for students to literally make this leap within the context we're discussing. It's very different in a studio, where one is oscillating between a variety of different things... **One is still learning a language...** Exactly. They are learning technique and questioning what they know. But a set of parameters, which in the case of the studio are the expectations of the program, the means of production available to students, etc., can help students learn to tactically address these issues.

In your practice, how do you deal with the fact that all three of you are traveling quite a bit, and there's a staff to manage and sustain? It depends on the nature of the project we're working on and the time frames. There is a tendency—a clear way we try to direct those within the office—to find out what the conditions are, separate out the issues, find out what's at play... We don't begin with a formal idea; it begins with research. And then ultimately the design process is one of give and take, in which the three of us work to draw out and look at multiple variations that would never have been conceived of from the start. The hope is that in that process we're not sketching the final product but rather setting up the conditions. Then we engage the people working with us to develop it. But you need to set up the research and define what's at play first. **You're almost operating on the level of a confederacy, but not for the sake of being a confederacy. It's more participatory.** In fact, it is optimistic. There is something productive and projective about these things. In a positive sense they can generate possibilities, potentials, and pleasures **...which is the best sense of an artistic practice. It is also a commentary on contemporary conditions. The abstraction of the architect as something other than a citizen enjoying or not enjoying contemporary conditions seems to make commentary a little bit hollow. You have to be inside the culture and its traditions in order to step back productively and offer critique. Certainly, in your office you're right in the middle of it all [points to office window at sidewalk level].** Well, we know a lot about peoples' kneecaps.

Interview with David Lewis, Paul Lewis, and Marc Tsurumaki was conducted in New York City in 2005 by Jon Dreyfous and Craig Mutter. It was revised by email in 2008.

Gregg Pasquarelli, Christopher Sharples, Coren Sharples, and William Sharples of SHoP

We're five partners with three names, and everyone hears that we're married and twins. But what's really most important is that all five of us have very different backgrounds. This is very important. It became a founding principle of our office, in the sense that we all had other careers before we went into architecture—and that, I think, allowed us to freely adapt other methods of problem solving and try out alternative business models. **Even using the term business model has been unusual for architects...** I guess so, although it seems normal to us. Corey (Coren) comes from a really strong business and marketing background. Chris and Kim (Holden) are more fine arts; and Bill is an engineer. I'm, embarrassingly, a finance guy. That's why I have the tie on. [laughter]

Also, Bill and Chris have an unbelievable knowledge and appreciation of the history of aerospace and aircraft design. That's a big thing for us. Another thing about this practice is that we were all friends in school. Chris was living in Japan, but four of us were in the same class together at Columbia. We all did very different work in school. So it wasn't like we all came together because we said hey, we all like the same style. Probably, the most important thing that brought us together was our dissatisfaction with professional practice. We thought, how can we attack this profession by creating a new kind of business? How is it possible to do this a different way? Those questions were way more important than aesthetics. **There's a dissatisfaction among our peers that sounds similar. Can we ask you about where that dissatisfaction comes from? Does it go all the way back to your school days?** Way back in 1987, I picked up an *ENR* (*Engineering News-Record*) magazine

and there was a trade article in there about Frank Gehry's fish project in Japan. The article was basically a warning to contractors. They were basically saying that if you deal with architects doing avant-garde work you're going to get screwed. I was in the construction industry at the time working for one of the largest construction companies in the United States—a very high-end firm. But we were cultured engineers, we went to art school and knew our architectural history, so to read an article warning engineers against innovative architecture just seemed wrong somehow, especially since the buildings our company produced were less than inspiring. You would never see architects on site, and that was something we questioned. It's interesting that while we were growing up we saw all these grand projects in various phases of construction in New York City and Philadelphia, so the idea of *making* was always something that was deeply embedded in our psyche. But as I watched our company's projects go up, I grew more and more dissatisfied. Two years of my life were spent watching this building go up, and the architect was not engaged in the process, and it was mediocre. That was really disturbing. **One could say market forces are what's behind that.** Well, maybe it was also a lack of management in the relationships between the teams that were working together on these projects. But then we went to architecture school and different things were happening there. So much so that when we came back out, we realized there was a real disconnect between the academy and the profession. There was an ethos in the 1980s among academics that led to the idea of *paper architecture*. A lot of our professors may not have had the opportunity to practice or produce buildings, so they were really promoting the idea that pure architecture was more about the idea than the building. The projects that were commissioned came out of competitions, and this was really frustrating to me at the time.

I remember it was almost like a badge of honor not to have your license. Exactly, it was almost like reverse discrimination… [laughter] **And nobody talked about it among our peers when we were in school. I mean, we acknowledged it but it wasn't seriously discussed.** On the other side were the practitioners, the people who were building. Most of these people were on the commercial side, completely commercialized entities, and so there seemed to be no way to enter into this world. It was an either-or, and we were like, it needs to be an *and*. It needs to be an *and* on several planes. That's what brought us together. Well, that, and we got some jobs. But we all had that same attitude. Let's build a good practice that's both professional and interesting. Let's also make an environment that's great to work in—as opposed to a sweatshop, which we've opposed since day one. We've never had an unpaid intern ever. We want the interns coming in to value their professional work, which goes for the academy too. When we teach studio, we teach building technology, construction technology, but we also stress professional practice.

It must be a relief to students. I remember listening to a Glenn Murcutt lecture in 1991, where he was talking about pragmatic things like the orientation of the building, and we were like whoa, that's refreshing! Yeah, students get excited to connect with the world of practice. We've asked students to write a pro forma for their building, and to link the pro forma to the financial aspects of actual construction. We're a performance-based operation, as opposed to a stylistic one or phenomenological one, so for us things like pro forma models are critical in feeding the whole design process. **You talk about spreadsheet knowledge, or database knowledge. But you also talk about phenomenology or at least about more abstract things. How does that conversation take place? Does it happen in the studio?** I think a lot of theory is useful. We all read, we all teach, we know our interests. Maybe the best way to explain it is to say that when we're in the academy we're the professional guys, and when we're in the profession we're the academic guys. For example, when formulating the theoretical concept for a building, we start by talking to the subcontractors about how they would connect two pieces of metal or wood. And then when we're out in the field, we talk to the guys about why the building is doing what it's doing in terms of its theoretical premise.

What about the day-to-day practice in the office itself? It's a back-and-forth. We don't start a project by searching for a concept. The project is generated by parameters. We really focus on the parameters of the problem, like site, program, budget… **And is that what you mean by performance-based practice?** Yes. The opportunities for design are embedded in and unearthed by all these parameters. If you look at the site, the zoning envelope, and so on, there is an immediate parallel practice of asking how all this affects the design, how we can utilize it to do something great. **So is it opportunistic?** Well, aesthetics enter in too. I go back to the aerospace industry where Kelly Johnson always said, "if it flies pretty good, it probably looks pretty good too."

You know, the Lewis brothers (of Lewis.Tsurumaki. Lewis) have said they find poetry in rules. That's exactly right. Al Latour—who was (Eero) Saarinen's engineer and Louis Kahn's engineer and who still gives lectures, by the way—once said the reason why Louis Kahn could call you on a Friday afternoon and get you to come over to his office in Philadelphia on a Saturday morning was because he engaged everyone in the experience. It's about going into a construction site or region and understanding how things are made and what resources are available to you. Really you have to build a tectonic language out of the materials at hand. There is an architecture already embedded there. That's what (Alvar) Aalto did, and what (Álvaro) Siza still does to some extent. There are architects out there who represent a regional as opposed to a stylistic approach to architecture. **Where does Frank Gehry stand with respect to that idea?** Well, I think Frank Gehry— and correct me if I'm wrong—identifies himself more as an artist and sculptor, and that may go back to his relationships with artists in the 1960s and '70s. What has made him so powerful in architecture is that he has had to overcome so many constraints in the construction industry—and don't get me wrong, there is something great in that—but basically I see most of his buildings as sculptural. **So how do you characterize your approach?** A real driving force for our work over the last few years has been this desire—which I think comes out of this performance-based modeling idea— for program, surface, and structure to all blend into a singular thickness. In a way, this idea is both functionalist and post-structuralist. There's a lot of (Gilles) Deleuze there. There are also a lot of unbelievably practical issues there as well. **You mention Deleuze but don't bring it up as a kind of intellectual crutch. It remains hidden; it informs things but isn't made literal.** The firm essentially started when Bill and I decided to work together as housing partners at Columbia. There's this housing studio semester where you're supposed to work in teams. It's the single most traumatic event of your three years there where you're forced to collaborate. So he and I were housing partners, and we had a pretty difficult semester where we really struggled because that was the year Deleuze's *A Thousand Plateaus* was first published. Bill and I and this guy Ed Keller were the only three guys reading this book, and we didn't know what the fuck it meant. So we went to Bernard Tschumi and said, "This is supposed to be the school about theorists, who here knows this stuff?" He said they'd just hired this guy out of (Peter) Eisenman's office named Greg Lynn, and he was supposed to know what this stuff is about. We struggled through it and we ended up making a "de-territorialized" housing project. We never made that again. [laughter] **One less plateau…** [laughter] We threw everything out—with seven days to go—and started all over again. We were like fine, now we know we can't do that. Let's start over and just do a really good housing project. And you know what? That's how the practice started.

So to come back to this performance-based approach in your work, how did that develop? Well, the symbiotic relationship of surface, structure, and skin was really explored in the P.S.1 project (MoMA/P.S.1 Young Architects Forum competition). That project was really the first five-year plan for this office. Obviously there was no mechanical work or controlling environments there, but that was the first time we were able to deal with and manage those things together, and also to produce the drawing set and make it ahead of schedule and under budget. Our competition was done in three days. It took two weeks to select the group and we only had six weeks to design and build it. That was in 2000, and we got 50,000 dollars and did it for 19,000. We gave the other 31,000 to the students who put it together. **And how does that relate to the Camera Obscura project?** That was the next logical step for us. It's what followed the Versioning and Porter House projects. The Porter House project had this custom rain-screen facade panel system, where each panel was unique and had its own number. But the Camera Obscura had something like 1,400 individual pieces and composite relationships, which were all put together on site by a contractor.

Your projects range in scale from these small interventions to larger urban scale strategies. A good example is the East River Waterfront proposal, which is a composite of many smaller projects. Could you talk about how the office addresses projects at different scales, particularly in relation to the scale of the city? Every project requires a different solution.

It's not necessarily the case that an aggregation of small components makes for a big impact. That's one way to approach a project. Sometimes it's the right way to go, but other times you need a big grand gesture.

As you've mentioned you're not promoting a stylistic bent or formal language. There also doesn't appear to be a particular market you're targeting. It seems like the premise of much of your work is developing the practice itself. Exactly, the theory of the office is the practice. Again, we are the academics in the profession and the professionals in the academic world. The most theoretical thing is the practice. It's all encompassing, it's holistic, it's a general practice. We compartmentalize, we don't pecialize, and I think that may be a pre–World War II attitude. What we've found is that older architects, the old guys… **You mean those 35 and older.** [laughter] No, I mean those 70 and older—they love us. And I think it's because they remember when architects used to practice like this. But they're also really in tune with the new technology. They're like, that's awesome, how can I get one of those machines? That's how we got to working with Harry (Henry) Cobb (of Pei Cobb Freed), and now he's got a 3D printer and it's all because we all got excited about the process of working together. He's been teaching us a hell of a lot in terms of what he had to deal with in the 1950s and '60s.

How do you think this great divorce within the profession, between theory and practice, happened? Well it's a very long political story. But, partly, it came from things like the academy's focus on theory, and its privileging the model of winning competitions rather than executing buildings. And the profession here does not support research in the academy, which does happen in Europe. **If you were to defend the academy, or that era, what would you say were the lessons learned from that period?** Oh, I don't think we're against the academy. I'm just saying that's one of the factors that led to the split. I think the institution was hugely instrumental in bringing critical thinking and critical theory back to the profession of architecture. **You said *brought back* and not *invented*.** They didn't invent it. They brought it back. It just got repackaged. In the 1970s, modernism had become formulaic, it had become about the production of big glass boxes. It became product-oriented and had to be reinvented, so it was important that the theorists brought back the avant-garde. Architects in the 1970s weren't working on the social project. Architects in the 1920s were designing sanatoria or libraries. Now an architect cannot even touch a hospital unless he or she is a specialist.

↘109 A:2, 140, 141 B:43, 159 A:3

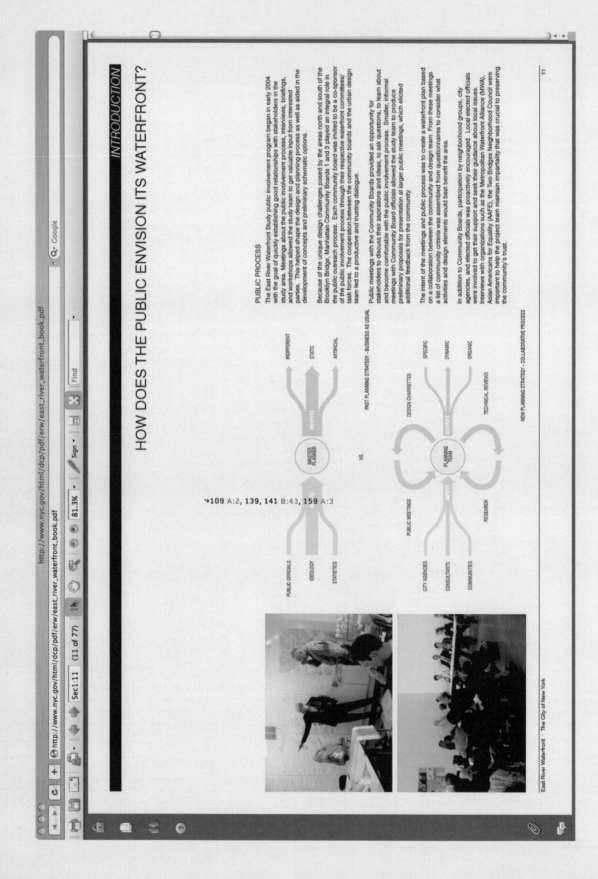

HOW DOES THE PUBLIC ENVISION ITS WATERFRONT?

↳109 A:2, 139, 141 B:43, 159 A:3

PUBLIC OFFICIALS
IDEOLOGY
STATISTICS

MASTER PLANNER

OUTPUT

NONEXPERT
STATIC
ARTIFICIAL

PAST PLANNING STRATEGY - BUSINESS AS USUAL

VS.

CITY AGENCIES
CONSULTANTS
COMMUNITIES

PUBLIC MEETINGS
DESIGN CHARRETTES
TECHNICAL REVIEWS
RESEARCH

PLANNING TEAM

SPECIFIC
DYNAMIC
ORGANIC

NEW PLANNING STRATEGY - COLLABORATIVE PROCESS

PUBLIC PROCESS

The East River Waterfront Study public involvement program began in early 2004 with the goal of quickly establishing good relationships with stakeholders in the study area. Meetings about the public involvement process, interviews, briefings, and workshops allowed the study team to get valuable input from interested parties. This helped shape the design and planning process as well as aided in the development of concepts and preliminary schematic options.

Because of the unique design challenges posed by the areas north and south of the Brooklyn Bridge, Manhattan Community Boards 1 and 3 played an integral role in the public outreach process. Each community board was invited to be a co-sponsor of the public involvement process through their respective waterfront committees/ task forces. The cooperation between the community boards and the urban design team led to a productive and trusting dialogue.

Public meetings with the Community Boards provided an opportunity for stakeholders to discuss their aspirations and ideas, to ask questions, to learn about and become comfortable with the public involvement process. Smaller, informal meetings with Community Board officials allowed the study team to produce preliminary proposals for presentation at larger public meetings, which elicited additional feedback from the community.

The intent of the meetings and public process was to create a waterfront plan based on a collaboration between the community and design team. From these meetings a list of community criteria was assembled from questionnaires to consider what activities and design elements would best benefit the area.

In addition to Community Boards, participation by neighborhood groups, city agencies, and elected officials was proactively encouraged. Local elected officials were involved to get their support and seek their guidance about local issues. Interviews with organizations such as the Metropolitan Waterfront Alliance (MWA), Asian Americans for Equality (AAFE), the Two Bridges Neighborhood Council were important to help the project team maintain impartiality that was crucial to preserving the community's trust.

That brings up the social mission of modernism. How does the issue of social responsibility factor into your practice? It does. We were down in Mississippi on day nine after Katrina hit, and we had a building completed in a matter of weeks. I wouldn't claim we were philanthropists, but we were and are interested in taking care of the people around us—and that includes our immediate environment. We're interested in creating a culture where people are happy to come to work. Our turnover is very low. I think we've lost five people in nine years. We're about 80 people now. People don't leave. **How is the office organized?** We don't have job titles and there's not a studio system here. It's not like there's Corey and her project managers, and Chris with his, etc. It doesn't work that way at all. At a minimum, there are two partners on every project, but usually there are three or four and it always shifts and moves. Clients like that. They have more than one person they can talk to. There's one person who's the typical point person for phone calls, but in meetings it could be any one of us that shows up to a presentation, and they're totally comfortable with that. Also, the staff works on at least two projects at a time, and they're continually moving and shifting back and forth, so you're always working with different people. We recently expanded and added more desks and took hours to do the seating chart. We took all the names and made sure everyone had the opportunity to work with someone different. There's not a formal Monday morning team meeting per se, other than power meetings, where all five of us meet and check in with each other. But every day we have a continuing conversation about what's happening on projects. Which is why we had to add three more conference rooms down here, so people could continually keep pinning things up and have running discussions.

How many projects are running right now? And how are the projects evolving in scale? We have about 14 right now, at a wide range of scales. We have a few projects that are over 100 million dollars. And the East River Waterfront project will probably be 200 million when it's done. In China we have a public project coming up that will be the next step for the Camera Obscura, translated to a much larger scale, but it's all tied to a similar process.

On many of these projects, there's an element of testing or innovation that you're introducing into the process. Things like methods, materials, and technologies that a client has likely not worked with before. How much time have you spent testing innovations? How much effort is required to convince a client that the innovation really works, and to invest in innovation? Basically, you're unfairly unqualified before you've done something and unfairly overqualified after you've done something. That's the whole game. We're still answering questions like, well, you did a 10-story condominium building which was very successful, but can you do a 14-story rental building? It's always this fight, chicken and egg, you can't direct a Hollywood film until you've directed a Hollywood film. To do it the first time once, that's the best and continual fight.

How do you deal with your fee structure? How do you review proposals? Do all the partners review them? Because if so, it sounds really time consuming. Firstly, fee structure is based on a percentage of the estimated cost. And then it's a set number. So the budget varies and it doesn't change. If the scope changes, then the fee is renegotiated. So that's the way we avoid that problem. Regarding our reviewing proposals, it is very time consuming, but there's your base contract and then there are adjustments. And then, Corey over here, can take on Virgin Atlantic's lawyers. She's like, I'm going to learn every architectural contract inside and out.

Well, it's just that you get these contracts and you know if you show it to a lawyer they're going to tell you not to sign it, and 20,000 dollars worth of legal fees later, you decide you really want the job anyway. We try to get the most we can out of the base contract and then negotiate a fee for the rest of it. **How do you decide what kinds of projects and clients to pursue?** We choose clients in a number of different ways. We definitely don't want to be specialists; we want a blend of avant-garde and practical, a blend of profit and loss, and a blend in scales. We're willing to take a project that might not be our first choice, as long as we feel it opens up new territory for us or gets us to a new scale. But in any successful project, at the end of the day, it's about the relationships between everyone involved, and it's about putting together good teams. If you have a good team and everyone respects and trusts each other and there is good open communication, it can be a great project no matter what. And if you don't have that, it can be terrible no matter what. It's something we've had to learn the hard way, but over time that's something we've come to focus on. **Can you give an example of this dynamic you're describing?** Well, when we started working on the East River Waterfront

→139, 140, 159 A:3

project, we'd seen 40 years of master planning go nowhere. We knew right away if we didn't embrace the organizations and bureaucracies that basically rule the river, then we were going to become part of that 40-year master-planning graveyard. But when you embrace those things, you have to realize that you're dealing with frustrating inefficiencies. You have to be tenaciously persistent. **How do you deal with that?** The thing is, you're operating on multiple scales, from community boards that can be as small as six people to a huge roomful of city officials, and everyone has a different desire, a different goal they're after. Your first job is to go in and listen and ask questions. Crafting what questions to ask, and to whom, is actually a really important challenge for us. This is one reason why you see all the problems over at Ground Zero (the World Trade Center construction site). The architects are really the people who need to stimulate the dialogue that sets up the design criteria. They're the organizers and composers of that process. If the architects disengage, then organizations like the Police Department or the Port Authority, or other disparate parties come in, and eventually no one is talking to each other anymore. The architect is the conduit through which everything should pass. Another point is that when the architect says: this is what the project should look like, the game is lost. And yet the process is not about design through consensus. That's a totally different thing, that's total compromise. In fact, we really believe that compromise is a result of not understanding all the forces at work. If you're actually building your argument to satisfy everyone's requirements, then the solution gets beyond the aesthetic, and you can get the design you actually want.

Do you find any disadvantages in being identified with technology? Sometimes early on in our career they called us the "avant-cheap" architects, which we sort of took as a compliment. **Sometimes working with clients, we notice that they can be surprised by our attitude as architects, in the sense that we really want to get this thing built most efficiently, that we care about cost, as if we were the owners of the project. It sounds like you've got that sort of attitude as well…** Yes, and we've been deeply rewarded for it. I don't know if you know this, but we've actually taken equity positions on a lot of our projects. One of the things we've learned is, if the client knows you're on the line as much if not more than they are, the equation suddenly changes. Suddenly, it's not about you as the architect trying to spend their money. The dynamic shifts, so that we can say, look we want to use this laser cutter to make 4,000 parts. It's going to make a really great design and it's going to cost less money, and then they respond, "Okay." There's no debate. That's a huge thing. Now we have positions in a half dozen other projects. It's not just about building cheaper, though. It's more about using design technology to build something better for a reasonable cost, as opposed to indulging every whim that we have. That kind of indulgence—not working with any parameters—turns us off. Again, we refer a lot to the aerospace industry. When people ask us who our influences are, we say Burt Rutan and Kelly Johnson (American

aerospace and aircraft engineers). Rutan was able to get a guy into space for 10 million dollars, compared to NASA's 100 million. It's true that NASA enabled Rutan to do a lot of his experimentation from 1948 onward, but at the end of the day he built the space station for a lot less. We also look to Johnson, the founder of Lockheed Martin's Skunk Works, and his 14 Rules of Management as a model for understanding how you move from the process of design to the procurement of parts, fabrication, and actual assembly. Those are the kinds of models we aspire to. Our whole argument is, we do good design for the same price or cheaper. Again, it doesn't have to be either-or, either value or design. You can have both. You get more architecture for your money. **How do you test it out?** We use technology to achieve variety, but we take advantage of economies of scale. For instance, if you have a complex design where someone has to cut all of these shapes by hand, that could get very expensive. Whereas if you have a machine reading digital files to cut those parts, it can cost the same, whether or not ↳241 A:2 you cut 500 of the same shape or 500 completely different shapes. Then if you can standardize the labor component, which is how that thing gets assembled, you can do something that's got complexity and interest. It responds to function or program or context at the same cost as if you said, well, it has to be a box and it has to be a square and all the components have to be the same. It's not complexity for complexity's sake though; it has to respond to the needs of the project. Standardization provides efficiency for sure, but formal standardization is not necessarily better. The fabrication has to be standardized for reasons of efficiency, but the actual components don't have to be. One of the concepts we set out to test was the Camera Obscura, because ↳101 A:1, 196–199 that was a public works project and was going out for a low bid. Previously, we'd had a number of R&D (research and development) projects where we had more control because we were doing it as design-build, or because it was a private project where we were partially the clients. But Camera Obscura was a project that was going out to public bid, and we wanted to test the feasibility of making this project entirely from a computer model. We wanted to create shop drawings and specifications and assembly instructions directly from that model, and do it without violating the rules of the public bid process. We did find a way to do it within the confines of the public works rules, and it came in under budget. It led us to think about process in new ways, writing specs and creating documents in a new way. The only traditional drawings we used were those produced for the city review process.

Do you write your own specs? We have a spec writer who we work with to develop and modify them for public sector bids. For instance, one mantra in the public works sector is you can't sole source, you have to write a three-manufacturer specification that shows how everything you do will be available out of a catalog. Instead of listing three brands from which component x can be bought, in our case component x exists on a digital file. We list three fabricators they can go to in order to get the parts cut. For a contractor, it's the same thing as buying out of a catalog. If not for the Camera Obscura project, our contracts with East River and with FIT (Fashion Institute of Technology)—which involves the Dormitory Authority of New York State—might not have developed the way they did. FIT had a standardized system in place for doing curtain walls for obvious reasons, and they wanted some assurance that the kind of documents going out to bid would follow a prescribed method. They wanted a track record. And we used the Camera Obscura project as a model that allowed them to begin to understand how this process with the computer can begin to allow us to break with some of those conventions. **So you were able to use this small project as leverage?** Yes, and when we met with their quality assurance people in Albany, we laid out a strategy for how we wanted to do the FIT curtain wall system, involving the production of a three-dimensional file from which all other documents would be extracted. As with Camera Obscura, we put out a digital package to three qualified fabricators to let them bid on it and build a mock-up and base their bid on that mock-up. This way we were able to solidify the most complex part of the contract very early on, and in a way that allowed them to engage and make changes. This was all a direct result of breaking with the standardized government procurement process.

You're giving a small example of how the whole profession could potentially change. Yes, and I'll give you one more example. It's something the office has spent the last eight months investing in. We did three competitions last year whose concepts were based on performance, and we won them in large part because we've been working on and investing in this, and in large part because of our collaboration with Buro Happold. What we're doing is trying to embed green performance strategies into our buildings as they're developed. We're always being asked to make promises about performance, before we even know how we'll follow through with them. We'd like to be able to make these promises with some initial analysis, so we started speaking with the Stevens Institute of Technology in New Jersey and discovered they were studying software that can help in this regard. It addresses many facets—not only parametric—but environmental, structural, three-dimensional modeling… And we've started looking

at how we can bring this in at the feasibility and schematic phases. **Isn't this similar to what Gehry Technologies (GT) is doing?** Yes, but I think we're more interested in what happens before you even get to the management phase of the project. The management model is about extracting data out of the computer in order to get it built in real life. But I'm talking about how I can also change the model parametrically and use technology to generate design criteria. The dilemma is this: no matter how qualified or talented your engineering consultants are, ultimately, you can't manage their people. You can't tell them to do this model or make that model. They have a fee for schematic and feasibility service and they're only going to use up so much of that time on thinking outside the box. What we want is to be able to go into our engineer's office already having done these models ourselves, knowing that what we're giving them in terms of digital information is something that will allow them to start their work at a higher level. We want to see this happening in structural issues, as well as environmental ones. And this really requires a different kind of person in the office too. That's not to say we hire a technician who just does these models. No, the kids that are going to Stevens now are architects, mathematicians, biologists… They're similar to the kind of classmates we had, except the focus of their commitment is to understand how to communicate in the industry and how to manage. We're paying three full-time scholarships for Stevens students interning here, and we actually have three kids from our office taking scripting classes there. Just to add to what Bill is saying, the key here is not just one piece of software. To us they're tools, so we use this software to solve this problem, that software for that one, and so on.

We asked Dennis Shelden of GT whether he might think about turning Digital Project (software application based on CATIA and developed by Gehry Technologies) into open source software… Yes, Rhino (modeling software) representatives came into our office a few weeks ago. They're sending us scripts, we're making comments and sending them back, and 24 hours later they're posting them online. We're talking about who's going to own the scripts, and Rhino says, we'll post the scripts, and if you want to own them, own them. One of the problems with Digital Project is that there's no open-sourcing interface. But Rhino wants to own the whole market if they can. And they're trying to do that by selling 500-dollar packages to students, and making source readily available. **It must make Autodesk (foremost design software company, producing AutoCAD among others) quite nervous.** The problem is: how can you commit to just one software? At one point, all five of us sat around trying

to decide which software we were going to spend 150,000
dollars on, and finally we realized we weren't going to do
that. We were going to build a realm in which you can
start to engage all these different software. It has to do with
the scale of the project. Some projects are all-encompassing
like Camera Obscura, and with many projects we pick
and choose which software makes sense for them. **Can you
comment on practicing in the United States versus
Europe or Japan?** I don't know, I think everyone has a
grass is greener scenario. Europe has great quality material,
and in Japan the contractors have so much integrity. Then
you go lecture in Japan and they're like, oh, you have so
many new materials to work with. And in Europe they say,
you're so free to try all these new things. Here it's such a
hierarchical system. I think this office—if we had to make
a choice—would choose to work in the United States,
because it's fertile in terms of us being able to impact and
influence a position. **You know, one motivation for doing
this book was our discomfort with Rem Koolhaas's
call in *Content*, to "Go East!" i.e., to Asia. We felt
in some ways this was an abdication of responsibility,
and that in America there are a lot of things going
right. It's not a homogenous movement, to be sure,
but something promising is happening.** I agree.
I think it's this generation that's doing it. It's not about
style, it's not something you can readily point to or identify.
For instance, it took us an hour to bring it up today, in
this conversation, to talk about where we're going. It's not
something that's easily digestible and consumable, but it's
happening. Maybe by the time everyone realizes it, the
revolution will be over. And in a way maybe that's a good
thing. The contractors and unions are resisting, but it's too
late, it's all going to change.

*Interview with Gregg Pasquarelli, Christopher Sharples,
Coren Sharples, and William Sharples [Kimberly Holden
not present] was conducted in New York City in 2005 by
Jon Dreyfous, Elite Kedan, and Craig Mutter and revised
in 2008.*

↗97 A:1

3 Degrees of Felt MY Studio/Meejin Yoon

Alice Tully Hall **Gehry Technologies** consultant
Architect: Diller Scofidio + Renfro with FXFOWLE Architects

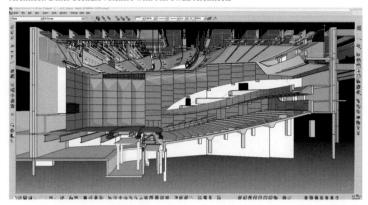

Arthouse **Lewis.Tsurumaki.Lewis**

↘26, 99 A:1

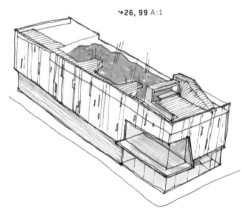

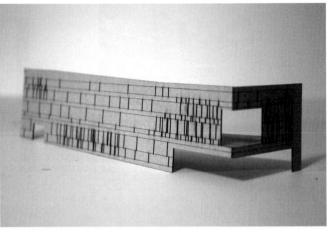

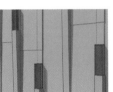

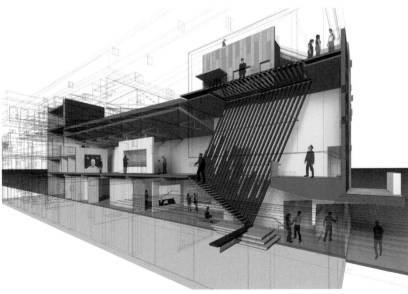

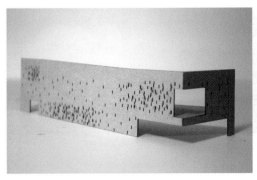
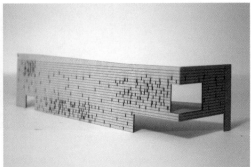

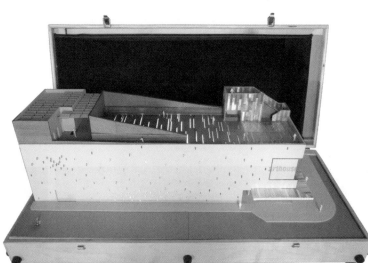

↗50, 83, 99 A:2, 242–243

Avra Verde Residence **MARCH/Chris Hoxie** consultant
Architect: Rick Joy Architects

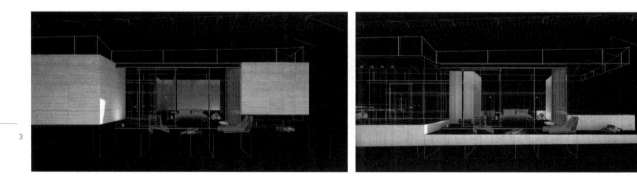

1

2

3

↗100 A:1, 244–245

Beijing National Stadium **Gehry Technologies** consultant
Architect: Herzog & de Meuron

1

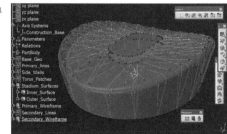
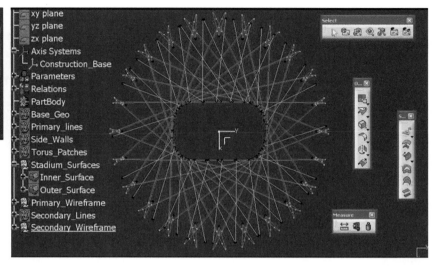

2

↗51, 100 A:2, 194 A:1

Bornhuetter Hall, **Lewis.Tsurumaki.Lewis**

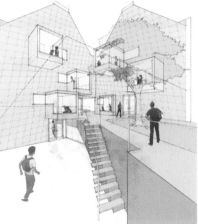

3

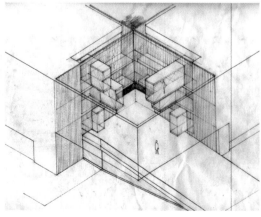

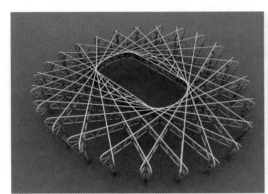

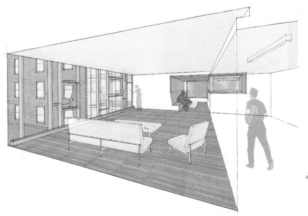

1

2

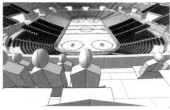

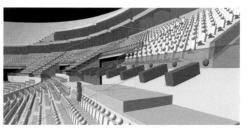

3

↗ 52–53, 101 A:1, 142 B:32, 196 A:1, 241

Camera Obscura SHoP

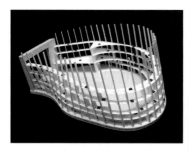

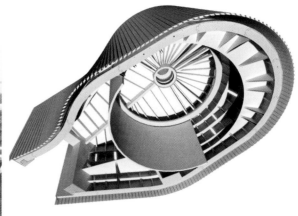

Brooklyn Arena—Atlantic Yards Gehry Partners

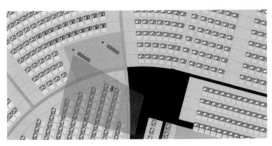

↗54, 104 A:2, 200 A:1, 231, 247 A:2

3

Canopy: MoMA/P.S.1 nARCHITECTS

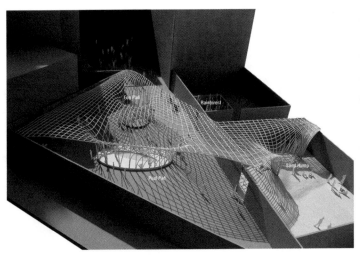
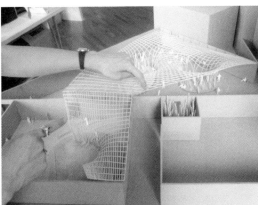

↗88 B:33, 105 A:1, 248

China Central Television Headquarters (CCTV) **Front** consultant
Architect: OMA

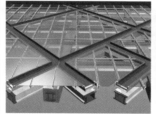
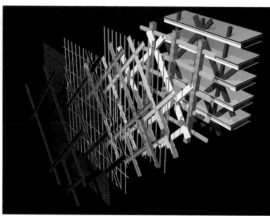

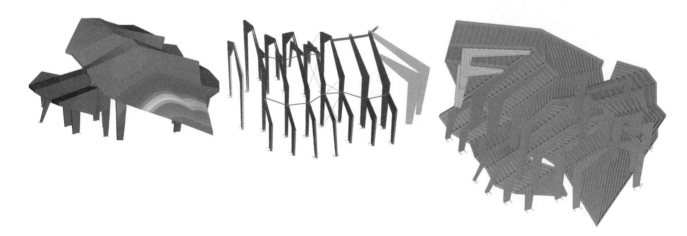

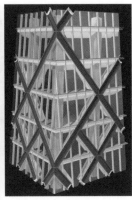
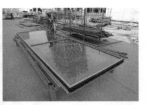

***D Gallery* Front** consultant
Architect: Point B Design

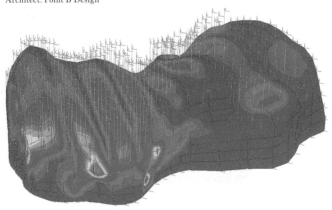
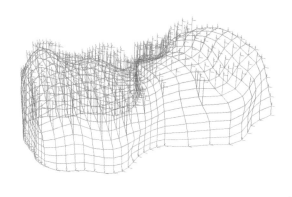

↗107 A:1, 204 A:1, 250–251

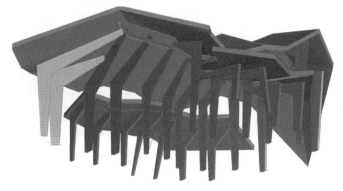
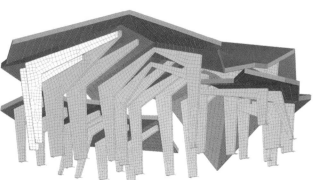

1

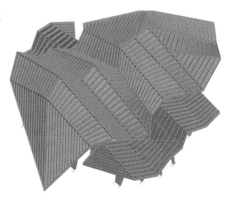

↗12, 56–57, 108 A:1, 190 A:1, 252–253

***Dark Places* Servo**

2

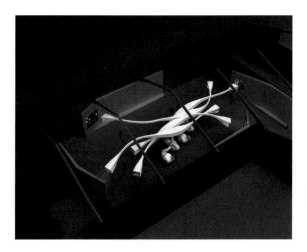

3

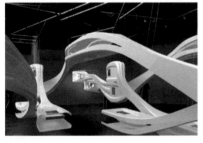

1

↘108 A:1, 211 A:1

2

3

MOCK-UPS AND RENDERINGS   158

↗109 A:1, 214 A:1

***Dee and Charles Wyly Theater* Front** consultant
Architect: REX/OMA

↗109 A:2, 139–140, 141 B:43

***East River Waterfront,* SHoP**
with Richard Rogers Partnership and Ken Smith Landscape Architect

↗129 B:21

Eavesdropping **Lewis.Tsurumaki.Lewis**

↗60, 110 A:1, 254–255

Fluff Bakery **Lewis.Tsurumaki.Lewis**

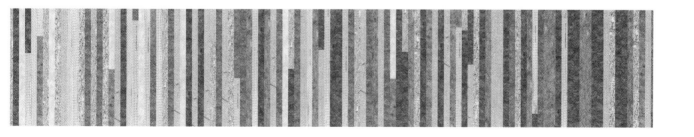

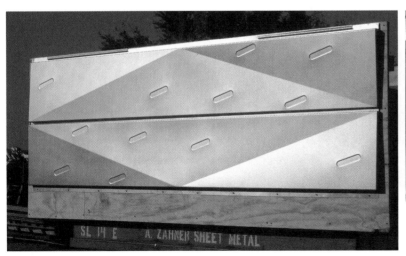

↗111 A:2, 276 A:23

High Line 23 Front consultant
Architect: Neil M. Denari Architects

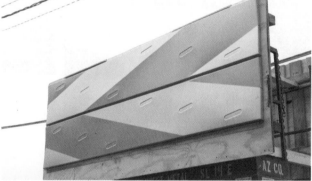

↗112 A:1

Honda Advanced Design Center George Yu Architects

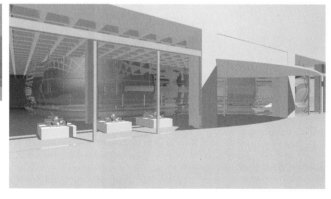

A   B   C   D

1

2

 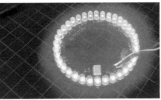 

3

↗66, 114 A:1, 180 A:27, 220 A:1, 259 A:1

LoRezHiFi MY Studio/Meejin Yoon

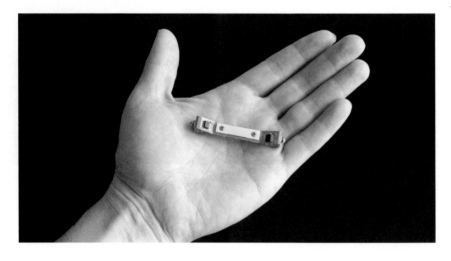

↗67, 118 A:1, 235 A:43

MaxStudio.com George Yu Architects

↘235

↗68, 120 A:1, 178 B:28

Möbius Dress MY Studio/Meejin Yoon

1

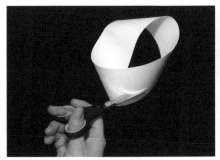 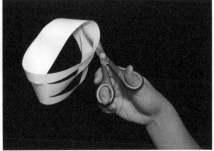 

2

3

Olympic Sculpture Park MARCH/Chris Hoxie consultant
Architect: Weiss/Manfredi

1

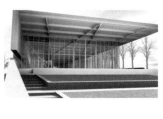

2

3

1

2

↳69

3

→70, 121 A:2

***One Island East* Gehry Technologies** consultant
Architect: Wong & Ouyang (HK) Ltd.

1

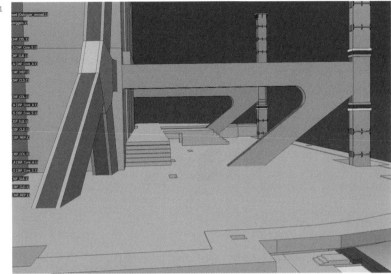

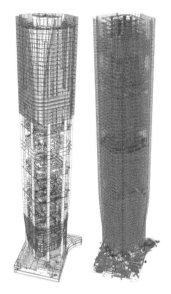

2

3

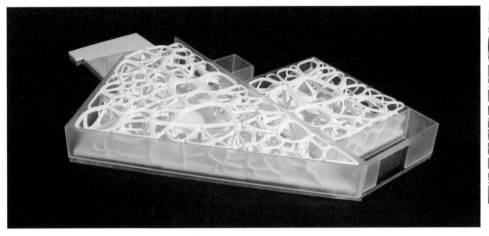

↗122 A:1

P.S.1: LOOP MY Studio/Meejin Yoon

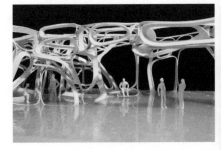

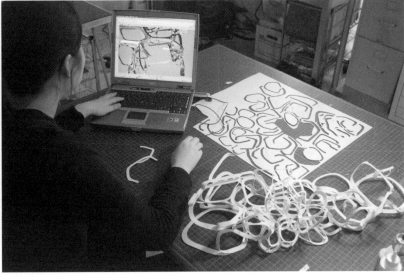

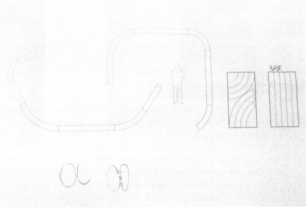

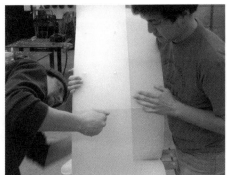

1

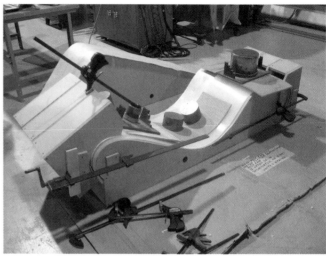

2

↗ 123 A:1, 239 A:38, 275 A:9

Sensorium, George Yu Architects

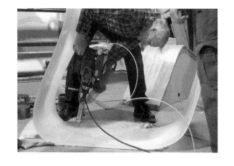

3

↗ 239 B:13

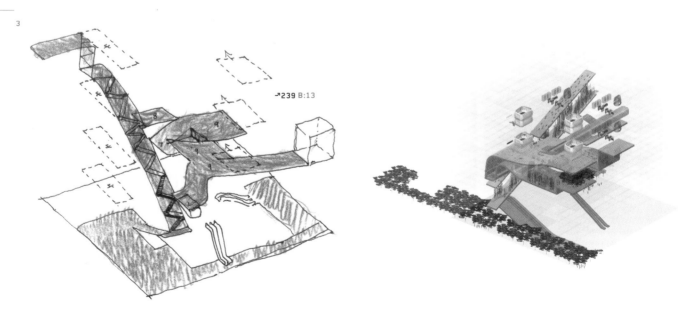

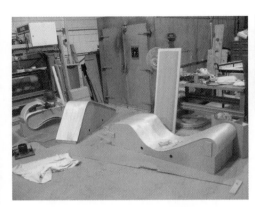

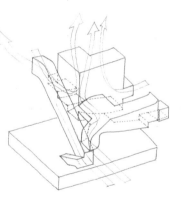

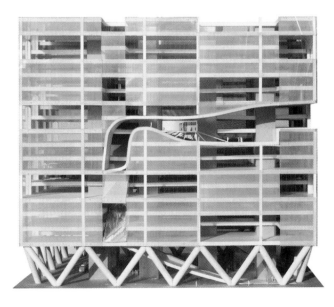

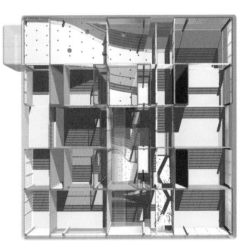

↗71, 88 A:48, 122 A:2, 264 A:1

Seattle Public Library **Front** consultant
Architect: OMA/LMN joint venture

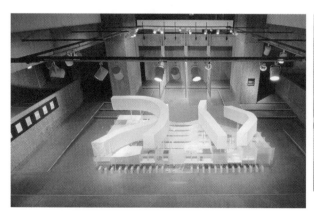

↗72–73, 124 A:1, 266–267

Shop Lift: Rethinking Retail, Transcending Type George Yu Architects

Weatherhead School of Management Gehry Partners

↗76–77, 126 A:1, 179 B:3, 224 A:1, **268**

White Noise/White Light, MY Studio/Meejin Yoon

1

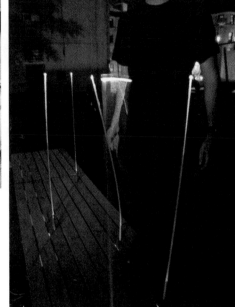

2

3

Meejin Yoon of MY Studio

We wanted to talk to you about your academic work, and how that turned into your professional work. Some projects that come to mind are ones you did at MIT (Massachusetts Institute of Technology), particularly your textile and clothing projects. I began teaching at MIT several years after graduating. Prior to that I had been practicing in a rather analog mode. The digital was not a large part of my undergraduate or graduate education at Cornell and Harvard's GSD (Graduate School of Design). But teaching at MIT changed all that. My first semester there, I enrolled in a popular Media Lab course called How to Make Almost Anything with Neil Gershenfeld. The class is essentially a crash course in fabrication and electronics tools and covers Design Tools, CAD CAM (computer-aided design and manufacturing) fabrication tools, microcontroller programming, machining, and so on… The course culminates in an individual fabrication project, and mine was the Defensible Dress. I had been thinking about the project before I took the class, but the class really equipped me with the skills and tools to properly realize it. It was an opportunity for me to synthesize a number of longstanding interests. I wanted to engage the scale of the body and test the way the human body interacts with space. The dress was made of aluminum rods mechanically attached to a series of servo motors, which were controlled by a microcontroller and an IR (infrared) sensor. It was a bit of an ad hoc construct made from off-the-shelf fabrication and electronics components.

But more important than the project was what I got out of the course. Technologies that I assumed were out of reach in terms of cost and expertise were suddenly demystified and accessible. The do-it-yourself ethos was also a really important influence on me. I was exposed to a whole generation of students who teach themselves new skills constantly through software tutorials, online help, and Google, and who can make almost anything overnight by ordering off-the-shelf components and materials from Digi-Key and McMaster.

My formal architecture education didn't really teach me how to build. We made drawings and notations for building. We worked in representations of architecture. The Media Lab course introduced me to a completely different model of education—a kind of personalized focus on making through fabrication and testing during the design process itself. **What you're describing is a personal paradigm shift.** Yes, absolutely.

Your Cornell education and MIT education represent two very different strands of thinking. Maybe you could talk more about Cornell. For me, Cornell was a really solid design education, which placed a lot of emphasis on form-making and modernism. It's a school where postmodernism never happened, and though it was committed to design ideas, the products of design—models and drawings—were privileged aesthetic objects in their own right. In the urban design program at GSD, by contrast, we weren't designing objects, but strategies. We were taught to think about design in terms of strategies and tactics for development, which was a real transition for me. When I left Cornell I was really interested in large-scale design projects, but oddly enough by the time I left GSD I was interested in small-scale objects such as books and concept clothing.

What I got from MIT was a shift in my thinking about design and fabrication. The attitude there is if you have an idea you have to prototype it, test it, and make it again. Another thing was the attitude toward the design product. At MIT quality is not assessed in terms of how beautifully crafted the project is or even how well it acts as a vehicle for the idea, but by potential impact. This comes from a completely different way of understanding the role of testing, prototyping and R&D (research and development).

How does that manifest itself in the way you teach design? While I'm very process-oriented, the studio is not only about process. It's about how you frame the question. It's about teaching each student to frame their thesis relative to the scope of the studio. They have to develop a process for themselves that pushes their specific project forward. This lab approach forces students to test ideas, to really prove their thesis as well as evaluate it and repeat it. **So it's about learning how to develop a personal method?** Yes. Or developing a design language out of the thesis project itself. And then, depending on the nature of the studio problem, the design language evolves from there. I think that's really important. One thing I learned consistently from Cornell, GSD, and MIT is that you have to become very facile in different design processes, methods, and languages and learn to move skillfully between and beyond them. But I think an interesting characteristic of my work—and one I sometimes wonder about—is the absence of any recognizable style or signature. I sometimes ask myself if breadth and depth are mutually exclusive, or rather if one can continue to expand one's interests and still contribute to the field. In the academy, there is a lot of pressure to focus your research agenda and make it hyperspecific. It's like a branding exercise in some ways, since the agenda gets attached to you and becomes your signature. The more narrowly defined, the better, because the easier it is to prove that you're on top of the field. I've often worried that my work is too wide-ranging in scale for this reason—from artist's books to clothing to installations to urban design. I feel external pressure to commit myself to just one area, but I'm unable to do it. **Well, what about the Eames duo (Charles and Ray Eames)?** Yes, I always use them as a model. They worked in film, designed exhibitions, and built furniture and architecture. For them, design was a way of living. They were always engaged in research and didn't limit themselves to just one medium. **Back when I studied history, you could specialize in 16th-century English theology and market yourself very effectively in terms of publishing. But to my mind architecture is different, or should be. The question is how do you respect the profession's interdisciplinary nature and still market**

yourself successfully? I recently had an exhibition of my work at the Wolk Gallery at MIT. And I have to say I think everyone should be required to do an exhibition of their work ten years after graduating from school. Seeing your work together on one wall, you're forced to critique yourself—not just each project individually but as a whole. It's interesting to see what issues keep resurfacing. It becomes clear there is a research agenda that appears as threads through the work, despite differences in scale or medium. I like to think of my work as part of a larger research project. I like to think larger issues arise out of the specificities of a particular project, that they feed in organically, moving both forward a little at a time. Don't get me wrong. I don't use a client's project to push through my own agenda. Each project has its own parameters and motivations, but there is definitely a negotiation going on between the specific site, program, scale, and materials of the particular project and a larger research agenda. **So what did you discover?** Recently, my portfolio was reviewed for the Rome Prize and one of the committee members made a comment I found interesting. As he was looking through the portfolio, he said he felt like each of the projects was formally distinct, but that there was a kind of invisible ink signature that you could sense through all the projects. For example, both the Möbius Dress and the 3 Degrees of Felt project (for the Aztec Empire exhibition at the Guggenheim) were projects that examined a continuous surface in space. The Möbius Dress took the spatial loop of the Möbius strip and adapted it for wear on the human body, so the dress operated in relation to the body. Whereas 3 Degrees of Felt operated in relation to the artifacts and curving interior space of the Guggenheim.

↳120 A:1, 166 A:1

A Möbius strip has one continuous surface and one continuous edge. I was curious to understand the relationship between a single-sided surface and a single edge as a spatial idea. I began the project by cutting the Möbius strip. I cut toward the edge and then a second time along the middle, unraveling the strip in order to understand its spatial logic. I made a life-size Möbius strip from two yards of industrial felt fitted with two zippers of 72 inches and 144 inches. Because of the geometry, this created two interlocking loops. The Möbius strip is one-sided, one-edged, and has zero orientation, so it was important that the material I used have no hierarchy: no warp, no weft. I chose felt because it's a seamless material created through friction. Structured only by the body, it twisted and turned, from a continuously evolving surface, as it unraveled. The spatial loop created the appearance of two intertwining bands of fabric that met at points around the hips and torso. The dress was meant to challenge clothing's absolute adherence to conventions of interiority and exteriority. It's an inherently inside-out and outside-in garment—a dress that's worn to be unworn.

The Aztec Empire exhibition at the Guggenheim was
→49, 97 A:1, 145 A:1
also made from a continuous surface using felt, but the logic behind it was different. I was asked to collaborate on the exhibition design by Enrique Norten of TEN Arquitectos. What we wanted to do was create a singular but non-uniform experience, for which there were two interrelated challenges: First, there were over 450 Aztecan objects of varying scales that we had to accommodate. Second, we had to operate within the constraints of Frank Lloyd Wright's unique museum interior. In studying the collection of artifacts and the space of the museum, we quickly learned that not all of them would fit along the ramp. So in order to accommodate all the objects, we began to bend the display wall, folding it in and out of the bays to expand the linear square footage of display by approximately 50 percent. The ribbon wall was then slit at various heights so that we could bend and peel the wall to create gaps for artifacts. The Aztecan artifacts had a wide range of requirements, so this wasn't easy. Some of them required UV protection, some required security glass, somewere designated "stars" and had to be situated prominently. Locally, it was clear what we had to do to accommodate the object—pull back where security glass was required, compress circulation to foreground a star object, etc. But every one of these cuts in the wall had repercussions down the road, so it was equally clear we needed to have a system.

I wanted to develop a system that would allow us to
→193 B:1
model each object in Rhino (modeling software) and link it to information about the object's specific requirements. A series of plug-ins and scripts were written by Stylianos Dritsas, a recent MIT graduate, to test a sort of low-tech parametric generative design process without using high-end parametric software. Once the definitions were assigned, a script generated the wall along with the different sized pockets for objects. As objects were rearranged, deleted, swapped out, and redefined, the script allowed the wall to regenerate itself. The undulation of the walls acted to conceal and reveal the objects, but this had to work in both directions since, some people start from the top of the ramp and some start from the bottom.

We tried to hide or efface the Guggenheim's structural bay system in order to create a kind of inner liner along the continuous circulation. The walls were made of a dark, thick felt, transforming the classic white wall interior. By absorbing light and sound, the felt wall transformed the space into a deep, mute envelope. It's impossible to tell from photographs, but the acoustic dampening of the space altered your experience of the museum's whole interior in a subtle but powerful way.

Could you talk more about some of your interactive projects, like White Noise/White Light. How was that
→76–77, 126 A:1
generated? White Noise/White Light, or WN/WL, was one of nine interactive installations at the Athens 2004 Olympics. It was commissioned through a design competition called Catch the Light. I was invited to compete because someone on the selection committee heard about a small interactive project I did at the Architectural League called the Pleated Wall. The Pleated Wall was made of a series of projections or protrusions on a vertical plane that would respond to the viewer's approach—pulling back to invite you in and pushing out once the view had departed. White Noise/ White Light was an outgrowth of this project, but turned on its side—literally as well as conceptually. The competition design brief requested that the proposed installations along a designated route in Athens record and play back the sounds of the city to visitors. In response, I proposed collecting all the sounds of the city and playing it back in such a way that one experienced a field of white noise. The idea was to create a kind of absence of sound through sound. What I found interesting about the concept of whiteness— white light being the full spectrum of color and white noise being the full spectrum of frequencies without differentiation—was the idea of total accumulation and the relationship of the multiple to the singular. By adding many frequencies, I could create a condition whereby all of them and none of them were measurable or understandable.

The project consisted of approximately 400 semi-flexible fiber-optic strands (a material typically hidden in our floors and walls and cities that only exists to transmit—whether data or light). The fiber optics were arranged in a grid and were made to transmit a response one-to-one with the movement of people through the field. Activated by a passerby, they transmitted light from white LEDs below the deck platform, while the speakers emitted noise. The volume of white noise and the intensity of white light were controlled by means of a custom microprocessor designed by Matt Reynolds, an electronics engineer. I met Matt through the How to Make Almost Anything course. He was a PhD candidate at the Media Lab and was the teaching assistant during the microcontroller phase of the class. For WN/WL, he worked with us to develop the electronics; each stalk unit contained its own passive infrared sensor and microprocessor, which used a software differentiation algorithm to determine whether a person was passing by.

The original intention was to take thousands of sound samplings of the city, filter and isolate all the frequencies, and then remix them in equal amounts together. But due to our various constraints we had to manufacture the white noise electronically based on a physical phenomenon called Johnson noise. Johnson noise is created from the thermal motions of electrons in a resistor carrying current. So in the end we did not record and remix, we created the sound by putting electrons in motion.

In a way, the project was conceived as a sort of measuring device, recording the movements of people through the field. But what was actually more interesting in the end was the way it induced behavior. People would run through it, jump, wave their arms, and twirl. Through quantitative multiplication, it created a qualitative effect that not only recorded activity but generated it. Cycling between input and output in order to measure the body, the crowd and the city, the field became an unpredictable aggregation of movement, light, and sound. In the end it created a kind of saturated inhabitation, rendering the concept of *white*, in all its undifferentiated completeness, material.

It was an amazing opportunity. Basically, I was given the chance to take an idea that originally existed at the scale of the circuit board and realize it at the scale of the urban plaza in Athens. It's always gratifying to imagine moving through something you design and then actually getting to do so. We had tight budget constraints coupled with the inherent logistical problems with building something overseas, so I do think the MIT attitude of anything-is-possible helped enormously.

Tell us more about the project you're working on in Washington DC. What is it exactly? LoRezHiFi is our nickname for it. The formal name is Sound Grove: Light Stream. It's an interactive sound-and-light installation on the sidewalk and in the lobby of a building on Vermont Avenue. The street is abnormally wide. The sidewalk is 41 feet, 25 of which is given over to a parking zone. Though it is officially public space, the zones were historically used by property owners for landscaping, which was originally, of course, seen as an amenity. But over the years increasingly little has been done with the area—a few planters, and the rest is paved over for parking. We took this wide swath of sidewalk as an opportunity to create an interactive landscape that would engage the public.

The project consists of two parts, the Sound Grove and the Light Stream. The Sound Grove is essentially a grove of touch-sensitive stainless-steel poles that are 12 feet high and three inches in diameter. It was conceived of as literally an urban musical instrument. The poles are arranged in a four-by-five grid, and each pole is divided into four segments divided by a Lexan diffuser. Each segment, when touched, triggers a sound, and when released, the sound fades away. We worked with sound composer Erik Carlson (from Area C) to compose each of the sound segments. Each segment is very simple, consisting essentially of a single sound and a pause that repeats. But each segment is also slightly different from

the others, so as to avoid repetition. One difference from White Noise/White Light is that the poles are networked together, so each pole knows if another pole is activated. We worked with Carlson to create a kind of family of sounds so that when you let go of one sound segment, another segment on a pole in the distance would be triggered to play a sound and then fade—like an echo. We had to develop in-house an interface to study and test the sounds in time and space. Lisa Smith, a member of our office, developed an interactive Flash site where we could upload sounds for specific segments and test them with each other in various configurations and sequences. This site facilitated collaboration between Erik Carlson and members of my studio.

The Light Stream portion of the project is based on a series of interactive LED nets visible from both sides. The nets are suspended between two layers of glass. The LEDs are held in place by wires, and each net acts as a dispersed screen that receives a video feed in the form of either a text, graphic, or image. When seen together, the three LED nets stream text and images with overlays of video feed—in real time—of the building's surveillance cameras, creating what we call a digital shadow. As you approach the net, it responds by digitally casting your shadow in the matrix of LED pixels. On one side the shadow is created by pixels that light up in the shadow profile, while on the other the shadow is created by pixels that turn off.

Was the technology pre-engineered? What existing technologies did you use? We began by examining existing technologies and products such as Color Kinetics' iColor Flex SL, Barco's Mi-Pix, Sensacell's Module T64 and Glas Platz's LED power glass. These are all prepackaged LED technologies that are addressable. But in the end none of the products did exactly what we wanted them to—or if they came close, they were packaged in a way that didn't match our design intent. We decided to do a custom designed LED net. We're working with Will Pickering of Parallel Development to design and fabricate the LED portion of the project. He came up with an ingenious way to create an armature for the LEDs. Essentially, the armature is the heat sink for the LEDs suspended on four wires that allow each one to respond to the behavior of the viewer. The electronics design is so intelligent and yet minimal.

There seems to be a lot of research going on right now in interactive design. Why is that, do you think? What's valuable about interactivity? I mean it's easy to say that when the participant is involved it's a positive thing, but what's valuable about it to you personally? I think partially it's about play, and creating a sense of play in the urban environment. It can be a moment

in your experience when you engage something unfamiliar,
something that makes you more aware of your context and
surroundings. For me, what I love in these projects is the
tactile quality. The sounds come from touching, or brushing
up against this physical thing.

**To me *play* is a philosophically suggestive term.
But it's worlds away from the standard issues that
get brought up when people talk about generative
or algorithmic design. I almost think it's a political
difference. What do you think?** As architects, we use
the term *play* interchangeably with *tolerance* in tectonics.
We allow for play between two materials or joints, for
example. Play is the gap or the space between that allows
for difference. I do think the notion of play is philosophically,
politically, and socially suggestive. Maybe it's because
these days what's more interesting than the orchestrated,
choreographed effects of architecture is architecture's
potential for inducing new atmospheres and behaviors,
unscripted effects and unprogrammed events—a kind of
re-examining and revisiting of architecture's potential to
construct, as much as the requirement that it be constructed.

*Interview with Meejin Yoon of MY Studio was conducted in
New York City in 2005 by Jon Dreyfous and revised in 2007.*

Dennis Shelden
of Gehry Technologies

It seems that there is an agenda in your work based on a dissatisfaction with contemporary American building means and methods. Yes. But I think that dissatisfaction is a reflection of or an amplification of the dissatisfaction of a lot of professionals in the building industry. There's a sense that the professions of design and building are less than what they could be, that the procedures of contemporary practice have obscured the intentions and ambitions of practice, and that change is needed. Our agenda at Gehry Technologies (GT) is in a sense purely about the potential of technology to serve as a catalyst for that change.

Is it a mix of software capabilities and a new kind of consultancy? We've taken on both software development and the application of technology to practice through consulting. The business model continues to evolve, but in some ways I'm really not sure you can do one without the other. We've found it difficult to get the industry to adopt changing technologies without providing significant consulting on the ground. Also, I don't think you can develop paradigm-changing technologies unless your organization is directly involved in projects that are themselves striving to affect the paradigm.

How does this affect the design process? Are you advocating a different form of design practice? There is a strong design agenda in our work, but I think we have a different take on what exactly design is. I see design in the broadest possible terms, including the development of both means and methods, as well as the processes of project

execution. So to my mind conventional design comes in a little later than you might think. You have to look at the overall process and take into account all of the stakeholders; you have to understand their individual and composite design intentions, and only then can the classical view of the architect as designer take hold. The architect can be the conductor—or at least a conductor—but only if the process is set up correctly.

Our work—and the technology we develop—is sometimes characterized as being about the design-to-fabrication pipeline, and though that's certainly a critical component, the characterization, I think, is too narrow. Certainly, there are many contemporary projects where a consideration of *making* is deeply integrated into the design intent. You simply cannot realize much of contemporary architecture—at reasonable project costs, or while maintaining control of the design intent—without a deep understanding of means and methods being embedded in the pre-tendering design phases of the project. This has sometimes involved alternative models of design and project delivery, where fabrication knowledge is incorporated into the design before the project is tendered. It has often required that there be some role for fabricators—or at least incredibly knowledgeable engineers—in defining the system logics as part of the design intent.

And this, I think, pretty much goes to the heart of what's significant for our practice: there needs to be dramatic change to the process and roles required to realize ambitious projects. New processes are creating openings for design, and technology is providing a catalyst for rethinking conventional ideas about the building process, including

who is responsible for which aspects of it. And by rethinking process there's tremendous opportunity for all stakeholders to get something new out of the equation.

In terms of the actual design, the tectonics and the technology, there is definitely a sense that the processes of building are increasingly converging with those of manufacturing. Many systems that historically have been built on site out of rough materials are being pre-manufactured and assembled. A lot of contemporary architecture—standard and nonstandard—is concerned overtly with issues of systematization and manufacturability. There's no necessary demarcation between old and new here; there's simply a very rapid movement toward increasingly componentized building. The technology has been a big part of this process, especially in nonstandard architectural projects, since they're almost impossible to site fabricate; the pre-building and assembly of these projects requires incredible planning and control of construction geometry. Digital tools have been a big part of this evolution, since the confidence required to pre-build complex geometrical components and then have them assembled on site is hugely important. Consider for a moment the sorts of tools professionals have had historically to document and control projects. **How do you define generative form?** That's a fairly difficult question. To my mind, no design passes through digital operations without being fundamentally altered by it. And yet, at the same time, computers have shown absolutely no capacity for independent design. I think we have to first precisely define what we mean by *design*. One could say that one designs a winning chess strategy, and of course computers have proven more than up to the task. But the truth is computers only traverse solution spaces; they don't define them. Computers don't have the capacity for synthesis, which is a key part of the design process; it requires that one frame the problem in the process of designing the solution.

It's clear that, given a well-defined problem and set of operations, digital algorithms can run along and generate form. So for me the question is this: other than the obvious advantages of efficiency and precision, what's the payoff in terms of design? And, perhaps even more specifically, what's the advantage to the designer? How does it shape his or her original intention? At the heart of the debate concerning generative design, of course, is a philosophical mystery about where the design intent comes from.

I have to say, a purely formal exploration of the digital has not had a traditionally big role in our work, and I think there are a number of reasons for that. In part, we just don't see it as our role. I don't believe designers need Rube Goldbergian devices to come between them and their products, for example. On the contrary, a lot of our technical development efforts have been concerned with making otherwise incredibly complex building-performance issues compelling and evocative, so that designers can reach through complex system issues while working out their own designs. Ultimately, I think design intent comes from a whole host of sources that just don't lend themselves to the sort of closed form—or computable—representations that enable generative techniques to function. But another reason is purely economic. Nonstandard architecture can require an enormous amount of fabrication-level detail, often developed through a fairly complicated fabrication logic. By *complicated*, I certainly don't mean relative to the complexity of the rules of engagement of a building in its cultural context—these issues are, I believe, still largely beyond the computable or at least the automatable—but large, complicated rule sets nonetheless. And these systems have engineering performance requirements to meet, unit costs to hit, fabrication equipment methods and constraints to support. Our technology can solve problems like that, because they're well defined, they have well-defined goals that are appropriately and efficiently addressed through computation. **But playing devil's advocate: if you set up intelligent parameters, won't it be interesting to see what computational systems lead to formally?** I think it's an intriguing question, and I guess there's another potential model of computation, or problem solving, where the solution defines the problem, or the problem and solution evolve together. It can certainly be a compelling experience to watch your design grow based on a set of instructions you provide.

But to me, the computer is not a black box—with a lot of knobs on it—that just magically makes things appear. The results of computation are directly traceable to the logic inside, and that logic is readily available to anyone who has the inclination to look. Computers are incredibly useful when they're properly and deliberately instructed; they're most effective when given localized, well-defined problems. And architectural intent is generally beyond that scale, so it requires human intervention along the way. The complexity that can be independently generated in terms of design intent is, in my view, still relatively limited.

What if the design is directly sculptural or spatial? What if we have an unabashed interest in the geometries of hyperbolics colliding, for example, and want to extract those forms. Or what if I'm just interested in the idea of the torus? Then I think the tools can be incredibly empowering. Don't get me wrong, I'm not advocating a rationalist approach to design; I'm advocating a rationalist approach to computation in design. Because computation is a really lousy, really limiting tool for performing non-rational operations and a really great tool for logical ones, I think it should be applied to the latter rather than the former. There are other, perhaps more worldly tools that should be used for those aspects of the design process that are not intrinsically computational.

But you mentioned the geometries of hyperbolics and, again, that's where I start finding things more interesting. For example, the work of Mark Bury on (Antoni) Gaudí's Sagrada Família in Barcelona comes to mind. He's spent a lot of time working on Gaudí's forms using parametric approaches, and, in his analysis, the forms of the Sagrada Família are forms that result from operations of linear stone cutting tools swept in space. The resulting forms are hyperbolic paraboloids, which of course are rational, computationally generatable forms. They just happen to bind the formal inspiration with the built environment directly, through a set of geometrically encoded intentions. Parametric geometry techniques are incredibly well suited for these sorts of forms and intentions.

One of the interesting things about parametrics, though, is that we can codify these shapes in terms of geometrically founded logics. But that in itself is not enough. The question quickly becomes how you control and direct these rule sets as a designer. The interaction should be compelling, evocative, and transparent to the designer. The designer should be able to guide the tool toward a solution that gives him or her intellectual and operative power over the algorithms. Here at GT, we've sometimes been able to develop approaches to tectonic problems that are inherently prerational. That is to say, the tool is driven by the designer to produce forms that are by definition constrained to satisfy a given performance criterion. No matter what he or she does, the design product resides in the space of feasible forms as defined by the system requirements. In other words, if you give designers tools with great flexibility they can produce designs that are both their own and yet which fall within an agreed-upon space of making and creating. That's an outcome that is guided by engineering and yet totally in the hands of designers, and as such it can generate really powerful ideas. **But who's making the rules?** We do. [laughter] Or the world does. Seriously, though, it comes from a dialogue between stakeholders. More often than not, our job is to translate the stakeholders' statements into an operative form, and of course, ideally, to make the nature of that digital rendition as compelling, transparent, and faithful to their intention as possible.

Perhaps, the most profound examples of this dynamic—and an analog one at that—has been the role of paper in physical model making. Paper and other sheetlike materials are a really important part of Gehry's process, and the tectonic argument for this is that paper materials generate forms that at full scale have certain constructability efficiencies—namely, they can be produced out of sheetlike materials without stretch forming. From the perspective of fabrication efficiency, you might argue that this adoption of, or acceptance of, the constraints of paper forms has had a huge contribution to the success of Gehry's practice. And of course there are likely other embedded design intentions in these forms as well, but that's sort of beyond my scope…

I mean, imagine for a moment the phenomenological power of that sheet of paper during the modeling process. Just think of the broad spectrum of fabrication, construction, economic, and formal consequences that follow from the designer playing with that sheet of paper. During my earlier years with Gehry's practice, I was one of several people wrestling with what it meant to translate that paper quality into digital form. That experience was incredibly influential and left me with some lessons I'll never forget. One was an incredible respect for the physical and material world and the embedded knowledge of physical things. A simple sheet of paper is incredibly knowledgeable about its nature, and in many ways the digital counterparts—with all their gigaflops and megapixels—fall far short of that kind of intrinsic knowledge in the world. Another was how to insert a design interface into complex circumstances. The physical world, when you stop to think about it, has an incredible user interface. A sheet of paper guides the designer—even as the designer guides the paper—in ways that are natural, direct, transparent, and yet at the same time very much constrained toward its solution. I've continued to look for digital approaches that might embody something like this elegance.

In earlier days, NURBS (non uniform rational b-spline) modeling exhibited none of these characteristics. I think everyone who's worked directly with NURBS curves or surfaces initially had to ask themselves, why are the control points not on the surface? And from an intuitive perspective, it's a pithy question—they should be on the surface. But from an algorithmic perspective, it makes complete sense, though for reasons that are too complicated to explain here. In the interim there have been a number of tools built on top of the NURBS mathematics that allow you to manipulate surfaces with more intuitive tools, but also less directly, and potentially more obscuring of the intrinsic nature of the form.

Do you think there's a valuable lesson in the way open-source code has developed? Is collectively rewriting and correcting code something you could provide? Could sharing the development of parameter functions be a way of setting up an architectural project? There are really interesting unsolved questions regarding authorship, intellectual property, and responsibility around the development, distribution,

↘59, 75, 121 A:1, 175 A:3

and consumption of parametric models. For example, contemporary parametric tools can already support the notion of a parametric typical detail, which is provided as part of design documents in a more or less conventional detail drawing. It describes a general set of rules that can be applied to a local set of building conditions during construction. But there are tons of unresolved issues around this, both procedural and technical. For instance, how would the engineer control, and so take responsibility for, a detailed design if it takes on a life of its own in another party's hands? How would the engineer be compensated? Is there a market for this sort of parametric IP (internet protocol)? Should engineers increasingly become software developers? Of course there is a market for single-family house plans already on the internet, and the notion of parameterizing these housing plans has already been pursued by several internet companies.

There is also the question of interoperability. Parametric components require, like any file format, an encoding. But that's not the end of its development. It develops further as the software gets adopted and used by design professionals. The problem is that since there is still not a shared language for describing the behaviors of buildings and their components, certain discrepancies and incongruencies can arise between the way the software gets encoded and the way it gets used by the profession. GT is a strong supporter of IFC (industry foundation classes) and other standards organizations that are seeking to remedy this problem for this reason. But it's easy to see how difficult the task is. Even if you define a common language, you can't be sure that something hasn't been lost, that the expressive capacity of that language isn't somehow artificially restricted.

But your question is intriguing. Are there architectural equivalents to open source? I think you could consider the American two-by-four system a kind of open-source system. It encompasses a basic set of simple parametric rules like 16-inch O.C. (on center) framing, nominal versus measured sizes of timbers, and so on. Other specialized conventions for trusses, plywood, etc., have unfolded from there. It's a unifying open standard that's been adopted throughout the industry. It's flexibly adhered to by designers and product manufacturers alike. And it has clearly revolutionized the building industry in terms of manufacturability, efficiency, and simplicity with flexibility. The question is: will digital tools follow a similar path and provide similar efficiencies as the physical standards? And, perhaps even more intriguingly, will there be new physical standards—the next generation of the two-by-four system—corresponding to advances in information IP systems? **Could you use this approach for urban planning? Some of the material could just be about zoning, for example.** Yes, I think the

technologies are increasingly lending themselves to project knowledge on a vast scale. A number of reasons come to mind. First, technology is increasingly tipping the scale from prescriptive to performance-based codes, i.e., agencies have the capacity to dictate the desired result directly without having to resort to "cook book" approaches to describing performance intentions. So parametric building codes—where the end result is dictated, not just the rules for getting there—seem like a plausible direction in the future for urban planning. Second, the technical capabilities for handling truly vast data sets are becoming increasingly available. Agencies and large owners like the GSA (General Services Administration) are starting to require building models as part of the deliverables for design and permitting. I think we will very soon see tools that are able to handle city-scale aggregations of design information down to the rebar level, i.e. at any useful level of detail, along with capabilities that make processing, consuming, and simulating information possible. Finally, one can see the increasing convergence of design information with the real world, and, soon enough I'll bet, we'll see a direct connection between design data at the urban scale and the actual performance of facilities like cities.

Let's talk more about the process aspects of GT's work. How do you see technology innovation changing practice? Profoundly. I have two things to say about this. First, my personal interest has always been to try to look at building in the broadest possible sense, to search for some kind of unified design process. Early on, I became very interested in the engineering and performance aspects of practice. I came to respect the engineering and architectural approaches to practice, both of which I would characterize equally as design—even though most engineers and architects would beg to disagree. As part of this inquiry, I've always seen digital techniques as a potential unifying force, well before the tools really had the sort of collaborative capacity they do now. As the technology has matured, I think it has become more obvious that this is the true source of the technology's power and interest for design professionals.

My second interest has been the development of GT as a viable business. In this regard, I've been influenced by Silicon Valley and other businesses that I've been involved with professionally. I have a profound respect for how economics influences our lives, as both individuals and professionals. In design, they're still often seen as corruptive of professional values, or at best as something to be left to the harsh realities of the real world. But if you look at many innovative firms like Front or SHoP, they have interesting business models, where they are producing process innovations alongside unique design offerings to create new ways of providing value.

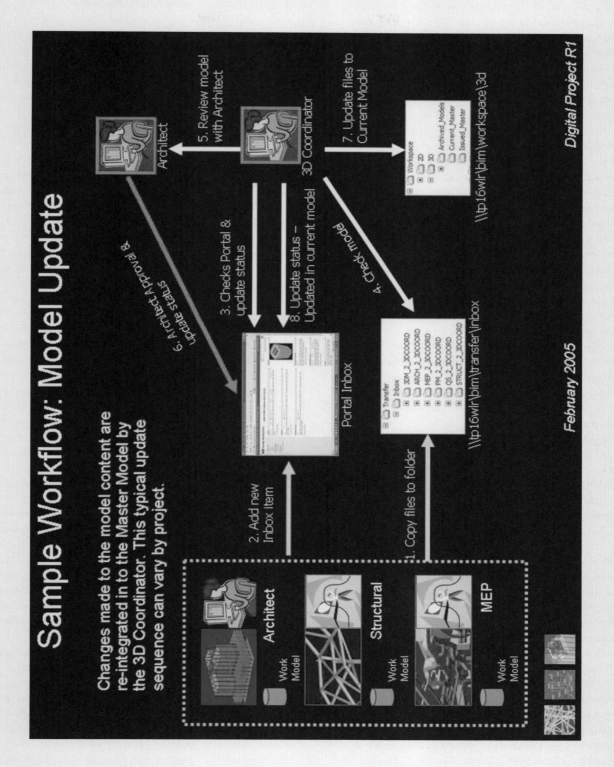

Sample Workflow: Model Update

Changes made to the model content are re-integrated in to the Master Model by the 3D Coordinator. This typical update sequence can vary by project.

5. Review model with Architect

Architect

3D Coordinator

7. Update files to Current Model

6. Architect Approval & update status

3. Checks Portal & update status

8. Update status – Updated in current model

4. Check model

Portal Inbox

Workspace
- 2D
- 3D
- Archived_Models
- Current_Master
- Issued_Master

\\tp16wlr\bim\workspace\3d

Transfer
- Inbox
  - 3DM_2_3DCOORD
  - ARCH_2_3DCOORD
  - MEP_2_3DCOORD
  - PM_2_3DCOORD
  - QS_2_3DCOORD
  - STRUCT_2_3DCOORD

\\tp16wlr\bim\transfer\inbox

2. Add new Inbox item

1. Copy files to folder

Architect

Work Model

Structural

Work Model

MEP

Work Model

Digital Project R1

February 2005

Viewed from these two perspectives—integrated practice and economics—you quickly find that conventional building delivery, as it is currently practiced, is incredibly inefficient in delivering value. Just take a long hard look at the process of building, how design fits into this process, the value it generates, where other value is created, and how alternative aspects of building delivery can capture additional value. There is definitely some room for improvement. *Value* is a funny word and, like it or not, one of the only common currencies for measuring value is currency. Many of the things that are of interest to designers—design control, practice opportunity, financial compensation, to name but a few—come only with value, and more often than not that requires a classic business calculus, weighing risk versus opportunity and the like.

It's strange that the exercise of determining where and how value is created is such an alien concept to the building trade. I mean, it's such an integral part of almost any process involved in the creation of goods, or the consumption of services.

Can good design create value? Of course. In fact, the value of high design, signature design, branded architecture, whatever you want to call it, has never been higher. You see firms like Asymptote or Zaha Hadid—once small design firms but with distinctive design offerings—exploding with work internationally. There's certainly a technological component to these firms' capacities to operate internationally. On the performance side, LEED (Leadership in Energy and Environmental Design) certification is showing great value to owners, both as a statement of citizenship and as a bottom-line driver to facilities; and I think the argument is beginning to take hold that some increased investment in performance design is worth the cost in terms of the intangible and tangible financial value of facilities.

At the same time, the production components of design are being increasingly commoditized, through outsourcing and automation. Firms are not going to be able to subsidize the design phases of projects through compensation for documentation, because this historical value equation is being increasingly inverted. There is a really fundamental shift happening in the design professions, which I think really needs to be understood and considered by professionals. The impact of technology, of course, is central.

While I think there are a number of exciting opportunities within the existing professions, our primary concern at GT is with the demarcations of professional roles—in particular, to the processes that bind building delivery together. This is interesting to us, in part because it's so under-explored and open; it's one of the areas in which orders of magnitude of new efficiency and value are still possible. This is all very much outside conventional ideas about the scope of architecture and design, but it's very fertile ground for innovative firms. Our role has been typically situated between existing professional roles—as the technical methodology drivers, and as the information architects, managers, and coordinators. **Clients must be part of this, right? And they have to be expecting a payoff for participating in these processes?** Absolutely. Owners need to be involved in changes to process, partly because they're the ones with ultimate overall control if they elect to take it, and partly because it's their building. They're the ultimate recipients of potential additional value and should therefore have a very active role in shaping this value. I think we could make the whole design process more transparent to the owners; they could have a much bigger role in design decisions than they do now, including decisions regarding building performance, project scheduling, cost options, and so on. Some owners have had difficulty taking on this positioning—particularly those who aren't continually doing new projects and aren't equipped to assume this increased responsibility. But many are, and the role of GT and others, I think, is to first define the potential value, and then work with the team to minimize risk, real and imagined, as well as help incrementally realize this value for owners and the rest of the team.

Our most successful projects have been where the owner has really understood the potential and so has driven the project from the top. We have owner-clients who will claim savings of more than 10 percent of the cost of construction by making an investment—both financial and in terms of institutional engagement—in technology. And I think this is just a point of departure. There is simply so much unrealized value in building, and we are just now beginning to really understand that. **But this is not the transformation of the construction industry we're talking about, or is it?** Yes. Clearly there's a transformation occurring, perhaps at a slower pace than some of us would like, but arguably as fast as the industry can consume it. I think it will be a revolution through evolution. **But in order to get to the bottom of what's really driving this revolution, don't we need a deep understanding of history in terms of what it means to build in America? If you look at Gehry's early residential projects, they trace and deconstruct what the building blocks of American construction are. Can new technologies push that critique forward? And how can smaller firms take advantage of these new means of executing design and construction?** Look, it's happening. We should go back to the position of the architect in all of this. The architect is a generalist who is orchestrating all the different specialists. Over time, this role has sort of stopped working in American architectural practice. Specialists and construction managers often have greater say in the feasibility of a design or building approach than the architect. For many of our clients, this is their main motivation for working with us—the ability to effect control over design intent through construction, by being able to clearly demonstrate the feasibility and rationale of the design as it plays out in the field—to be treated, as Gehry would put it, as an "adult" in the conversation about building delivery. The question of whether this agenda is of interest to architecture seems to be still a topic of debate in the profession, but I think the answer is becoming clear: constructability, project finance, software, and other areas of value in the building supply chain can and should be of interest to architecture as such. For smaller firms, obviously their capacity for pursuing these opportunities is limited, but many smaller firms are still taking on pieces of the puzzle, and not finding it particularly onerous to do so. I think the reality is that many firms are finding the gap between doing their work the same old way and doing things a bit more advanced is not as big a hurdle as it seems from the outset.

And yet sometimes it seems like you can produce a quality product and the market just doesn't follow.
True. But it does seem like the building industry really may be at a true tipping point this time. Certainly change is coming dramatically these days, and on all fronts. At worst, there will be enough to keep you in the game. We get a lot of great feedback about what we're doing. During the dot-com boom, you had these incubator companies that provided capital and operational support for emerging technology companies. That's what a practice or even a studio may offer in this century. That's what I would like to build. I'd like GT to be an idea- and initiative-generating organization, organized around the mission to positively affect a whole profession and an industry that we all care about.

Interview with Dennis Shelden of Gehry Technologies was conducted in Los Angeles, California, in 2005 by Jon Dreyfous and continued by email in 2008.

David Erdman of Servo

Could you talk about the Dark Places exhibition? The
project came to us three years ago through Joshua Decter.
He's an independent curator who teaches curatorial design
at Bard. He was out here interviewing several architects
to design a show called Dark Places that was to be loosely
themed around film noir and its impact on urbanism in
Los Angeles, using the works of artists like Cathy Opie,
Cindy Sherman, John Baldessari, Vito Acconci. He
was looking to work with an office that could help make
the content of the show impact the architecture. So the
resultant display method is not a white cube, it works much
more violently and aggressively with the art, and that's
partly due to Joshua's sensibility, but also the content. **So
the spatialization is not neutral, but there's also a
participatory or interactive element too, right? Do you
have a lot of experience with interactive design?** We
haven't done interactive design per se. We always collaborate
with other people, and on this project we're working with a
team from MIT (Massachusetts Institute of Technology) who
also teach at UCLA (University of California, Los Angeles)
in the design media arts department. **What's the venue?**
It's the Santa Monica Museum of Art, and the space is a
big Butler shed. It's been a really interesting experience
working with them and with Elsa Longhauser, the director
of the museum. **How did the original superstructure get
laid out?** These [gestures to model of installation] are from
studies just based on pick points in the ceiling and ways that
we could connect back up into it. There's a certain way to
balance these components, and it has to be a generic system
adaptable to any space when the show travels. There's a kind
of productive tension in the show between the installation

inflecting the existing space versus being something that
could be distributed in different configurations in subsequent
showings. Which is partly how the system developed. It's
what gave us these four strands, which means you could
partner them or install them singly, and then there's a system
of walls that will be discarded from each show, which kind of
peels off existing gallery walls to deal with frontal projection
orientations. There are front projectors and rear projectors
all built into the same component, but with a different screen
strategy so that we get some larger and smaller formatting
areas. The material for the components is an ⅛-inch-thick
plastic that's vacuum formed onto molds, and we're working
→156 A:3
with a different color plastic that's sandblasted and milky.

**How do you work with a structural engineer on the
integrity of these pieces?** You talk about shape, and they
begin to do analyses where they examine the shapes and
determine what the shear is going to be across the surfaces.
You load it up and you tell them what the material is, and
they figure it out. In this case, in the galleries we don't want
people touching this stuff—it's mostly above their heads on
the ceiling—because there's equipment in it and other things.
It's set up so that it can be hung in multiple configurations
and doesn't get in anyone's way. **Representing something
like this is a challenge. What kinds of tools have you
been using, not only in terms of software but also
in developing the drawings?** Well, we have to develop
storyboards for lighting effects and interaction, which is
a whole separate set of drawings from the technical drawings. And then we issue these to other consultants who,
in turn, issue drawings back to us, which are more formal

schematics, like how you'd actually wire it to get power and other things built into the system. →208 A:1, 210 A:1

A lot of architects wish they were in exhibition design, if only because of the kind of prototyping you do. Prototyping is more common in Detroit and aeronautical industries, or even theme park industries, where products are made. Those products make money, and architecture tends to spend it. Your work seems to be in a zone that's architectural but more at the scale of product. Well, it comes out of the entertainment industry. Part of why we're able to do it is that the set-building industry in LA is substantial in lots of ways, including construction and lighting effects. UCLA, Caltech (California Institute of Technology), and Art Center (College of Design, Pasadena) all have very strong interactive design programs right now, which are taking the place of MIT and that legacy of spatial computational design. It's a kind of design that's relevant to Detroit or anywhere on the east coast. Not only is it cheap—the sets are normally expendable, for example, they're sometimes used for one shot in a movie—it's fast too. You call set builders up and they're like, do you need this tomorrow? [laughter] No, we need it in a couple of months. And then they tell us to call them when we're ready to go. They say we'll get it to you in a week; we don't want to know about it until you're ready to go into production. **When you were in architecture school did you think you'd be heading down this road? I mean, it's not a traditional architectural practice.** Not at all. **It's interesting because it's never linear, you work through the material, the material speaks to you, and then you work your way back to the conceptual...** And on every project, we've been able to spend a lot of time fabricating stuff at full scale, whether it's the prototype or the final thing itself. Our earlier work consisted more of raw experiments, kind of analogous to (Peter) Eisenman's House VI drawings or (Daniel) Libeskind's Chamber Works drawings, which are experiments in mutation, in technologies of perspective and site that were kind of raw, and they were just what they were.

What are the origins of Servo? We all met at Columbia. I was there with all three partners at one point in time, but we all met in New York. And Marcelyn Gow and I had worked together quite a bit in school in the mid-1990s. Marcelyn and I finished together in 1998, Chris Perry finished in 1997, and Ulrika Karlsson finished in 1995. And Marcelyn and Ulrika had spent the early 1990s in Berlin, and all four of us had been talking about doing work together. Marcelyn got an opportunity to do a show in Berlin, and so in the spring of our last year at Columbia we decided

to put something together as a group, and do so in a way that reflected how we wanted to work as a group. So instead of four of us as individuals showing proposals, we thought we'd do some research on different models of practice and figure out a way to make the one-time collaboration work over a longer period. That was kind of the launching point. **And this is concurrent with Ocean, right?** Yes, well, I went to college at Ohio State, and I was in Jeff Kipnis's studio in my last year. I was familiar with the people at Ocean, and I think this is a little bit different in that the members of Ocean are all physically apart and don't work together as a team necessarily. They're an open-ended network of artists and architects, and they're more competition-oriented. Also, SHOP is four people, married couples, one city. Whereas we're living in four different cities but still trying to find a way to work together as a unit. I do think LA and Stockholm have brought a whole bunch of resources into the practice that we couldn't have gotten as four people in New York.

Why did you move to LA? First and foremost to teach. And then the office was running, but I was working out of school for the first two years before we had a space out here on Lincoln. Our idea was to draw on all these tropes from our respective discourse networks. There is this interesting history between Europe and the States, between East Coast and West Coast, and our different locations reflect the different personalities we bring to the group. One of us is a radical construction guy, one's a radical theorist, one's more politically minded—you can make all these stereotypical associations... **Like members of a band...** [laughter] And so we were looking for that concoction to naturally produce a different way of reading the work, and a different way of developing it. It was also supposed to be opportunistic. You could exploit local opportunities simultaneously. You could exploit and explore different avenues that could allow somebody to do work that might be more difficult in New York. **But there really aren't many practices that work this way, are there?** In architecture, there are some shared similarities with Archigram and Team X and Mark Wigley's historical explorations of those collaboratives. Marcelyn is currently doing her dissertation on engineering and art collaboratives at the ETH (Eidgenössische Technische Hochschule, Zürich). In those cases there was a belief that the network could impact practice, but they weren't necessarily formed like ours. **Do you place yourself historically that way, following the lineage of Superstudio?** Well, there's the interest in the network and in computational design, and how that would begin to impact space and material. Both Marcelyn and I did independent studies at Columbia on the Situationists and other independent groups. There is a definite interest in alternate models of collaboration such as between art and architecture. The Situationists were overtly political. They certainly had political attributes, but in the case of Archigram, they were British and there were political attributes that were superficial…it was also part of a pop sensibility.

Have you found these analogs useful in creating your own practice? We certainly were aware of all of these groups. But when we started, we didn't sit down and say, this is how we're going to position ourselves. It's something we've become more aware of over time. But, again, the important issue here is that somehow the construction of the practice influences the construction of the work, both the spatiality and the materiality of it.

When you look ahead, how do you see that evolving? What kind of projects, what kind of a practice? I think we've been circumstantially fortunate. We've slowly progressed up in scale. The first works were more about what can you do with a CNC (computer numerical control) milling acrylic, and how can that be understood programmatically? And that led to things like a component of a project that fed lighting. So it wasn't a literal program, but it was storage and lighting and display cases; and there was an idea that you would have both a highly technical material thing paired up with an idea of a possible landscape that would filter through it. **A combination of material science and architectural conceptualizing?** Yes. For the first three and a half years we were working on commissions from curators. Our first projects like the Cloudbox and the one for Urban Issue in Berlin weren't even commissions. We had to go out and find funding for those, and they were quite small. We were very ambitious and were searching for things that we wanted to research and had a very long leash to do that. **You were basically responsible for yourselves.** Right, we had small solo shows. Then we kind of packaged all of that for the show at Storefront for Art and Architecture in New York, which also got us into the Young Architects Forum program. I consider that the first chapter, because we were working with these product lines. We were theorizing outside of clientele and really going off on a trajectory that we wanted to explore, which was one part fiction, one part pragmatic possibility. And then we started getting larger pieces commissioned by particular shows, like Lobbi_ Ports for the Cooper-Hewitt show and Archipelogics for Zaha Hadid's show.

I would say, there have been three chapters for Servo so far. The first chapter was very internal, the second chapter consisted of larger pieces that started moving into furniture and environmental installation, and more recently we started

getting client-based work, such as a house renovation and addition, which has moved us up in scale. **So getting back to your latest phase of freestanding buildings, how is this process working at that scale with all four partners?** Well, as we come into larger, more long-term development projects, we've had to outline a strategy for working at a day-to-day level. And what we try to do is start a project with all four of us in one place, spend a week charretting if we can afford to do that. **The other networks would say that's not even necessary. Do you find it necessary?** We do. I don't know what they're doing, but I think if you can't sit around and let it gestate, and look over somebody's shoulder and sketch something out, there's not an energy there that allows it to develop. At least for us. We can't find that energy over the phone or over the internet. **In some cases, the collaboration comes later, like Rick Joy's recent collaboration with Will Bruder, which has allowed Joy to jump up in scale. But your firm built the collaboration first.** We did. And that was not planned, it just happened to be the way things worked out. So we've had to try to find a way to keep that dynamic intact on the client-based projects. Part of that has to do with initiating projects with as many partners as possible, and then we typically like to have two people involved in a project from beginning to end. There's usually one person who is highly involved with the project on the day-to-day level, as well as all the design issues from top to bottom. And then another person, who is built into the schedule but not as heavily responsible, does a lot of the client interface, and they'll work together. **Collaboration is powerful because of the different points of view, but what is the upside of the geographic dispersal?** There are a couple of things I think are really good about it. There are resources that can be developed locally with each member. We have two hubs that have physical offices and two that don't, and those two that have offices have cultivated a whole lot of resources like any other office would, such as clients, fabricators, etc. And there's the aspect of far-reaching collective expertise that you gain by working in different places. I think we probably wouldn't be bringing to the table as much difference if we all worked in the same place. So there's a resistance there that can be very productive.

Interview with David Erdman of Servo was conducted in Los Angeles in 2005 by Jon Dreyfous and revised in 2007.

3 Degrees of Felt
Aztec Empire Exhibition
Guggenheim Museum
MY Studio/Meejin Yoon
with Enrique Norten/TEN Arquitectos
Script for exhibition wall pockets
Date: 2004

```
 1:version 1.0 class
 2:begin
 3:   multiuse = -1   'true
 4:   persistable = 0   'notpersistable
 5:   databindingbehavior = 0   'vbnone
 6:   datasourcebehavior  = 0   'vbnone
 7:   mtstransactionmode  = 0   'notanmtsobject
 8:end
 9:attribute vb_name = "googenpoint"
10:attribute vb_globalnamespace = false
11:attribute vb_creatable = true
12:attribute vb_predeclaredid = false
13:attribute vb_exposed = false
14:option explicit
15:
16:public guid
17:public owner
18:public layer
19:public link
20:public bit
21:
22:public polyline
23:public vertex
24:public segment
25:public distance
26:public parameter
27:public direction
28:public pocket
29:public vertices
30:
31:function create(object, parent)
32:   set owner = parent
33:   let guid = object
34:   let layer = rhino.objectlayer(guid)
35:   set polyline = nothing
36:   set link = nothing
37:   let pocket = vbnullstring
38:   let vertices = array(0)
39:
40:   vertex = rhino.pointcoordinates(guid)
41:
42:   bit = false
43:   set create = me 'update
44:end function
45:
46:public static function load(layername, googen)
47:   let layer = layername
48:   set owner = googen
49:
50:   dim objects: objects =
rhino.joinarrays(rhino.joinarrays(rhino.joinarrays(rhino.joinarrays(rhi
no.objectsbylayer("lowlow"), rhino.objectsbylayer("bottom")),
rhino.objectsbylayer("middle")), rhino.objectsbylayer("higher")),
rhino.objectsbylayer("toptop"))
51:   if (isnull(objects)) then
52:      owner.window.println ("err: the document contains no nodes")
53:      exit function
```

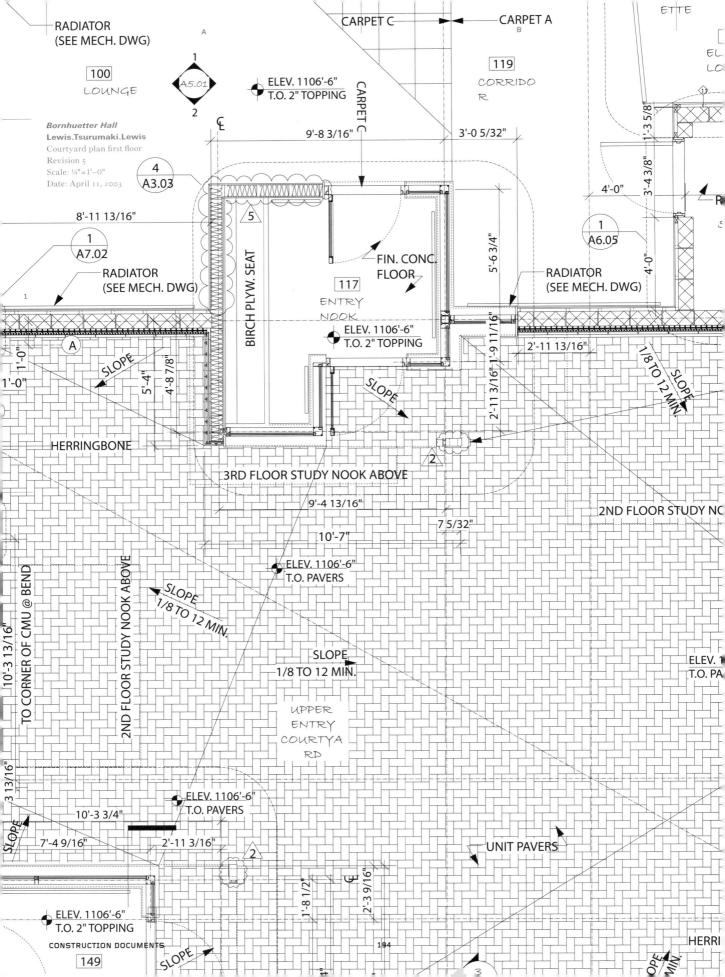

RADIATOR
(SEE MECH. DWG)

CARPET C — CARPET A

ETTE

100
LOUNGE

119

CORRIDOR

⊕ ELEV. 1106'-6"
T.O. 2" TOPPING

CARPET C

A5.01

Bornhuetter Hall
Lewis.Tsurumaki.Lewis
Courtyard plan first floor
Revision 5
Scale: ¼"=1'-0"
Date: April 11, 2003

9'-8 3/16"

3'-0 5/32"

4'-0"

4
A3.03

5

8'-11 13/16"

1
A6.05

1
A7.02

BIRCH PLYW. SEAT

FIN. CONC. FLOOR

5'-6 3/4"

RADIATOR
(SEE MECH. DWG)

RADIATOR
(SEE MECH. DWG)

117

ENTRY NOOK

⊕ ELEV. 1106'-6"
T.O. 2" TOPPING

2'-11 13/16"

2'-11 3/16" 1'-9 11/16"

A

SLOPE

SLOPE

1/8 TO 12 MIN.

5'-4"

4'-8 7/8"

1'-0"

1'-0"

HERRINGBONE

SLOPE

2

3RD FLOOR STUDY NOOK ABOVE

2ND FLOOR STUDY NO

9'-4 13/16"

7 5/32"

10'-7"

⊕ ELEV. 1106'-6"
T.O. PAVERS

ELEV. 1
T.O. PA

SLOPE
1/8 TO 12 MIN.

SLOPE
1/8 TO 12 MIN.

UPPER
ENTRY
COURTYARD

⊕ ELEV. 1106'-6"
T.O. PAVERS

TO CORNER OF CMU @ BEND

2ND FLOOR STUDY NOOK ABOVE

10'-3 13/16"

3 13/16"

SLOPE

10'-3 3/4"

7'-4 9/16"

2'-11 3/16"

2

UNIT PAVERS

1'-8 1/2"

2'-3 9/16"

⊕ ELEV. 1106'-6"
T.O. 2" TOPPING

HERRI

CONSTRUCTION DOCUMENTS

149

194

SLOPE

3

SLOPE
MIN.

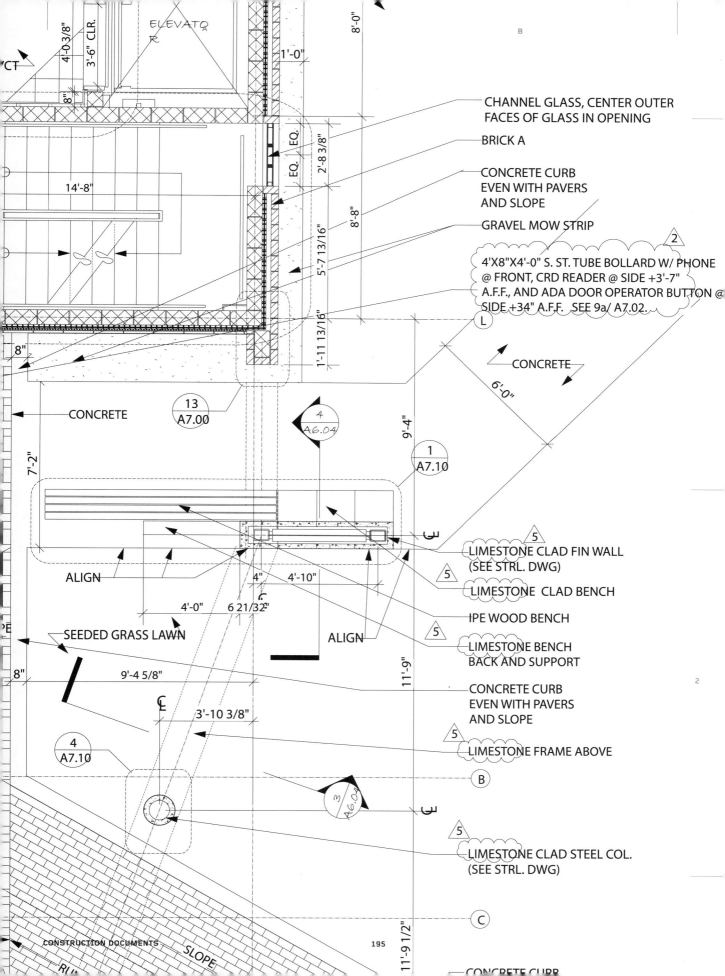

CHANNEL GLASS, CENTER OUTER
FACES OF GLASS IN OPENING

BRICK A

CONCRETE CURB
EVEN WITH PAVERS
AND SLOPE

GRAVEL MOW STRIP

4'X8"X4'-0" S. ST. TUBE BOLLARD W/ PHONE
@ FRONT, CRD READER @ SIDE +3'-7"
A.F.F., AND ADA DOOR OPERATOR BUTTON @
SIDE +34" A.F.F. SEE 9a/ A7.02.

CONCRETE

CONCRETE

LIMESTONE CLAD FIN WALL
(SEE STRL. DWG)

LIMESTONE CLAD BENCH

IPE WOOD BENCH

LIMESTONE BENCH
BACK AND SUPPORT

CONCRETE CURB
EVEN WITH PAVERS
AND SLOPE

LIMESTONE FRAME ABOVE

LIMESTONE CLAD STEEL COL.
(SEE STRL. DWG)

ELEVATOR

SEEDED GRASS LAWN

ALIGN

ALIGN

CONSTRUCTION DOCUMENTS

SLOPE

195

Camera Obscura
SHoP
Compression ring template layout
Scale: 1"=1'–0"
Date: September 1, 2004

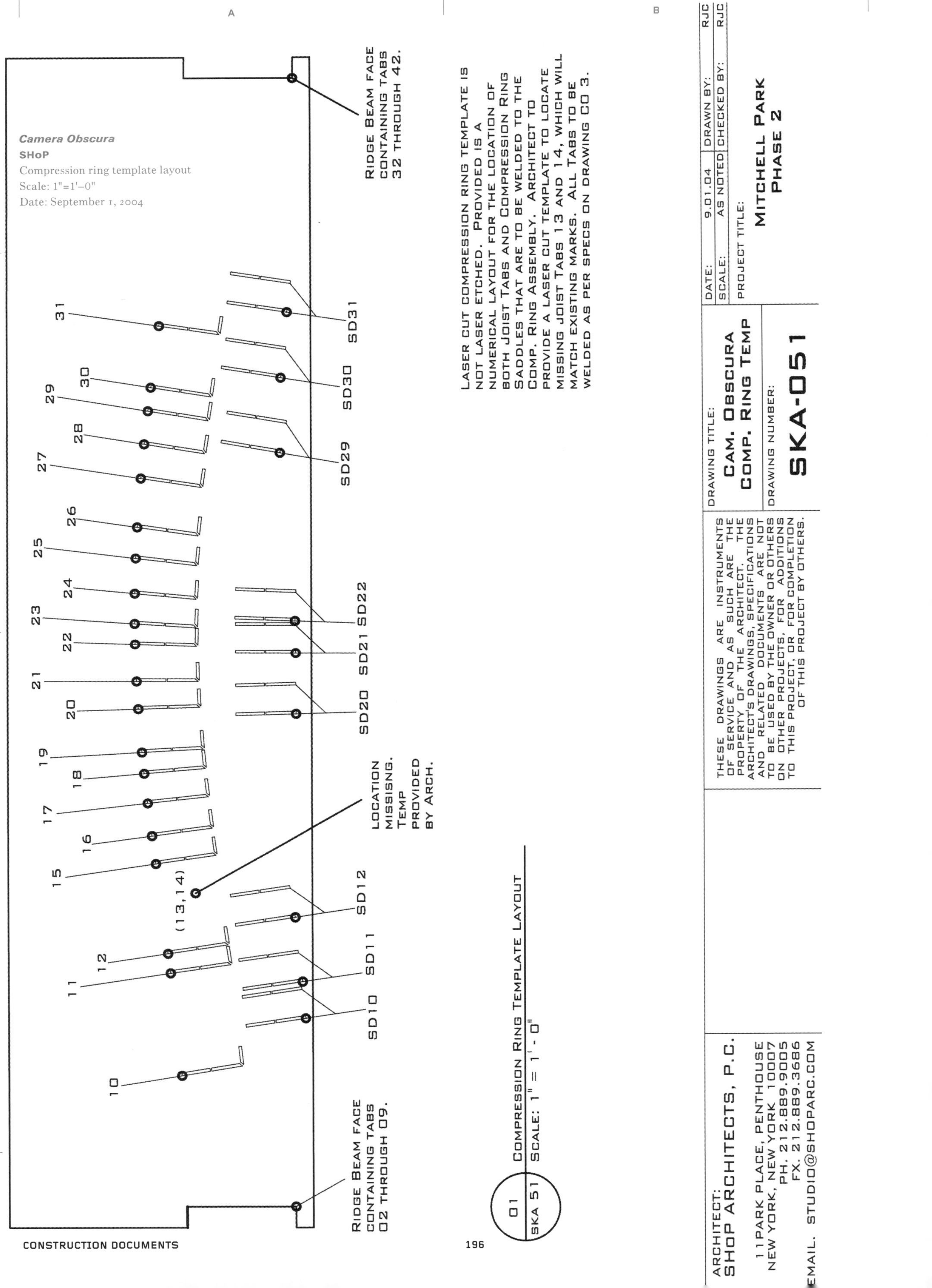

RIDGE BEAM FACE CONTAINING TABS 32 THROUGH 42.

SD31
SD30
SD29
SD22
SD21
SD20
(13,14)
SD12
SD11
SD10

LOCATION MISSISNG. TEMP PROVIDED BY ARCH.

RIDGE BEAM FACE CONTAINING TABS 02 THROUGH 09.

LASER CUT COMPRESSION RING TEMPLATE IS NOT LASER ETCHED. PROVIDED IS A NUMERICAL LAYOUT FOR THE LOCATION OF BOTH JOIST TABS AND COMPRESSION RING SADDLES THAT ARE TO BE WELDED TO THE COMP. RING ASSEMBLY. ARCHITECT TO PROVIDE A LASER CUT TEMPLATE TO LOCATE MISSING JOIST TABS 13 AND 14, WHICH WILL MATCH EXISTING MARKS. ALL TABS TO BE WELDED AS PER SPECS ON DRAWING CO 3.

(01) COMPRESSION RING TEMPLATE LAYOUT
SKA 51   SCALE: 1" = 1'- 0"

| DATE: | 9.01.04 | DRAWN BY: | RJC |
| SCALE: | AS NOTED | CHECKED BY: | RJC |

PROJECT TITLE:
MITCHELL PARK PHASE 2

DRAWING TITLE:
CAM. OBSCURA COMP. RING TEMP

DRAWING NUMBER:
SKA-051

ARCHITECT:
SHOP ARCHITECTS, P.C.
11 PARK PLACE, PENTHOUSE
NEW YORK, NEW YORK 10007
PH. 212.889.9005
FX. 212.889.3686
EMAIL. STUDIO@SHOPARC.COM

Camera Obscura

SHoP

Steel components assembly

Scale: NTS (not to scale)

Date: July 23, 2004

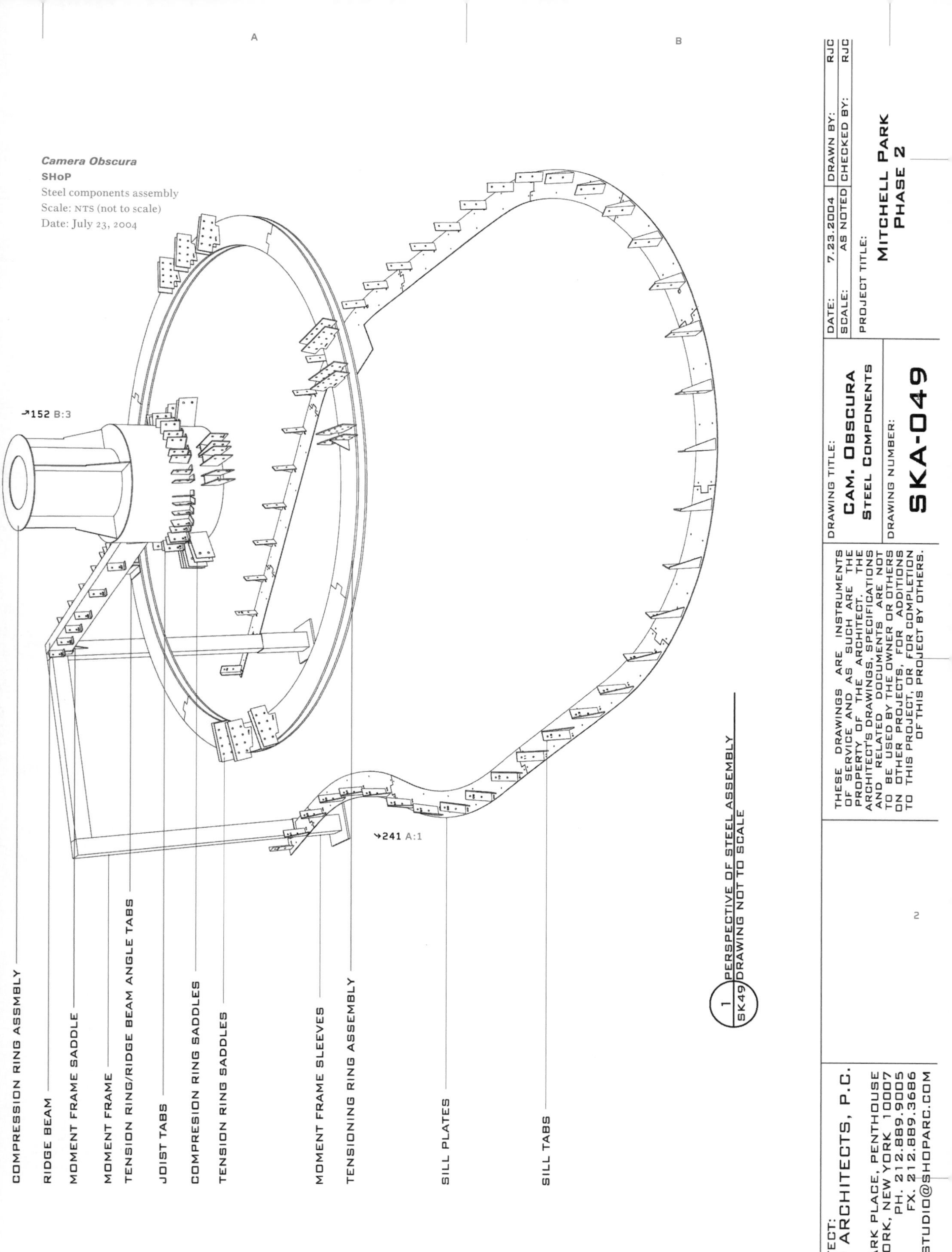

A
B
↗152 B:3
↘241 A:1
COMPRESSION RING ASSMBLY
RIDGE BEAM
MOMENT FRAME SADDLE
MOMENT FRAME
TENSION RING/RIDGE BEAM ANGLE TABS
JOIST TABS
COMPRESION RING SADDLES
TENSION RING SADDLES
MOMENT FRAME SLEEVES
TENSIONING RING ASSEMBLY
SILL PLATES
SILL TABS
1 SK49 PERSPECTIVE OF STEEL ASSEMBLY
DRAWING NOT TO SCALE
2
ARCHITECT:
SHOP ARCHITECTS, P.C.
11 PARK PLACE, PENTHOUSE
NEW YORK, NEW YORK 10007
PH. 212.889.9005
FX. 212.889.3686
EMAIL. STUDIO@SHOPARC.COM
THESE DRAWINGS ARE INSTRUMENTS OF SERVICE AND AS SUCH ARE THE PROPERTY OF THE ARCHITECT. THE ARCHITECT'S DRAWINGS, SPECIFICATIONS AND RELATED DOCUMENTS ARE NOT TO BE USED BY THE OWNER OR OTHERS ON OTHER PROJECTS, FOR ADDITIONS TO THIS PROJECT, OR FOR COMPLETION OF THIS PROJECT BY OTHERS.
DRAWING TITLE:
CAM. OBSCURA
STEEL COMPONENTS
DRAWING NUMBER:
SKA-049
DATE: 7.23.2004
DRAWN BY: RJC
SCALE: AS NOTED
CHECKED BY: RJC
PROJECT TITLE:
MITCHELL PARK
PHASE 2

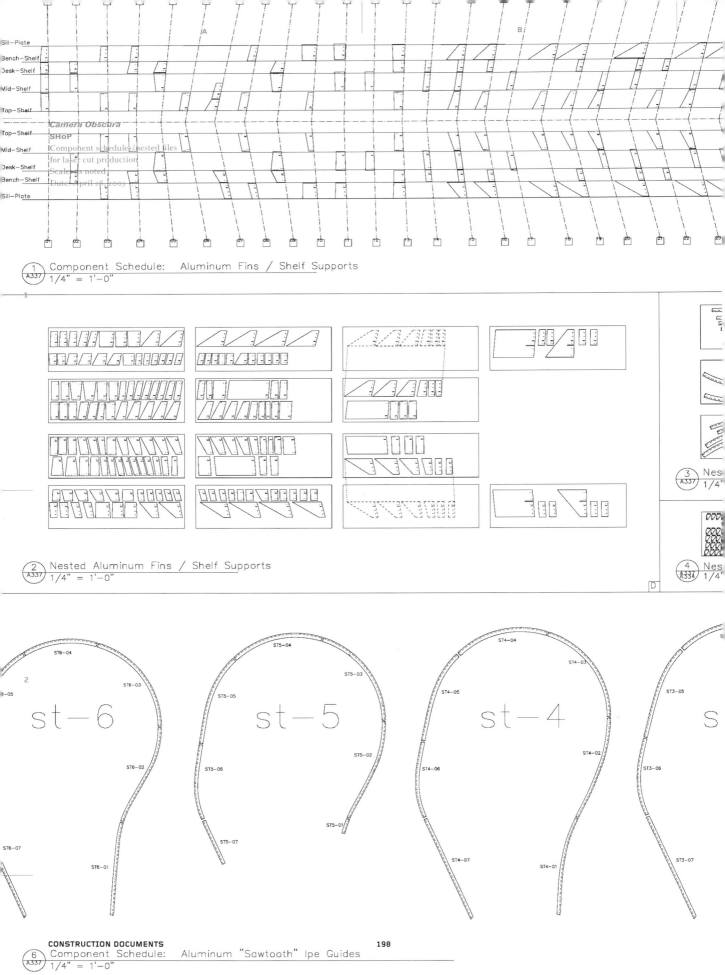

Sill-Plate
Bench-Shelf
Desk-Shelf
Mid-Shelf
Top-Shelf

Top-Shelf
Mid-Shelf
Desk-Shelf
Bench-Shelf
Sill-Plate

Camera Obscura
SHoP
Component schedules/nested files
for laser cut production
Scale: as noted
Date: April 28, 2003

A
B

1 **Component Schedule:** Aluminum Fins / Shelf Supports
(A337) 1/4" = 1'-0"

2 **Nested Aluminum Fins / Shelf Supports**
(A337) 1/4" = 1'-0"

3 Nes
(A337) 1/4"

4 Nes
(A334) 1/4"

D

st-6
ST6-04
ST6-03
3-05
ST6-02
ST6-07
ST6-01

st-5
ST5-04
ST5-03
ST5-05
ST5-02
ST5-06
ST5-01
ST5-07

st-4
ST4-04
ST4-03
ST4-05
ST4-06
ST4-02
ST4-01
ST4-07

s
ST3-05
ST3-06
ST3-07

2

6 **Component Schedule:** Aluminum "Sawtooth" Ipe Guides
(A337) 1/4" = 1'-0"

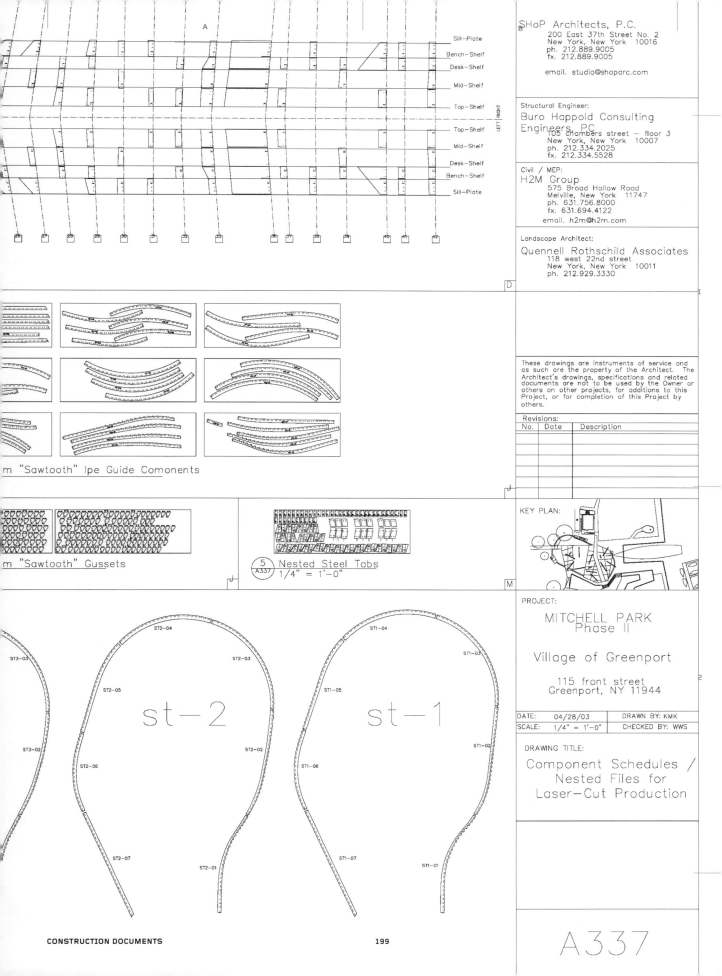

Sill-Plate
Bench-Shelf
Desk-Shelf
Mid-Shelf
Top-Shelf

Top-Shelf
Mid-Shelf
Desk-Shelf
Bench-Shelf
Sill-Plate

LEFT | RIGHT

A

m "Sawtooth" Ipe Guide Comonents

m "Sawtooth" Gussets

(5) Nested Steel Tabs
A337 1/4" = 1'-0"

st-2

st-1

SHoP Architects, P.C.
200 East 37th Street No. 2
New York, New York 10016
ph. 212.889.9005
fx. 212.889.9005

email. studio@shoparc.com

Structural Engineer:
Buro Happold Consulting
Engineers, PC
105 chambers street – floor 3
New York, New York 10007
ph. 212.334.2025
fx. 212.334.5528

Civil / MEP:
H2M Group
575 Broad Hollow Road
Melville, New York 11747
ph. 631.756.8000
fx. 631.694.4122
email. h2m@h2m.com

Landscape Architect:
Quennell Rothschild Associates
118 west 22nd street
New York, New York 10011
ph. 212.929.3330

Revisions:

No.	Date	Description

KEY PLAN:

PROJECT:

MITCHELL PARK
Phase II

Village of Greenport

115 front street
Greenport, NY 11944

DATE:	04/28/03	DRAWN BY: KMK
SCALE:	1/4" = 1'-0"	CHECKED BY: WWS

DRAWING TITLE:

Component Schedules /
Nested Files for
Laser-Cut Production

A337

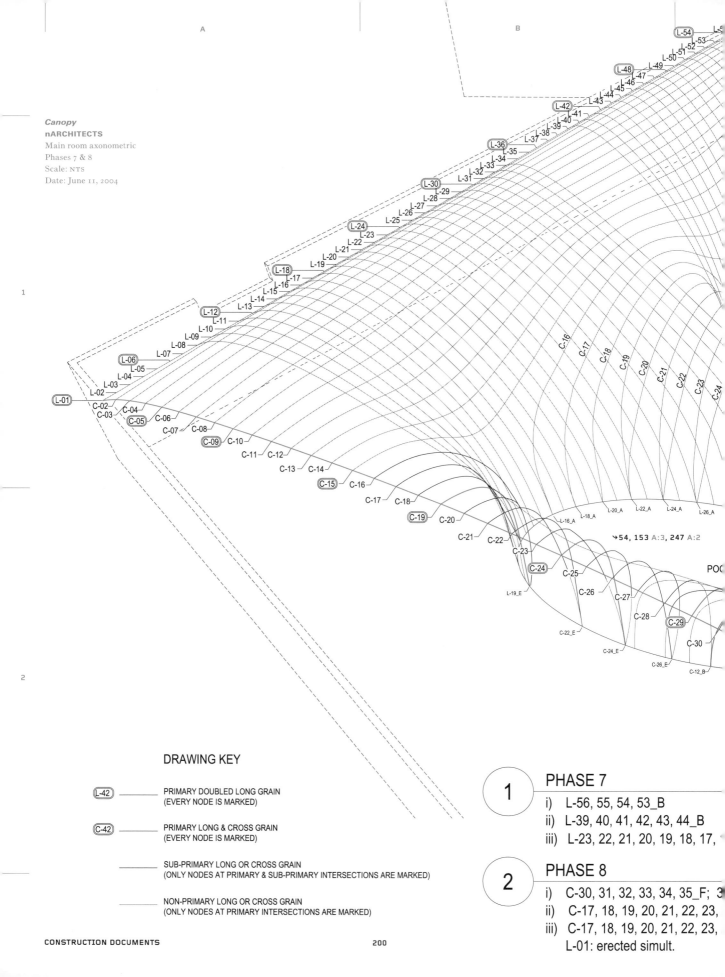

Canopy
nARCHITECTS
Main room axonometric
Phases 7 & 8
Scale: NTS
Date: June 11, 2004

DRAWING KEY

| (L-42) | PRIMARY DOUBLED LONG GRAIN (EVERY NODE IS MARKED) |

| (C-42) | PRIMARY LONG & CROSS GRAIN (EVERY NODE IS MARKED) |

SUB-PRIMARY LONG OR CROSS GRAIN
(ONLY NODES AT PRIMARY & SUB-PRIMARY INTERSECTIONS ARE MARKED)

NON-PRIMARY LONG OR CROSS GRAIN
(ONLY NODES AT PRIMARY INTERSECTIONS ARE MARKED)

① PHASE 7
i)   L-56, 55, 54, 53_B
ii) L-39, 40, 41, 42, 43, 44_B
iii) L-23, 22, 21, 20, 19, 18, 17,

② PHASE 8
i)   C-30, 31, 32, 33, 34, 35_F; 3
ii) C-17, 18, 19, 20, 21, 22, 23,
iii) C-17, 18, 19, 20, 21, 22, 23,
     L-01: erected simult.

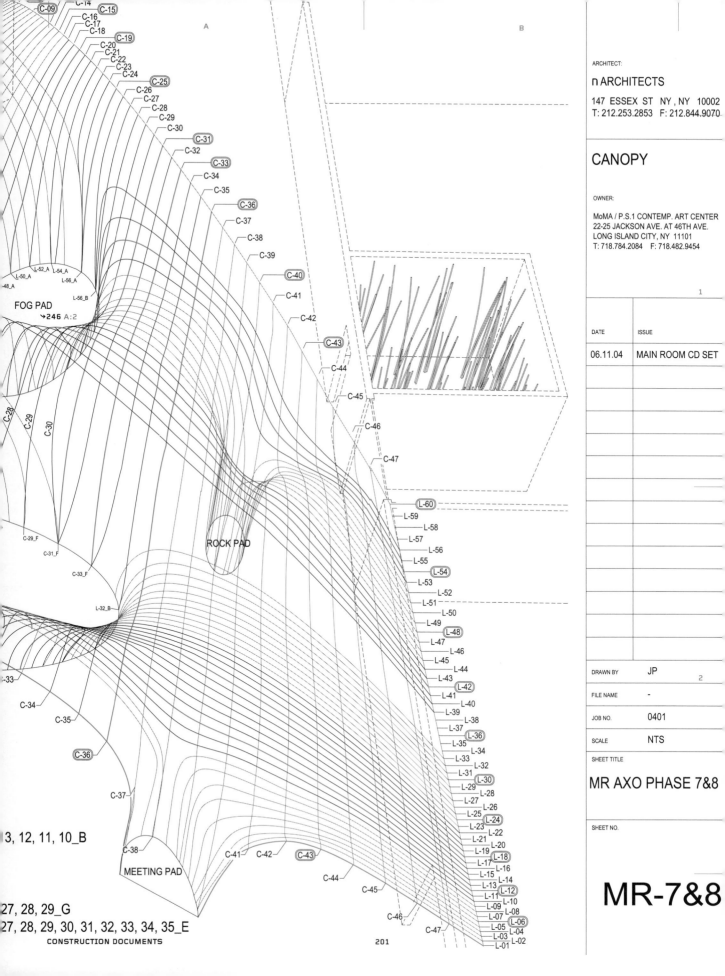

FOG PAD
→246 A:2

ROCK PAD

MEETING PAD

3, 12, 11, 10_B

27, 28, 29_G
27, 28, 29, 30, 31, 32, 33, 34, 35_E

CONSTRUCTION DOCUMENTS

201

ARCHITECT:

n ARCHITECTS

147 ESSEX ST NY , NY 10002
T: 212.253.2853   F: 212.844.9070

CANOPY

OWNER:

MoMA / P.S.1 CONTEMP. ART CENTER
22-25 JACKSON AVE. AT 46TH AVE.
LONG ISLAND CITY, NY 11101
T: 718.784.2084   F: 718.482.9454

DATE	ISSUE
06.11.04	MAIN ROOM CD SET

DRAWN BY	JP
FILE NAME	-
JOB NO.	0401
SCALE	NTS

SHEET TITLE

MR AXO PHASE 7&8

SHEET NO.

MR-7&8

1. USING THE PLAN, LOCATE THE GRIDLINE YOU ARE WORKING ON.
THEN CHECK THE BAMBOO LENGTH TABLE AND VERIFY THE SPLICE TYPE.
THE SPLICE TYPE (E.G. 3.2) INDICATES THE NUMBER OF SEGMENTS (3)
AND THE POLE CONFIGURATION (.2)

2. REFER TO THE SPLICE TABLE & AXONOMETRIC TO SELECT THE CORRECT
BAMBOO POLES FROM THE RACKS. SELECT ACCORD. TO DIAMETER & FLEXIBILITY.

Canopy
nARCHITECTS
Splice types
Scale: NTS
Date: May 26, 2004

1 1/2" - 1 5/8" DIAM.: BASE & TOP RAIL CONNECTIONS W/ LARGER CURVATURES

1 1/4"-1 1/2" DIAM.: BASE & TOP RAIL CONNECTIONS W/ SMALLER CURVATURES
& INTERMEDIATE CONNECTIONS W/ LARGER CURVATURES.

1" - 1 1/4" DIAM.: INTERMEDIATE CONNECTIONS
& TOP RAIL CONNECTIONS W/ SMALLEST (~7') CURVATURES

1" X 12'-18': FOR SPLICE TYPES 2.1 & 3.1

3. NOTE THE LOCATION OF THE THICK AND TAPERED ENDS.

4. SEAL BOTTOM AND TOP ENDS (12" MIN.) OF POLES
(EXCEPT BOTTOMS OF POLES @ RING BEAMS)

5. LAY THE POLES OUT TO THE REQUIRED LENGTH.
THE OVERLAP WILL BE MINIMUM 8', BUT WILL OFTEN BE MORE.
TRY TO KEEP THE POLES ON TOP OF EACH OTHER (TRY TO LIMIT 'TWISTING')

6. WRAP WIRES FIRST BY HAND AT LOCATIONS AS INDICATED BELOW.
POLES THAT TAPER TO VERY THIN TIPS MAY NEED MORE WIRE SPLICES)

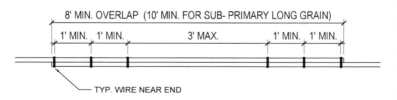

8' MIN. OVERLAP (10' MIN. FOR SUB- PRIMARY LONG GRAIN)

1' MIN. 1' MIN. 3' MAX. 1' MIN. 1' MIN.

TYP. WIRE NEAR END

7. USING AIRCRAFT PLIERS, TIGHTEN AND SNIP WIRE CONNECTIONS DOWN TO 1/2"
- TUCK SHARP END BETWEEN POLES. DISCARD WIRE ENDINGS IN A GARBAGE BAG.

8. USING PROFILE ELEVATIONS AND TAPE MEASURE, MARK OFF
INTERSECTION NODES WITH A PERMANENT MARKER.

9. ATTACH NEOPRENE TO BASE OF POLE ON COMPRESSION SIDE.

10. ERECT ARCH. 1-2 PEOPLE AT TOPRAIL; ONE TO TWO PEOPLE AT BASE.
INSERT POLE INTO BASE TUBE. OSCILLATE POLE BACK AND FORTH TO SWING
TOWARDS PERSON AT TOPRAIL. ATTACH ARCH TO STEEL TOPRAIL.

11. INTERSECTION NODES: USE ELECTRICAL TIES AS REQ'D TILL
POSITION IS CONFIRMED.

12. INTERSECTION NODES: USING BAMBOO TRIPODS, TEMPORARILY
SUPPORT CRITICAL POINTS AS NOTED (EVERY OTHER LONG & CROSS GRAIN
IN PHASES 1 & 2 HAVE CRITICAL POINTS THAT NEED TEMPORARY SUPPORT)

13. ONCE GENERAL SHAPE HAS BEEN APPROVED AND DIMENSIONS CONFIRMED,
ATTACH EACH INTERSECTION NODE WITH TYP. INTERSECTION WIRE CONNECTION.

14. SAW OFF EXCESS AT TOP RAIL TO MIDDLE OF WALL
AND SEAL WITH CLEAR END SEALER.

B

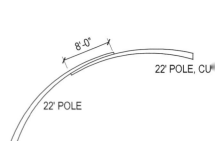

8'-0"

12' - 16' POLE

22' POLE

TYPE 2.1 (22'-30')
(1) x 22' POLE + (1) x 12' - 16' POLE

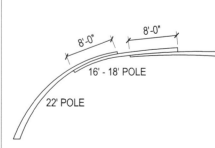

8'-0"

22' POLE, CU

22' POLE

TYPE 2.2 (30'-36')
(2) x 22' POLES

8'-0" 8'-0"

16' - 18' POLE

22' POLE

TYPE 3.1 (36'-46')
(2) x 22' POLE + (1) x 16' - 18' POLE

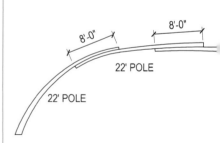

8'-0" 8'-0"

22' POLE

22' POLE

TYPE 3.2 (46'-50')
(3) x 22' POLES

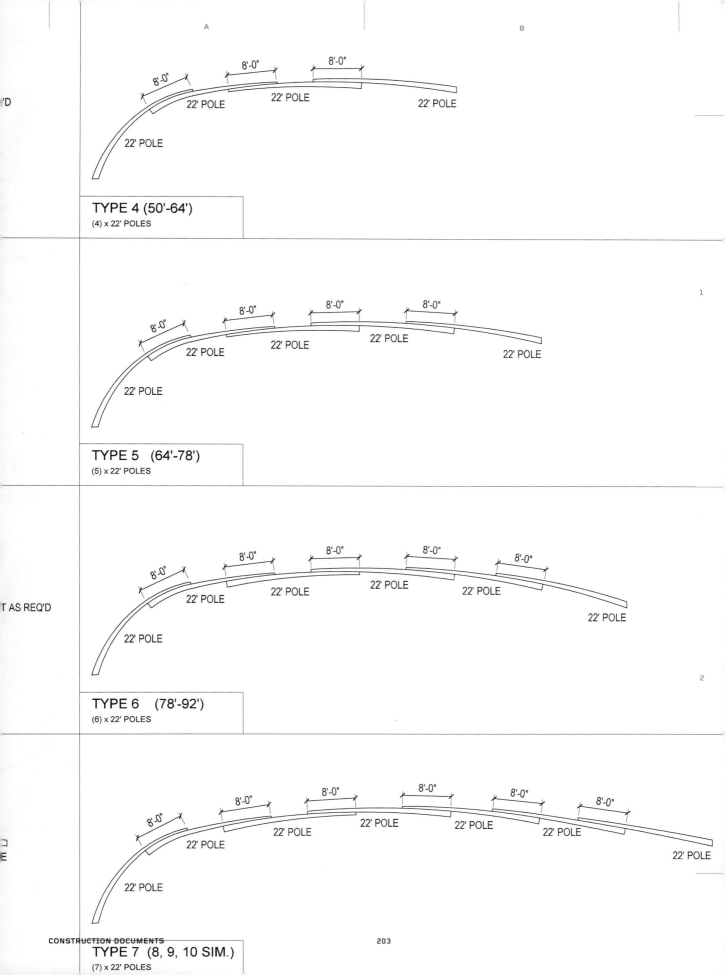

TYPE 4 (50'-64')
(4) x 22' POLES

TYPE 5   (64'-78')
(5) x 22' POLES

TYPE 6   (78'-92')
(6) x 22' POLES

TYPE 7 (8, 9, 10 SIM.)
(7) x 22' POLES

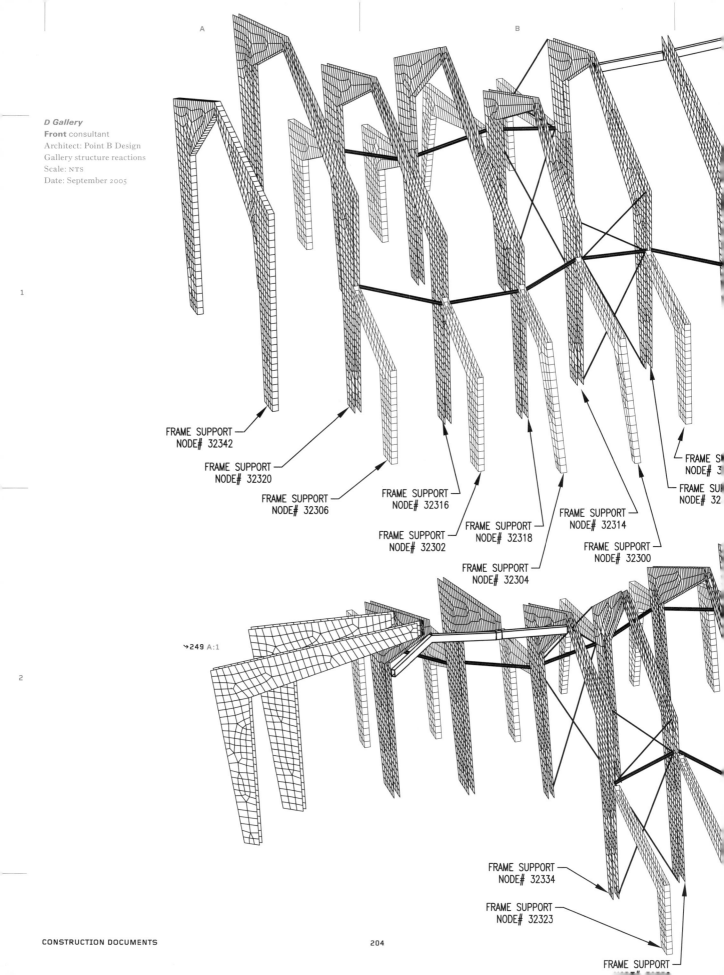

D Gallery
Front consultant
Architect: Point B Design
Gallery structure reactions
Scale: NTS
Date: September 2005

A

B

1

FRAME SUPPORT
NODE# 32342

FRAME SUPPORT
NODE# 32320

FRAME SUPPORT
NODE# 32306

FRAME SUPPORT
NODE# 32316

FRAME SUPPORT
NODE# 32302

FRAME SUPPORT
NODE# 32318

FRAME SUPPORT
NODE# 32304

FRAME SUPPORT
NODE# 32314

FRAME SUPPORT
NODE# 32300

FRAME S
NODE# 3

FRAME SU
NODE# 32

↳249 A:1

2

FRAME SUPPORT
NODE# 32334

FRAME SUPPORT
NODE# 32323

FRAME SUPPORT

RIDGE SUPPORT NODE# 32266

A

FRAME SUPPORT NODE# 32290

FRAME SUPPORT NODE# 32291

FRAME SUPPORT NODE# 32294

FRAME SUPPORT NODE# 32308

FRAME SUPPORT NODE# 32296

FRAME SUPPORT NODE# 32309

FRAME SUPPORT NODE# 32333

FRAME SUPPORT NODE# 32331

CONSTRUCTION DOCUMENTS
FRAME SUPPORT NODE# 32340

FRAME SUPPORT NODE# 32329

	Self Wt + DL			Live Load		
	FX (lbf)	FY (lbf)	FZ B (lbf)	FX (lbf)	FY (lbf)	FZ (lbf)
Node 32290	−557	0	6965	−440	0	5311
Node 32291	−332	0	2948	−232	0	1486
Node 32294	184	−232	395	119	−150	16
Node 32296	292	−358	948	243	−294	1056
Node 32298	86	−122	1650	78	−107	1601
Node 32300	−205	213	961	−298	324	1174
Node 32302	−211	205	1611	−132	125	1385
Node 32304	−432	473	1804	−428	476	1703
Node 32306	−479	521	2730	−395	431	2573
Node 32308	−1122	1279	8186	−804	917	4920
Node 32309	−651	742	5791	−436	497	3119
Node 32312	−40	18	4633	−23	3	2746
Node 32314	−49	68	4088	17	−14	2555
Node 32316	−238	272	3951	−183	210	2364
Node 32318	−51	58	3809	−23	27	2600
Node 32320	−142	161	3029	−100	113	1241
Node 32323	937	−617	1750	675	−433	1687
Node 32325	753	−759	2218	734	−762	2279
Node 32327	1406	−1457	3545	979	−1003	2827
Node 32329	582	−568	3131	408	−392	2675
Node 32331	286	−327	716	307	−350	−1062
Node 32333	1348	−1503	10480	1272	−1429	8301
Node 32334	−47	70	6522	−49	70	4525
Node 32336	−5	136	6874	−59	169	4765
Node 32338	65	−78	3110	25	−31	1762
Node 32340	−28	30	5104	−24	26	3445
Node 32342	−1469	1670	10980	−1319	1500	8526
	FZ (lbf)	MX (lbfin)	MY (lbfin)	FZ (lbf)	MX (lbfin)	MY (lbfin)
Node 32266	417	−29417	128	258	−21823	95

	Wind Suction			Snow		
	FX (lbf)	FY (lbf)	FZ (lbf)	FX (lbf)	FY (lbf)	FZ (lbf)
Node 32290	2808	3	−8301	−934	0	11789
Node 32291	4441	24	−8094	−511	0	27
Node 32294	26	657	208	153	−183	−261
Node 32296	369	619	−1230	464	−536	627
Node 32298	679	352	−2030	267	−322	1688
Node 32300	1113	−275	−1997	−98	97	794
Node 32302	1033	137	−1862	−59	45	1314
Node 32304	1022	−695	−2611	−187	209	1229
Node 32306	1261	−136	−3151	−310	339	1887
Node 32308	−2	4	1092	−1442	1644	6698
Node 32309	654	−738	−4343	−744	848	2997
Node 32312	41	1334	−12357	−71	49	3038
Node 32314	1711	−134	4344	87	−113	1510
Node 32316	562	−647	−2668	−104	120	2367
Node 32318	264	−302	−1744	43	−48	2687
Node 32320	548	−621	8461	−14	15	1767
Node 32323	895	1794	−2862	1125	−628	1833
Node 32325	−171	768	−1511	903	−884	2617
Node 32327	2130	−1269	767	1229	−1185	3083
Node 32329	1154	−605	−141	372	−281	2356
Node 32331	−360	414	15964	168	−191	−655
Node 32333	−2344	3125	−18030	625	−654	4396
Node 32334	1338	−351	−12715	−71	133	7901
Node 32336	640	471	−1025	−133	344	5568
Node 32338	711	−854	−2250	27	−36	1318
Node 32340	1068	−1238	−10539	−23	24	2605
Node 32342	3395	−3472	−14905	−926	1048	5823
	FZ	MY	MY	FZ	MX	MY

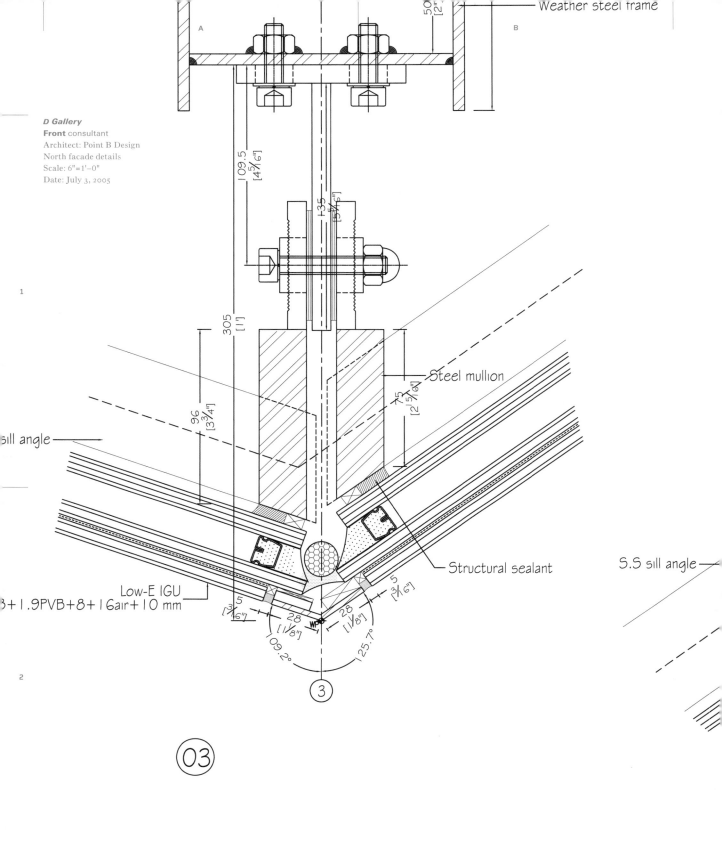

Weather steel frame

D Gallery
Front consultant
Architect: Point B Design
North facade details
Scale: 6"=1'–0"
Date: July 3, 2005

Steel mullion

sill angle

Structural sealant

S.S sill angle

Low-E IGU
8+1.9PVB+8+16air+10 mm

109.5 [4⅜"]
135 [5⅜"]
305 [1']
96 [3¾"]
75 [2¹⁵/₁₆"]
50 [2"]
5 [³/₁₆"]
5 [³/₁₆"]
28 [1⅛"]
28 [1⅛"]
109.2°
125.7°
WP

③

⓪3

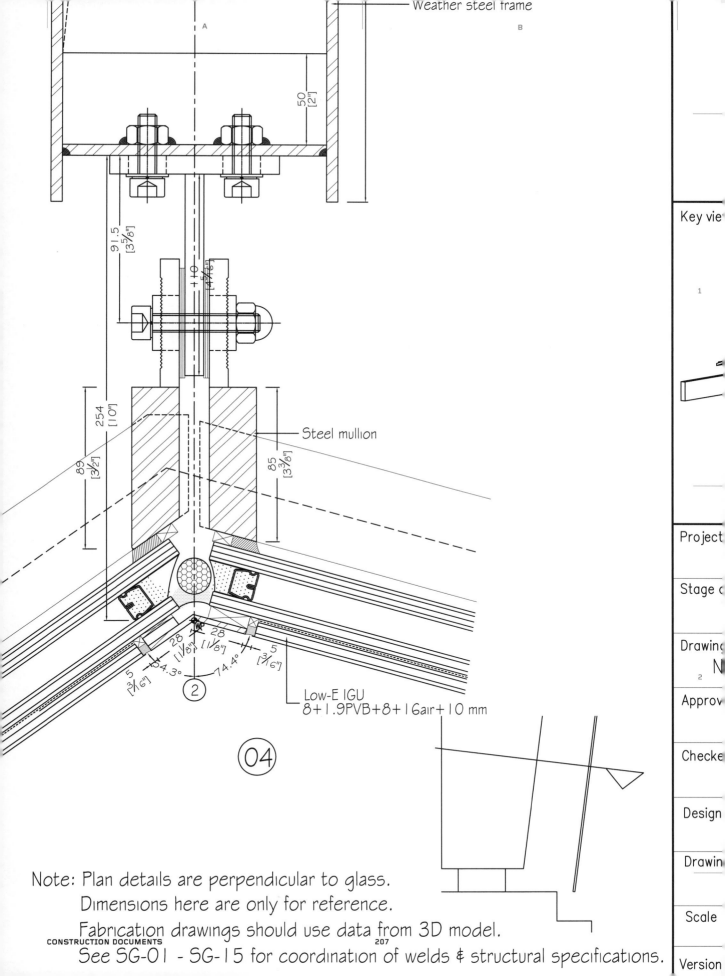

Weather steel frame

50 [2"]

91.5 [3⅝"]

⌀10 [4⅝"]

254 [10"]

89 [3½"]

85 [3⅜"]

Steel mullion

28 [1⅛"]   28 [1⅛"]

5 [3/16"]   5 [3/16"]

54.3°   74.4°

(2)

Low-E IGU
8+1.9PVB+8+16air+10 mm

(04)

Note: Plan details are perpendicular to glass.
      Dimensions here are only for reference.
      Fabrication drawings should use data from 3D model.
      See SG-01 - SG-15 for coordination of welds & structural specifications.

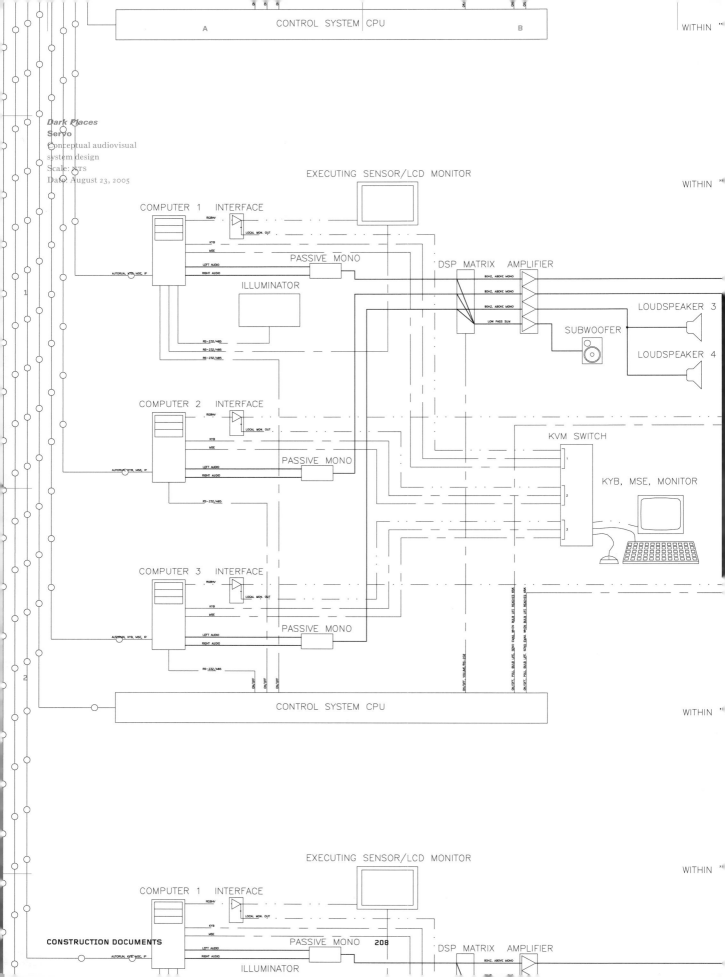

CONTROL SYSTEM CPU

A   B

Dark Places
Servo
Conceptual audiovisual
system design
Scale: NTS
Date: August 23, 2005

EXECUTING SENSOR/LCD MONITOR

COMPUTER 1   INTERFACE

RGBHV
LOCAL MON. OUT
KYB
MSE

PASSIVE MONO

LEFT AUDIO
RIGHT AUDIO

AUTORUN, KYB, MSE, IP

ILLUMINATOR

RS-232/485
RS-232/485
RS-232/485

DSP MATRIX   AMPLIFIER

80HZ, ABOVE MONO
80HZ, ABOVE MONO
80HZ, ABOVE MONO
LOW PASS SUM

SUBWOOFER

LOUDSPEAKER 3

LOUDSPEAKER 4

COMPUTER 2   INTERFACE

RGBHV
LOCAL MON. OUT
KYB
MSE

PASSIVE MONO

LEFT AUDIO
RIGHT AUDIO

AUTORUN, KYB, MSE, IP

RS-232/485

KVM SWITCH

KYB, MSE, MONITOR

COMPUTER 3   INTERFACE

RGBHV
LOCAL MON. OUT
KYB
MSE

PASSIVE MONO

LEFT AUDIO
RIGHT AUDIO

AUTORUN, KYB, MSE, IP

RS-232/485

ON/OFF
ON/OFF
ON/OFF

ON/OFF, VOLUME, RS-232

ON/OFF, POLL BULB LIFE, SEND EMAIL WHEN BULB LIFE REACHES 90%
ON/OFF, POLL BULB LIFE, SEND EMAIL WHEN BULB LIFE REACHES 90%

CONTROL SYSTEM CPU

EXECUTING SENSOR/LCD MONITOR

COMPUTER 1   INTERFACE

RGBHV
LOCAL MON. OUT
KYB
MSE

PASSIVE MONO

LEFT AUDIO
RIGHT AUDIO

AUTORUN, KYB, MSE, IP

ILLUMINATOR

DSP MATRIX   AMPLIFIER

80HZ, ABOVE MONO

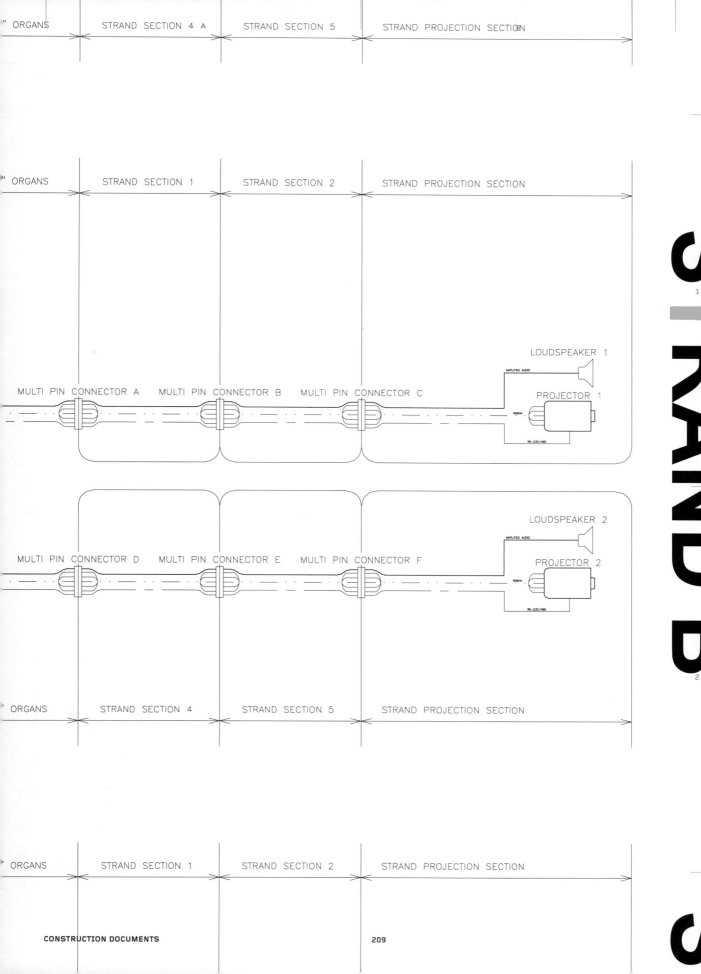

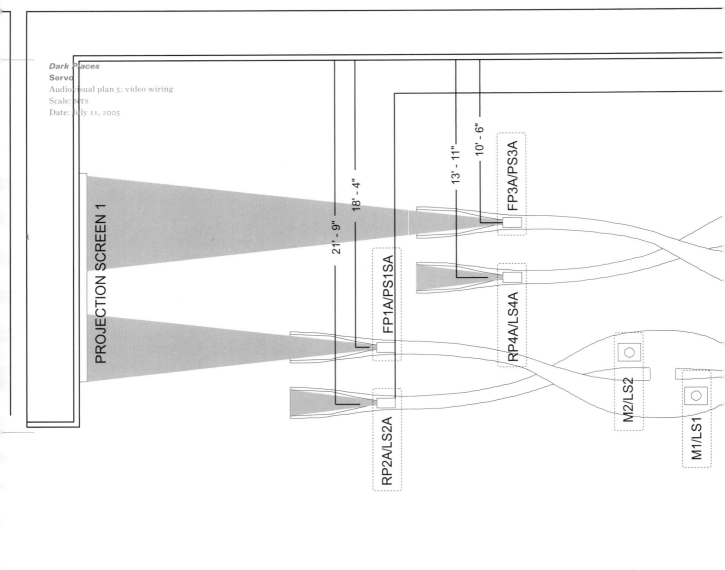

Dark Places
Servo
Audio-visual plan 5: video wiring
Scale: NTS
Date: July 11, 2005

PROJECTION SCREEN 1

21' - 9"
18' - 4"
13' - 11"
10' - 6"

RP2A/LS2A
FP1A/PS1SA
RP4A/LS4A
FP3A/PS3A
M2/LS2
M1/LS1

COMPONENTS

PROJECTORS - 8 TOTAL

FP1A - FORWARD PROJECTION UNIT 1 (NEC LT180)
FP2B - FORWARD PROJECTION UNIT 2 (NEC LT180)
FP3A - FORWARD PROJECTION UNIT 3 (NEC LT180)
FP4B - FORWARD PROJECTION UNIT 4 (NEC LT180)
RP1B - REAR PROJECTION UNIT 1 (NEC LT180)
RP2A - REAR PROJECTION UNIT 2 (NEC LT180)
RP3B - REAR PROJECTION UNIT 3 (NEC LT180)
RP4A - REAR PROJECTION UNIT 4 (NEC LT180)

MONITORS - 4 TOTAL

M1 - MONITOR 1 (VIEWSONIC 17" FLAT PANEL)
M2 - MONITOR 2 (VIEWSONIC 17" FLAT PANEL)
M3 - MONITOR 3 (VIEWSONIC 17" FLAT PANEL)
M4 - MONITOR 4 (VIEWSONIC 17" FLAT PANEL)

WORKSTATIONS
COMPUTERS - 12 TOTAL (1 AUDIO & VIDEO OUT PER)

WS1 - WS1A - WS1B - WORKSTATION 1 (SERVES M1/FP1A/RP1B)
WS2 - WS2A - WS2B - WORKSTATION 2 (SERVES M2/RP2A/FP2B)
WS3 - WS3A - WS3B - WORKSTATION 3 (SERVES M3/FP3A/RP3B)
WS4 - WS4A - WS4B - WORKSTATION 4 (SERVES M4/RP4A/FP4B)

ILLUMINATORS - 4 TOTAL

IL1 - ILLUMINATOR 1 (?)
IL2 - ILLUMINATOR 2 (?)
IL3 - ILLUMINATOR 3 (?)
IL4 - ILLUMINATOR 4 (?)

SPEAKERS - 12 SETS TOTAL - JBL CONTROL 23, AS PER
C.M. SALTER RECOMMENDATION, TOO LARGE - NEED NEW SPEC

LOCAL SPEAKERS = QUIET LOCAL SOUND, ONE PERSON,
VIA ORIENTATION

PROJECTED SPEAKERS = MODERATE BROADCAST SOUND,
MULTI PERSON, VIA ORIENTATION

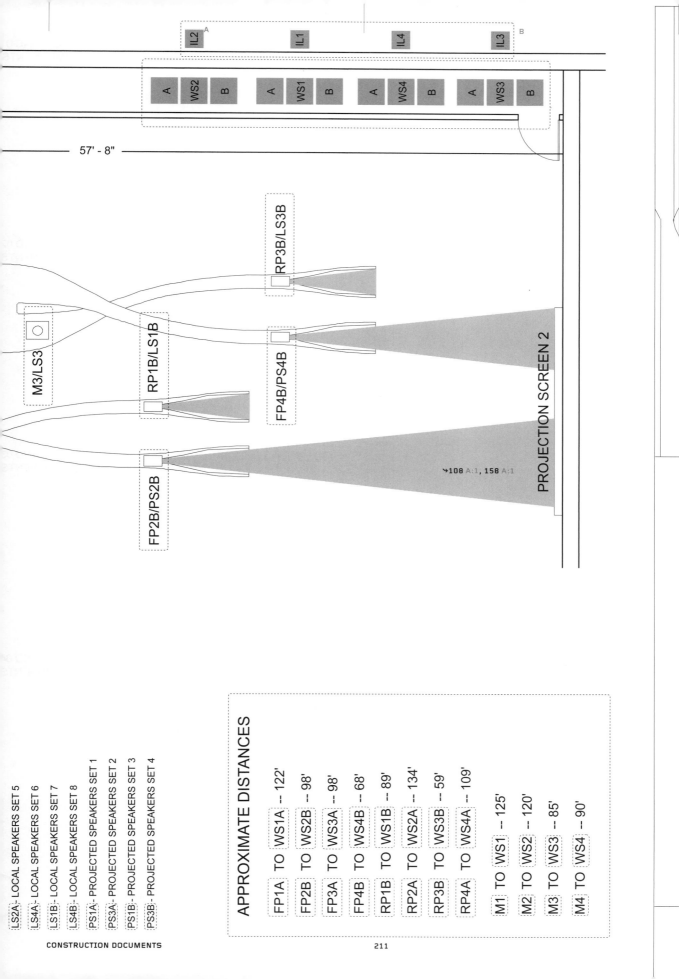

IL2 A   IL1   IL4   IL3   B

A WS2 B   A WS1 B   A WS4 B   A WS3 B

— 57' - 8" —

M3/LS3

RP1B/LS1B

RP3B/LS3B

FP4B/PS4B

FP2B/PS2B

PROJECTION SCREEN 2

↳108 A:1, 158 A:1

LS2A - LOCAL SPEAKERS SET 5
LS4A - LOCAL SPEAKERS SET 6
LS1B - LOCAL SPEAKERS SET 7
LS4B - LOCAL SPEAKERS SET 8
PS1A - PROJECTED SPEAKERS SET 1
PS3A - PROJECTED SPEAKERS SET 2
PS1B - PROJECTED SPEAKERS SET 3
PS3B - PROJECTED SPEAKERS SET 4

APPROXIMATE DISTANCES

FP1A TO WS1A -- 122'
FP2B TO WS2B -- 98'
FP3A TO WS3A -- 98'
FP4B TO WS4B -- 68'
RP1B TO WS1B -- 89'
RP2A TO WS2A -- 134'
RP3B TO WS3B -- 59'
RP4A TO WS4A -- 109'

M1 TO WS1 -- 125'
M2 TO WS2 -- 120'
M3 TO WS3 -- 85'
M4 TO WS4 -- 90'

CONSTRUCTION DOCUMENTS

servo
3008 Lincoln Blvd

DARK PLACES - AV PLAN 5
video wiring

SK-06

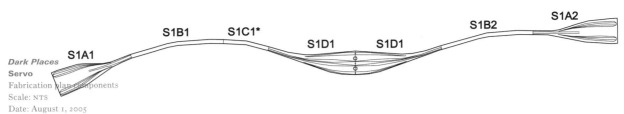

STRAND 01
CEILING COMPONENTS

Dark Places
Servo
Fabrication plan components
Scale: NTS
Date: August 1, 2005

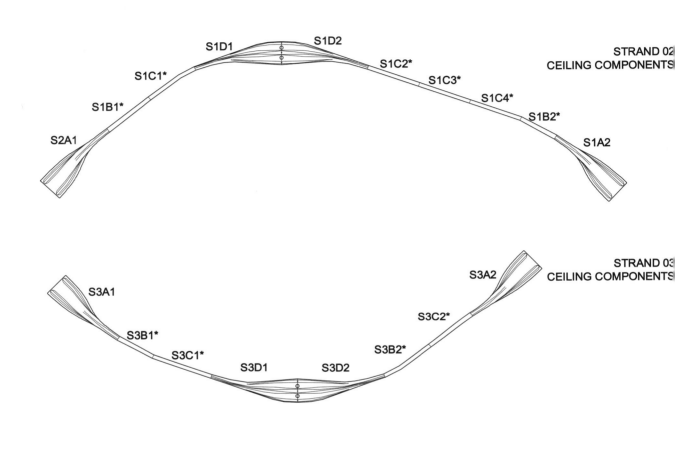

STRAND 02
CEILING COMPONENTS

STRAND 03
CEILING COMPONENTS

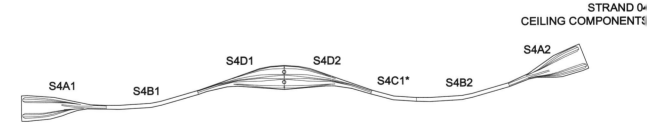

STRAND 04
CEILING COMPONENTS

2 STRAND PLANS 1—4
1/8" = 1'—0"

A

STRAND 01
GROUND COMPONENT

S1E1

STRAND 01
COMPONENT TOTALS
A-2
B-2
C-1
D-2
E-1
8 TOTAL COMPONENTS

STRAND 02
GROUND COMPONENT

S1E2

STRAND 02
COMPONENT TOTALS
A-2
B-2
C-4
D-2
E-1
11 TOTAL COMPONENTS

STRAND 03
GROUND COMPONENT

S1E3

STRAND 03
COMPONENT TOTALS
A-2
B-2
C-2
D-2
E-1
9 TOTAL COMPONENTS

STRAND 04
GROUND COMPONENT

S1E4

STRAND 04
COMPONENT TOTALS
A-2
B-2
C-1
D-2
E-1
8 TOTAL COMPONENTS

36 TOTAL COMPONENTS IN ENTIRE ASSEMBLY

TOTAL PART COUNT: 102
SEE FABRICATION SHEETS A5-2.2 TO A5-7.2
FOR MORE DETAILS

B

los angeles zurich stockholm new york

servo

3008 Lincoln Blvd
Santa Monica, CA 90405

FABRICATION PLAN
COMPONENTS

DARK PLACES INSTALLATION

OUND COMPONENTS 1—4

' = 1'-0"

A3-1.2

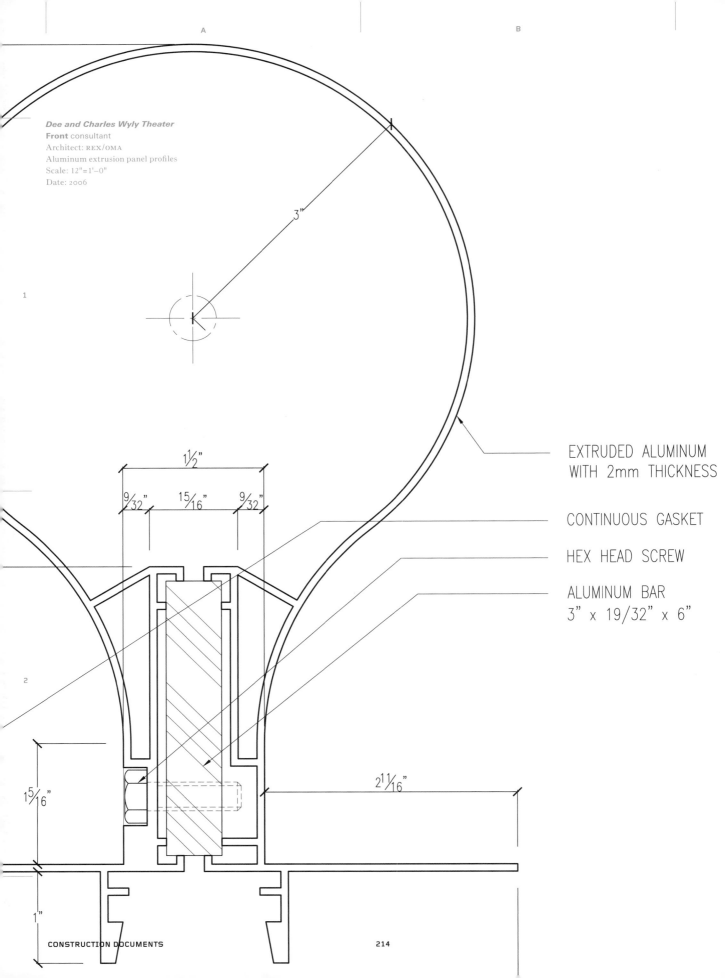

Dee and Charles Wyly Theater
Front consultant
Architect: REX/OMA
Aluminum extrusion panel profiles
Scale: 12"=1'–0"
Date: 2006

A

B

1

3"

1½"

9/32"   15/16"   9/32"

EXTRUDED ALUMINUM
WITH 2mm THICKNESS

CONTINUOUS GASKET

HEX HEAD SCREW

ALUMINUM BAR
3" x 19/32" x 6"

2

1 5/16"

2 11/16"

1"

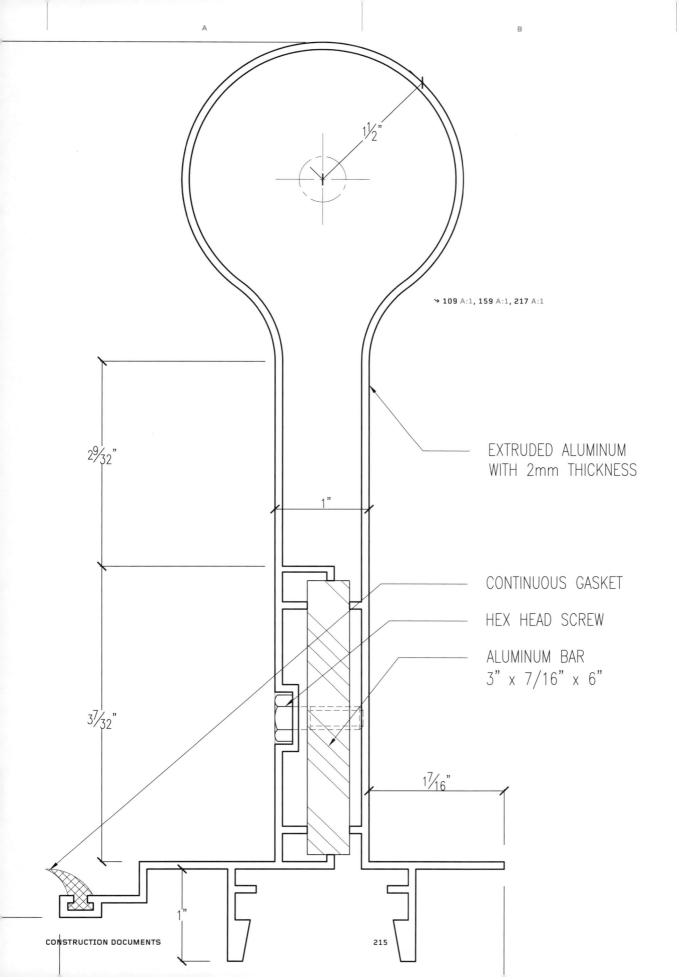

↘ **109** A:1, **159** A:1, **217** A:1

1½"

EXTRUDED ALUMINUM
WITH 2mm THICKNESS

2⁹⁄₃₂"

1"

CONTINUOUS GASKET

HEX HEAD SCREW

ALUMINUM BAR
3" x 7/16" x 6"

3⁷⁄₃₂"

1⁷⁄₁₆"

1"

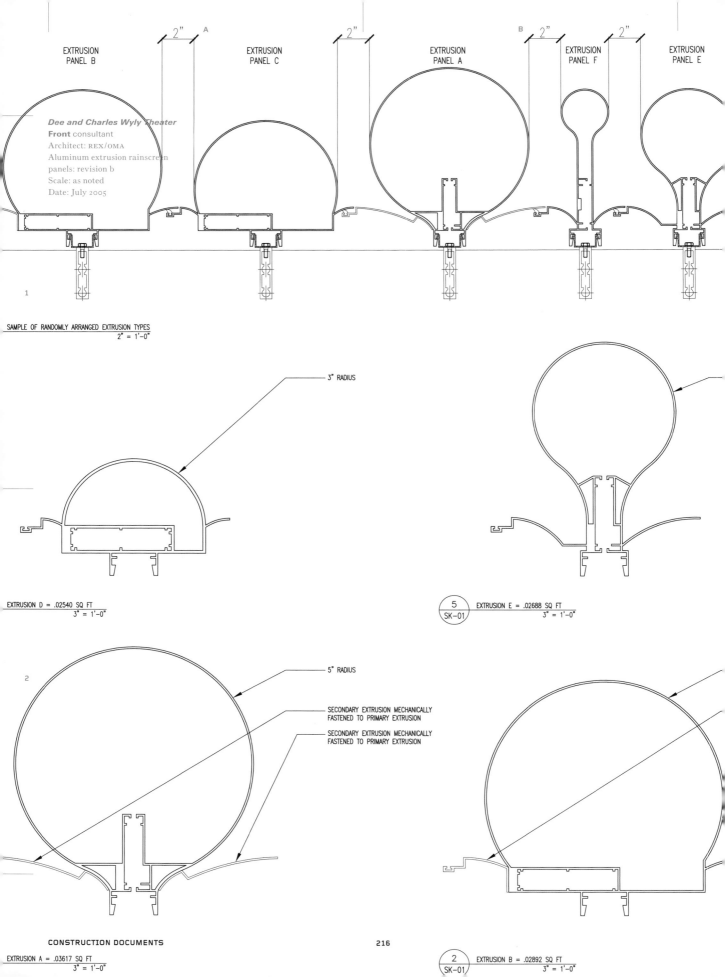

EXTRUSION
PANEL B

EXTRUSION
PANEL C

EXTRUSION
PANEL A

EXTRUSION
PANEL F

EXTRUSION
PANEL E

2" A

2"

B 2"

2"

Dee and Charles Wyly Theater
Front consultant
Architect: REX/OMA
Aluminum extrusion rainscreen
panels: revision b
Scale: as noted
Date: July 2005

1

SAMPLE OF RANDOMLY ARRANGED EXTRUSION TYPES
2" = 1'-0"

3" RADIUS

EXTRUSION D = .02540 SQ FT
3" = 1'-0"

5
SK-01   EXTRUSION E = .02688 SQ FT
3" = 1'-0"

5" RADIUS

SECONDARY EXTRUSION MECHANICALLY
FASTENED TO PRIMARY EXTRUSION

SECONDARY EXTRUSION MECHANICALLY
FASTENED TO PRIMARY EXTRUSION

2

EXTRUSION A = .03617 SQ FT
3" = 1'-0"

2
SK-01   EXTRUSION B = .02892 SQ FT
3" = 1'-0"

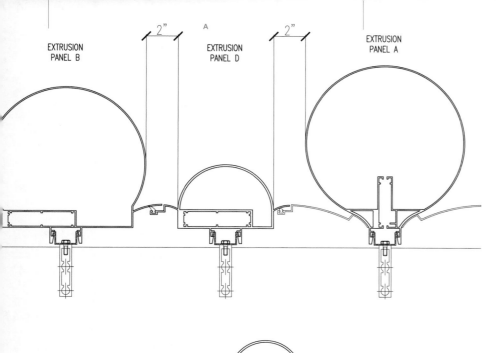

EXTRUSION
PANEL B

EXTRUSION
PANEL D

EXTRUSION
PANEL A

2"

2"

A

B

1

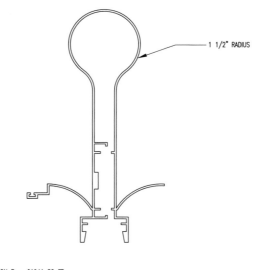

1 1/2" RADIUS

⑥ EXTRUSION F = .01941 SQ FT
SK-01   3" = 1'-0"

'S

RY EXTRUSION MECHANICALLY
) TO PRIMARY EXTRUSION

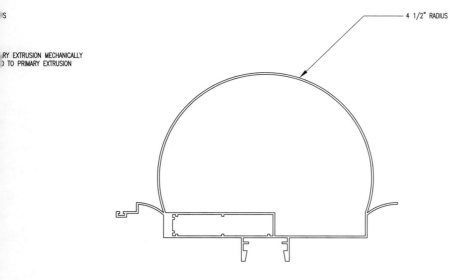

4 1/2" RADIUS

③ EXTRUSION C = .02515 SQ FT
SK-01   3" = 1'-0"

–	FOR COMMENT	JULY '05
NO	ISSUED	DATE

STAGE
NOT FOR CONSTRUCTION

FRONT INC
185 VARICK STREET SUITE 505 NEW YORK NY 10014
T212 242 2220 F212 242 2253

IN ASSOCIATION WITH

PROJECT   2
DEE & CHARLES WYLY THEATRE
DALLAS, TX

TITLE
ALUMINUM EXTRUSION RAINSCREEN PANEL
REVISION B

DATE	SCALE
JULY '05	MULTIPLE SCAL
PROJECT NO	INDEX
04017	
DRAWING NUMBER	REVISION NO
SK-01 Revision B	–

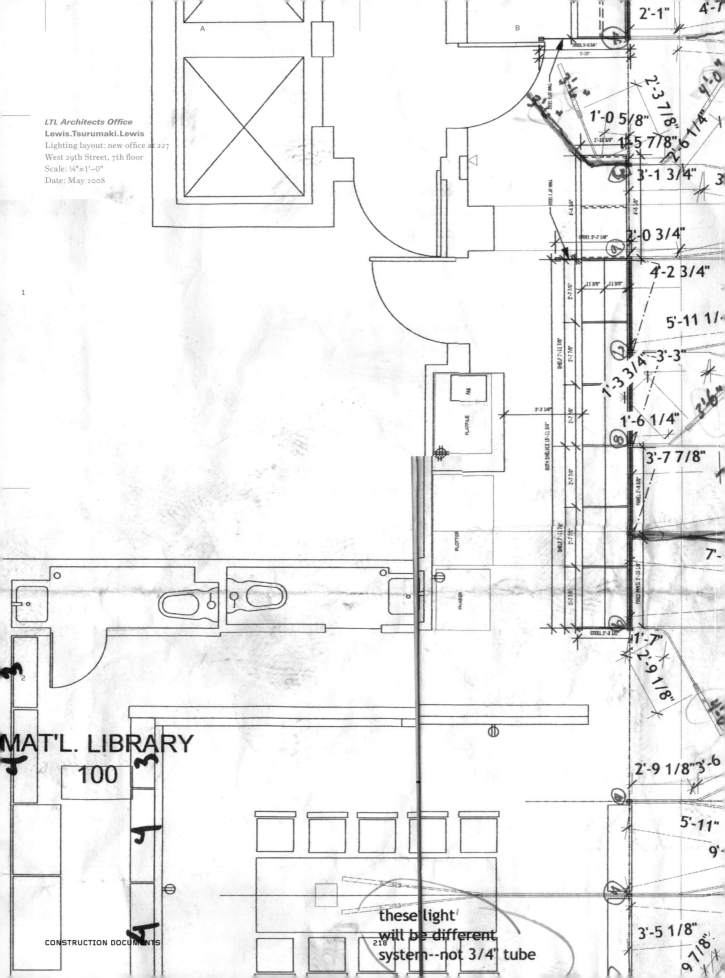

LTL Architects Office
Lewis.Tsurumaki.Lewis
Lighting layout: new office at 227
West 29th Street, 7th floor
Scale: ¼"=1'–0"
Date: May 2008

MAT'L. LIBRARY

100

these light
will be different
system--not 3/4" tube

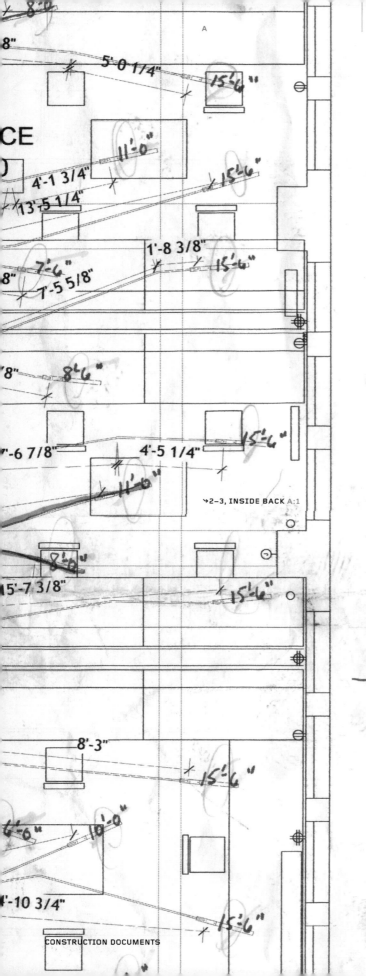

8"

5'-0 1/4"

15'-6"

CE
)

11'-0"

4'-1 3/4"

13'-5 1/4"

15'-6"

1'-8 3/8"

7'-6"
8"
7'-5 5/8"

15'-6"

8" 8'-6"

"-6 7/8"   4'-5 1/4"   15'-6"

11'-6"

➝2–3, INSIDE BACK A:1

8'-0"

5'-7 3/8"   15'-6"

8'-3"

15'-6"

6'-0"   10'-0"

4'-10 3/4"

15'-6"

30 LIGHTS

LENGTHS OF STEEL

15'-6"	10×
11'-0"	4×
10'-0"	1×
9'-0"	1×
8'-6"	3×
8'-0"	2×
7'-6"	1×
6'-0"	1×
4'-0"	3×
3'-6"	4×

60×   8" × 2" × 1/4 or 3/16"

PTD CRS STIFFENING PLATE

DUST COVER WITH VENT HOLES,
COVER WITH NO-SEE-UM
INSECT SCREEN TYP

LoRezHiFi
MY Studio/Meejin Yoon
Detail: rear lobby interactive light
vitrine fabrication
Scale: 3"=1'–0"
Date: December 21, 2005

DUST CAP TYP

TENSION BLOCK

PTD CRS TOP CHANNEL
SLOTTED AS REQD FOR
TENSION WIRES AND VENT

1

TENSION WIRES

LED NET 2.4" OC

EDGE OF GLASS FRAME BYND

2"X6" STL TUBE

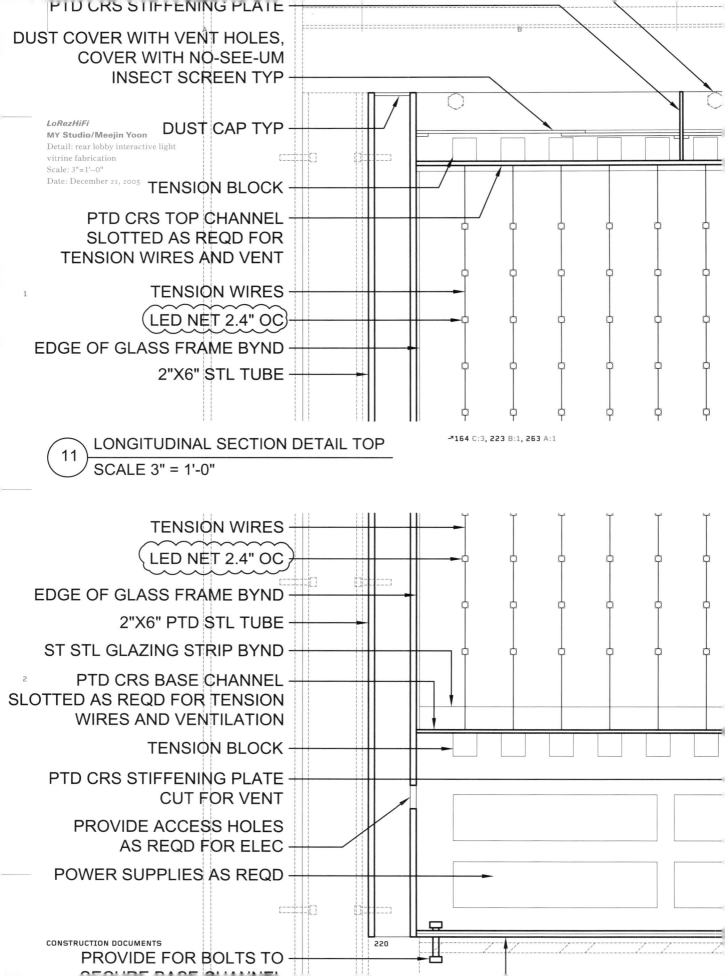

164 C:3, 223 B:1, 263 A:1

(11) LONGITUDINAL SECTION DETAIL TOP
SCALE 3" = 1'-0"

TENSION WIRES

LED NET 2.4" OC

EDGE OF GLASS FRAME BYND

2"X6" PTD STL TUBE

ST STL GLAZING STRIP BYND

2

PTD CRS BASE CHANNEL
SLOTTED AS REQD FOR TENSION
WIRES AND VENTILATION

TENSION BLOCK

PTD CRS STIFFENING PLATE
CUT FOR VENT

PROVIDE ACCESS HOLES
AS REQD FOR ELEC

POWER SUPPLIES AS REQD

PROVIDE FOR BOLTS TO
SECURE BASE CHANNEL

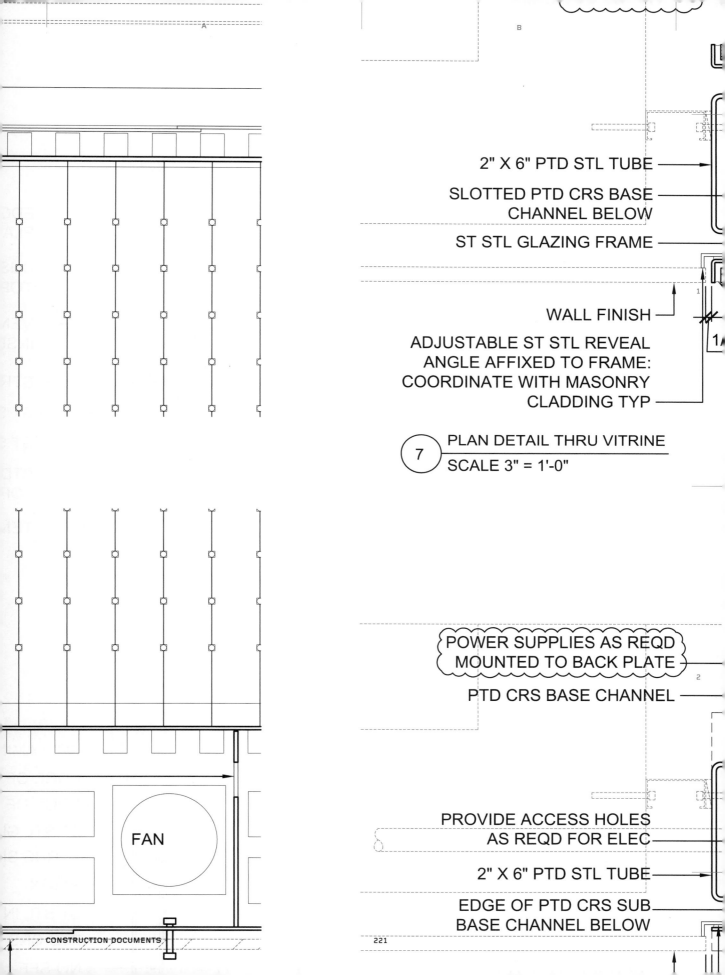

2" X 6" PTD STL TUBE ⟶

SLOTTED PTD CRS BASE ⟶
CHANNEL BELOW

ST STL GLAZING FRAME ⟶

WALL FINISH ⟶

ADJUSTABLE ST STL REVEAL
ANGLE AFFIXED TO FRAME:
COORDINATE WITH MASONRY
CLADDING TYP ⟶

⑦ PLAN DETAIL THRU VITRINE
SCALE 3" = 1'-0"

POWER SUPPLIES AS REQD
MOUNTED TO BACK PLATE ⟶

PTD CRS BASE CHANNEL ⟶

PROVIDE ACCESS HOLES
AS REQD FOR ELEC ⟶

2" X 6" PTD STL TUBE ⟶

EDGE OF PTD CRS SUB
BASE CHANNEL BELOW

FAN

⑩ LONGITUDINAL SECTION DETAIL BASE
SCALE 3" = 1'-0"

LoRezHiFi
MY Studio/Meejin Yoon
Detail: rear lobby interactive light
vitrine fabrication plan
Scale: 3"=1'–0"
Date: December 21, 2005

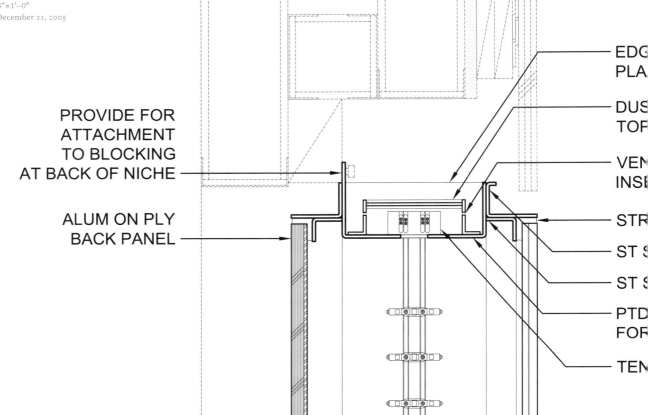

PROVIDE FOR
ATTACHMENT
TO BLOCKING
AT BACK OF NICHE ——

ALUM ON PLY
BACK PANEL ——

EDG
PLA

DUS
TOF

VEN
INSE

STR

ST S

ST S

PTD
FOR

TEN

⑨ LATERAL SECTION DETAIL TOP
SCALE 3" = 1'-0"

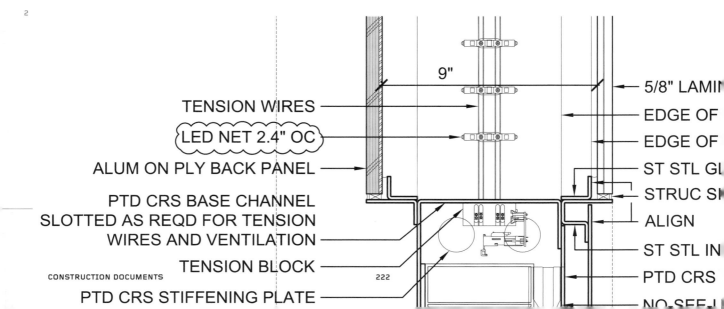

9"

TENSION WIRES ——

(LED NET 2.4" OC) ——

ALUM ON PLY BACK PANEL ——

PTD CRS BASE CHANNEL
SLOTTED AS REQD FOR TENSION
WIRES AND VENTILATION ——

TENSION BLOCK ——

PTD CRS STIFFENING PLATE ——

5/8" LAMIN

EDGE OF

EDGE OF

ST STL GL

STRUC SF

ALIGN

ST STL IN

PTD CRS

NO-SEE-

TD CRS STIFFENING
D

R WITH REMOVABLE
S, OPEN FOR VENT AT SIDE

RED WITH NO-SEE-UM
REEN

CONE TYP

GLAZING FRAME

ZING STRIP

OP CHANNEL SLOTTED
AND TENSION WIRES

LOCK

GLASS ACID ETCHED

BE BYND

GLAZING FRAME BYND

STRIP

SETTING BLOCK TYP

AZING FRAME

COVER PLATE

CT SCRN TO

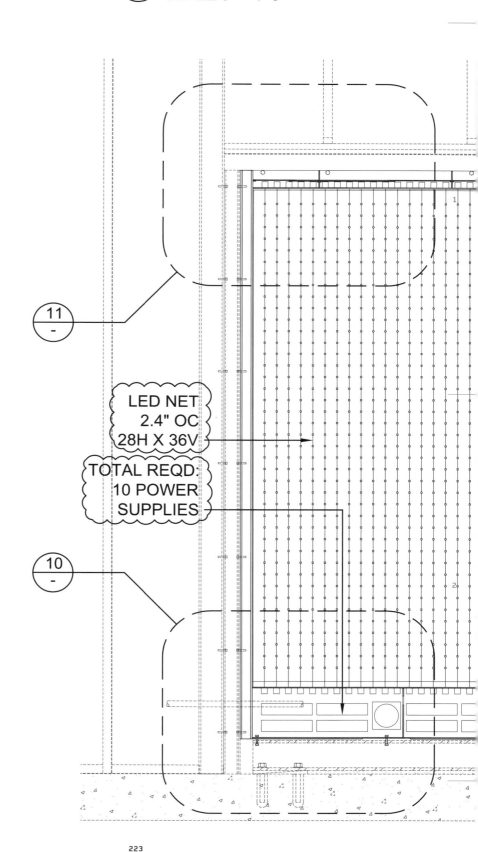

11 / -

LED NET
2.4" OC
28H X 36V

TOTAL REQD:
10 POWER
SUPPLIES

10 / -

| 5 | LONGITUDINAL SECTION |

White Noise/White Light
MY Studio/Meejin Yoon
Electronics details
Scale: NTS
Date: June 2, 2004

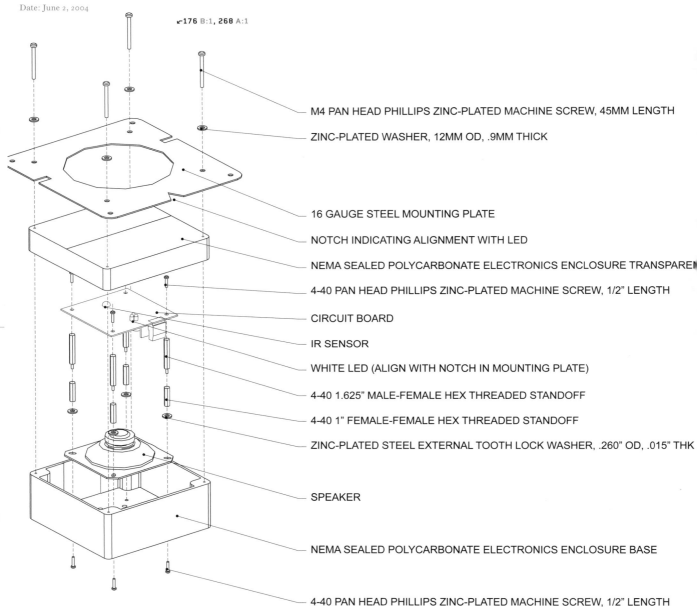

↙176 B:1, 268 A:1

M4 PAN HEAD PHILLIPS ZINC-PLATED MACHINE SCREW, 45MM LENGTH

ZINC-PLATED WASHER, 12MM OD, .9MM THICK

16 GAUGE STEEL MOUNTING PLATE

NOTCH INDICATING ALIGNMENT WITH LED

NEMA SEALED POLYCARBONATE ELECTRONICS ENCLOSURE TRANSPARE

4-40 PAN HEAD PHILLIPS ZINC-PLATED MACHINE SCREW, 1/2" LENGTH

CIRCUIT BOARD

IR SENSOR

WHITE LED (ALIGN WITH NOTCH IN MOUNTING PLATE)

4-40 1.625" MALE-FEMALE HEX THREADED STANDOFF

4-40 1" FEMALE-FEMALE HEX THREADED STANDOFF

ZINC-PLATED STEEL EXTERNAL TOOTH LOCK WASHER, .260" OD, .015" THK

SPEAKER

NEMA SEALED POLYCARBONATE ELECTRONICS ENCLOSURE BASE

4-40 PAN HEAD PHILLIPS ZINC-PLATED MACHINE SCREW, 1/2" LENGTH

2   ELECTRONICS DETAILS

Eric Bunge and Mimi Hoang of nARCHITECTS

Can we start with the Canopy project? It came out of the MoMA/P.S.1 competition, which has served as a springboard for firms that have won it, such as SHoP, to test ideas being developed in the office and to make discoveries over the course of the project's short implementation and duration period. Did that project confirm existing working methods for you? Did it present new possibilities of practice? Well, in terms of the implementation of our projects, we had always been interested in building and were directly involved in constructing and installing some of our projects. Canopy, however, was much bigger than our previous works. If we could talk briefly about discoveries made in that project, one of the more interesting ones was in the choice of using green bamboo, in that it's a natural material whose properties you couldn't really model. We'd met briefly with Arup (international engineering/consulting firm) about the project, but the structural properties were never modeled because its behavior, such as its curvature radius, is not really consistent.

So we planned the structure as much as possible. We modeled it three-dimensionally and mapped out all the profiles. But when we built it we realized that certain things were just different from the 3D model. And they were different in ways that we thought were much better than the 3D model. In our drawings and models we were so in control of the lines drawn and projected, but found that in reality the material had properties that were much more curvilinear, much more structural. For instance, it bowed out in areas we thought were going to be straight, and we had to insert two new dips in the canopy for structural reasons. All of

➷104 A:1

these things, we thought, made the project more rich and more varied in terms of the different scales of the spaces. So we became really interested in the new kinds of discoveries in construction that are not about a direct translation and not about a completely faithful translation but about opportunities that come up while you're building. I think this process can happen in any project but we were very aware of it during P.S.1.

And this process was very fast. Within a week of winning it we were already on site with some of the bamboo, and within the following six or seven weeks we were testing the material properties, the radii and so on. It underwent a transformation given those tests, but then, in fact, as Mimi said, that happened during construction, and is part of the loop that architects are not always able to complete from the initial drawings projected. That kind of feedback loop in planning and construction does happen for many architects on many projects, but for us, this ability to get direct response from what we'd drawn, and the unanticipated discoveries made during testing and construction was the most incredible experience. **The feedback that you're referring to, between the planning and the making, or between the logic set up in order to make something and the possibilities that emerge during the course of implementation, has become more abbreviated and direct in a lot of practices. In the case of P.S.1, this active feedback occurred between the structure you'd mapped out on computer and the direct trial-and-error process of construction on site. How did this dynamic shape the project, specifically?** In that project, for instance, we found that the bamboo

➷246–247

curvatures that we'd anticipated were too fragile, and we actually had to open things up and make the radii of the bending a bit bigger. So the project sort of inflated. It got a lot taller, in the form of arches to accommodate longer spans. And on a programmatic level we realized, having lived in this space during construction, that the two new dips introduced for structural reasons also introduced new scales of space, and also new scales of interaction. We named one of these areas the Meeting Pad and imagined that it would →54 serve that purpose. And we discovered that a given program can be rearticulated during the process of building. We were, in a sense, users in an incremental way, in a kind of unfinished project, so there was a kind of testing at that level too.

How was the process of making Windshape related to the experience of designing and building Canopy? It was similar in many ways, in the sense that we often spent about as much time planning on these projects as we did building, testing out every little step of the process and playing out all the steps of construction. Except that this was 6,000 kilometers away. But I think our attitude to Windshape was very different because of what we learned in Canopy. Maybe we were a little bit too cavalier with Windshape because of our successful experience with Canopy where we realized that we could design something, model it, and then anticipate another layer of design that would happen on site. There had been sections of the P.S.1 project that were moving in the wind, which we thought we could explore further.

So in the case of Windshape, we thought it would →127 A:1 be great to make something that would move with the wind, something that was very much a site factor and not in our control. There was also this idea that it was indeterminate and that we weren't completely in control of every single profile we'd designed. And we were drawn to the idea of making a structure that moved, and also weaving it with a material like string that would behave in a really dynamic way. A lot of this attitude actually came from observing what happened at P.S.1. So I think we went into Windshape with more unknowns that we anticipated, but which we thought we could work with. We improvised more with this project. For instance, many of the details we came up with, such as this initial kind of stitching of the poles, happened →269–271 on site. We improvised more also because the site was remote, in France. **So you didn't get to France until you were actually building it?** No, we went initially to choose a site. We were commissioned by the Savannah College of Art & Design (SCAD). They have a campus in Lacoste, France, where students spend a term. They have a yearly summer arts festival there, of which this commission was part. The previous years they had invited several artists, maybe

seven or eight, to do installations, but that year they decided to have only one major piece. What we actually designed were two pavilions, which served as a public meeting and event space for the town during the summer of 2006.

And as Mimi mentioned, we were a bit cavalier. The project came so close to failure 48 hours before the opening because of a huge windstorm. But it was actually great because we were able to rectify some structural problems just before the opening. There was a touch-and-go moment where we were wondering whether it would actually work. On these kinds of projects there's no chance to actually test these projects fully in advance, so that near-disaster turned out to be productive.

The two projects we've spoken about, Canopy and Windshape, both have a transitory nature, rather than the more conclusive nature of a building. They seem to be a kind of prototype for your practice. How have these projects informed the way you frame your practice? There are perhaps three threads or aspects of our practice that can be seen in these projects. One is our desire to do public work, or work that can be enjoyed by a larger public. Another is to make projects that respond to stimuli or to environmental factors that are not so fixed. And I guess the third is to develop innovative construction techniques.

Even though these installations represent a small portion of the sort of work we now do, they have set up a way of working for us. It's great to have these opportunities to build our own work. What we take from our design-build installations is an attitude to try to figure out how to build something and to develop a sort of construction logic. And I'm sure many architects do this with projects they build in a normative way. It's an attitude that is a subset of a larger ambition to join spatial invention with an interest in users and unpacking notions of program and typology.

I think maybe one other way in which those projects have been translated into subsequent projects is that we're interested in a very minimal attitude toward choosing technologies or materials that we use in our projects. It's not that we're interested in *minimalism* but we're interested in focusing on one particular thing that can serve many roles. So in the MOMA/P.S.1 project, which is a really wide-open program, you're basically told to provide for shade, for lounging, and for water to cool down, and that's about it. What we didn't want was to have one element be structural, another element be the seating, another element be the shade. We wanted one thing or one kind of system that would do everything. And I think that's an idea we try to push in a lot of our projects. Sometimes it's for economy's sake but mostly it's for the sake of invention. There's a kind of irrationality to it. In the case of green bamboo and string,

CANOPY P.S.1/MoMA 05.26.04
CONSTRUCTION SEQUENCE
to be updated periodically

	MAY 10-17 [10-14]	MAY 17-24 [17-21]	MAY 24-31 [24-28]	MAY 31-JUNE 7 [31-4] [5-6]	JUNE 7-14 [7-11] [12-13]	JUNE 14-21 [14-18] [19+20]
CREW	Core Team Begins			Bamboo Consultant Visit May 28th-29th; Helpers begin		
SITE MAINTENANCE	Irrigate live Bamboo (ground and leaves) daily	Water stored and erected bamboo poles twice daily; Clean up site daily; take trash to dumpster	Irrigate live Bamboo (ground and leaves) daily; Maintain Security Enclosure	Water stored and erected bamboo poles twice daily; Clean up site daily; take trash to dumpster; Maintain Security Enclosure	Irrigate live Bamboo every morning; Maintain Security Enclosure	Water stored and erected bamboo poles daily; Clean up site daily; take trash to dumpster; Maintain Security Enclosure
GEOMETRY	Survey North Edge Beam; Survey South Edge Beam		Survey Pool Pad decking	Survey Pool Pad decking		
TEMP. CONSTRUCTIONS	Build 12 adjustable tripods; Erect Scaffolding		Build North Edge beam w/5 tripods	Build South Edge beam w/5 tripods		
BAMBOO	Phase 1 of Sand Hump	Phase 2 of Sand Hump; Phase 1 of Main Space	Phase 3 of Sand Hump; Phase 4 of Sand Hump; Phase 2 of Main Space	Phase 3 of Main Space	Phase 4 of Main Space	Phase 5 of Sand Hump (doubled Cross Grain); Phase 5 of Main Space; Phase 6 of Main Space; Wrap Wire @ Nodes for Phases 1-4
WATER SYSTEMS	Rainforest: install temporary sprinkler + timer	Order and test rainforest irrigation system	Install Pool Pump	Install Rainforest Irrigation; Fog Pad: Install Pump, Copper Tubing / Plumbing	Install Fog Misting Nozzles	
FOAM	Order pool pump and fittings; Install fittings into foam	Glue foam together	Pool: Polyurea & install			
ELECTRICAL			Order Light fixtures; Test Lighting ideas	Install Electrical + Lighting to Pool Pad		
STEEL	Reinforce Sand Hump ring beam; Weld struts @ corner toprail locations; Install Steel Top Rails and Ring Beams	Weld tabs to fog pad; Purchase + install 8" channel @ rainforest threshold				
LUMBER	Compare decking options; Order framing lumber and decking		Framing & Decking: Fog Pad	Framing: Pool Pad; Decking: Pool Pad		Sand Decking
SAND						Organize Sand + Bobcat; SAND - JUNE 15TH
GENERAL					Clean / Sand Steel Bars	Paint Bars

they're not typical building materials. But the challenge we find really fun is to make it precise, to make it engineered.

In working with materials that are pliable and ephemeral and dealing with forces like wind and other kinetic modalities, it's like you're deliberately taking things that are impossible work with and challenging yourselves to extract an order and precision from them. But I think there's also a looseness that we're able to exploit, that if you were to try to build this with normative materials I think it would collapse or be blown over. **So could you say that in your process these nonconventional materials, combined with the aim of material economy, provide you with an opportunity to explore new properties, new forms, new experiences?** I think the search for material economy is part of a larger subset of a search for conceptual economy. I mean, one of the things we do most in the office is eliminate ideas.

We come up with so many ideas and we keep trying to cut out great ideas as much as possible so that some become dominant and take on more roles. Within that logic are these two concepts: one is that of the systemic approach. And the other is the search for variables. So, for example, in the case of the bamboo, its curvature performs in many ways—as a seat back or as a structural element, or as a support for a water nozzle, and so on. Maybe that ties back to our name, with this interest in variability and in controlling what those variables are on each project.

How does theory enter your practice? How does it inform your design? Or does it? Well, you'd mentioned the idea of critical practice earlier, and I've always thought that the term was very aloof and academic and, personally, I never connected to it. When our professors at the GSD (Harvard's Graduate School of Design) would invoke our ambition to be critical, I felt *critical* meant negative. I'd like to think of ours more as an *engaged* practice. **Many of the offices we've spoken with begin with the logic of constraints and conventions to reformulate projects...** I think that the idea of working within constraints is something that everybody thinks about nowadays. You know we all do that as a necessity. It actually doesn't interest me as a concept so much. I think what's more interesting is rewriting the constraints or redefining the problem conceptually, formulating the first questions. And that's a way of questioning program, typology, technology, site... All of these things just need to be rethought, through a new logic that you propose or project.

To what extent do your projects direct your practice? We can answer this a little bit more clearly now that we've had more time and projects to consider. It's a hard thing to answer when you're in it. Being in New York we've always tried to do public work as much as possible, and maybe that's why we have gravitated toward art installations. For us it's not about being artists—we don't pretend to be artists—but it's just for us a way to do public space. Or rather, a way for us to do architecture that is engaged in the public that would elicit response and interaction from the public.

For example, for Windshape, we were commissioned as artists, because it's an arts festival. And the commission was not to do a pavilion, it was to do an art piece. We were addressed as artists, and we said, okay, fine. But in our own terms we thought, how can we do an almost-building?

Where did the generating idea for Windshape come from? We had a lot of difficulties in the beginning. We had no idea entering into it what we were going to do or how exactly to approach it. We're not artists, and this site is a small town on the hillside in France that we'd never been to. At P.S.1 the parameters were more clear—it was clear who the client was, what the institution was, it was in the city we live and work in.

So we had to grab at something out of thin air—in this case literally the air. For us, the result is most definitely architecture, but a lot of people don't know what to make of it. We chose a site that was situated near the medieval fortress wall of the town and imagined extruding it up, as an inversion of the massive limestone walls, as well as a continuation, potentially, of an assumed or fictional archeology. **How did the wind come in?** Well, the wind was first. It came from studying the region and realizing that this wind, known as the mistral has a mythical presence in the south of France. Crimes of passion were forgiven during the mistral. It's a very violent wind. Everybody knows what it is. Our site was a hilltop overlooking agricultural fields. You can see those fields moving in the wind. When the wind approaches, you see it. It's a very potent thing. And also in contrast to the massiveness of this hewn-limestone town was this idea of creating an ephemeral double to this kind of medieval construction that would on the other hand assume some of the dynamic properties of the fields surrounding this town. There was a search for this spatial logic that would unite the landscape and the architecture of the region, in a way.

And you know, we would prefer to do permanent things... [laughter] But given that we've had the chance to do some ephemeral installations, I guess we see it as an opportunity to use non-building-like things and then make them almost-buildings. Knowing that it's not going to stand up for that long gives us the freedom to explore new possibilities. **So there is that interesting relationship**

between your installation work that tries to be building-like, and the more permanent building projects we looked at that embody ephemeral qualities, taking on temporality, malleability... Well, only one of them has actually been built so far [laughter]. Maybe that has more to do with uses and possible misuses— or *mis-users*, we call them—within a project. We have fun imagining what the expected uses are, what the expected fulfillments of the program are, and then comparing them to some of the unexpected uses or unexpected experiences that we can anticipate and optimize and possibly incorporate. For example, with Canopy, we thought about the identity of MoMA/P.S.1 as a museum, as a former school, as a rave venue, as a family/kiddie pool venue. And we thought through all its users and the huge range of scale and size of crowd, and created an environment that was in a way monumental but also intimate at the same time.

I wanted to come back to the idea of the prototype, as it's used now, not in reference to an archetype, but as part of a flexible, evolutionary process of working. In your case, there's a real-world component to the feedback between design and technique. This is in contrast to purely generative approaches in which feedback occurs in the computer. The latter can produce dazzling formal output, but the process itself can become overly formalistic, where, however masterful the technique, it's essentially a closed internal system. While that kind of advanced research is very valuable, it seems, ironically, conservative in relation to practices that work with hands-on or real-world feedback. For us, work that concerns itself primarily with the domain of computer-generated form and scripting is almost about a lack of courage. In the future, looking back, that work might be seen as a kind of academi-cism, like the late-19th-century academicism. Or as a kind of baroque that emerges from a fascination with tools and, in a sense, with craft and materials, which is legitimate and interesting at some level. But I think that purely form-alistic work is still kind of hermetic or myopic. I don't feel that the right questions are being asked. It's like a desire for instant gratification in terms of a formal beauty.

In another, more difficult way, these things could be arrived at by asking socially relevant questions—real questions that make sense to people in terms of the definition of what a project is, or of what our role as an architect is. There's a high risk of failure, but there might also be the potential for engaging issues of structure, material, economy, in conjunction with an examination of the culture and society at large. And do so from the get-go, rather than imposing a kind of formalism and trying to drive

a program out of software. We're much more interested in work that has some sort of resonance with the world at large—that is, beyond architecture. On the one hand we feel that architecture is already a rich and complex enough field that we don't need to borrow metaphors from other fields. At the same time, we want it to have cultural impact. **The danger of the generative approach is that it becomes trapped in a self-referential framework. But the tools are so powerful. Rather than being used as justification for an aesthetic desire, imagine if those techniques could be used to understand and to connect to the relationships within the real world. Maybe its this awareness, in general, that is needed to formulate a relevant theory of architecture now.** And it's also important to figure out from which platform or point of view one is critiquing what is perceived as the avant-garde. Our position is hopefully not a conservative one— that architecture as a profession should be reinforced, not dispersed, in order to try to create more radical architecture. On the other hand, there are some of our colleagues who are reaching some very interesting places using generative strategies, and they're playing an important role too. I don't think every practice has to be the same. It's just who we are and how we work together. I think we go back and forth between a very intuitive design process and a more conscious one where we're trying to state the parameters that are interesting to us, or the tools that we want to achieve with the project. It's kind of a constant tugging back and forth. Something that is extremely personal and abstract doesn't really survive in the office if it doesn't resonate with each of us, or with other members of the team. There's a universe out there of erased lines that's much larger than our office. [laughter] **But you know, that's a valid question, in terms of the labor it takes to produce a single project, and all the unseen residue of that output...** There are two ways to measure that: one is within a single project and the other is across a practice. How many projects get built out of what you've designed? Hopefully, lots. And that should be about performance and about hopefully answering the brief correctly to get the projects, and making sure that we're always tailoring our ambition correctly. That's a huge thing we're always discussing: What's the right ambition for this project? Where do we invent? Where do we make this economical? How do we get it built?

Interview with Eric Bunge and Mimi Hoang of nARCHITECTS was conducted in New York City in 2008 by Elite Kedan.

54, 153 A:3, 200 A:1,
226 A:2, 247 A:2

George Yu of
George Yu Architects

Can we start with your background before you arrived in Los Angeles? I have an undergraduate degree in urban geography from UBC (the University of British Columbia). I was really heading to work in planning in Vancouver, but during my urban studies I became more interested in the question of why modern architecture had failed, at least on a planning level. At UBC at the time, there was a Marxist bent or critique in the urban geography department. Projects like Chandigarh and Brasília represented the failure of modernism at the city scale. **So it was a critique of modernist planning?** You could say that it became a critique of modern masters more than anything. The favorite scapegoats were Le Corbusier, Mies van der Rohe, Frank Lloyd Wright… I became very curious and, more than anything, I was struck by the incredible beauty of Chandigarh, at least in images. So I decided to go into architecture after I graduated. The question was why, given that beauty, was there this complete failure urbanistically?

So then I decided to study architecture at UCLA (University of California, Los Angeles) from 1985 to 1988 and got a graduate degree. My biggest realization upon arriving was that architects at that time—at least my teachers—had completely abandoned the project of architecture. I had Charles Moore and Charles Jencks, and the first lecture given when I arrived was by Robert Stern and John Jerde. Stern and Jerde were showing work for the Olympics, and they had pasted graphics on their plans to hide Watts and Downtown LA. And I was struck by this complete abdication by architects of that particular urban realm, a territory that I thought was an incredibly powerful thing. If you took a look around LA at the time, you saw a lot of bad corner malls and shopping centers sprouting up all over the place, and it was all pretty depressing. But then Rem Koolhaas placed second at the Parc de la Villette competition and then not long after won three big competitions. All of this was around 1986, and in school that was practically not on the radar. There was this realization or hope that there was somebody out there taking on the urban question and the big problems, so I stuck with it.

What were your first work experiences? Thom Mayne had been on my thesis jury. After graduating I went to Morphosis. When I joined the office there were five people. I was the sixth. At that time, Morphosis was pretty unpublished and hadn't built much. The biggest projects were the Kate Mantilini Restaurant and the Medical Center (Cedar Sinai Comprehensive Cancer Center). The Crawford House was under construction, but other than that there were no completed freestanding buildings yet. The reason they hired me was because a Japanese real estate mogul had just hired them for several projects in Japan, including a golf course and a headquarters building for his company. I spent almost four years on the golf course clubhouse project right from the start. Two of those years were in Tokyo as the representative doing construction documents with the local associate architects. Morphosis was taking that leap from doing small-scale work to freestanding buildings and taking on larger issues.

What did you learn at Morphosis? Well, the transition was hard, because up until then it was a practice that was really concerned with surface finishes and details and

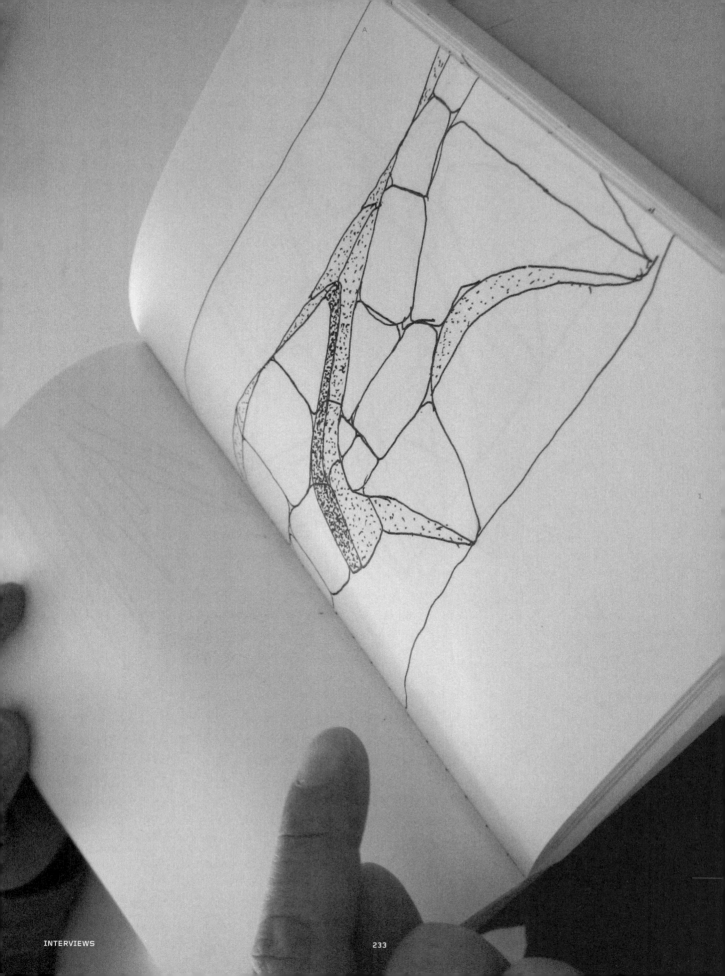

finessing every joint. And then suddenly, with that project, there was this jump in scale to a 40,000-square-foot freestanding project. The practice realized we couldn't draw the thing in the same way, we couldn't study it in the same way, we couldn't make MDF (medium-density fiberboard) models and paste models of every single joint and corner. We had to start thinking globally, and also we had to think about how it was connected to landscape, and how it was connected to a much larger context. The frame of reference shifted, and the moves changed.

A colleague of yours at Morphosis talked about how there was a shift in the firm in the late 1980s toward what he called camouflage buildings—buildings that started to inhabit the landscape rather than mark the landscape. Yes, Mayne was working on a house at the time that was the last gasp of the idea of ideal geometries inscribed in the earth, but I guess camouflage is a good word… **It brings to mind a different morphology.** That was one lesson—the thinking of a directed and different morphology where focus was placed on a project's feathering into, and simultaneously disturbing, its context. But more importantly for my subsequent development was the lesson about the dynamics of a practice, and how it could evolve. What it took to maintain focus and control, and at the same time transition and develop.

You know, Philip Johnson spoke at the GSD (Harvard's Graduate School of Design) in the late 1980s or early 1990s and—always looking to grasp new paradigms—he described a movement he was calling "The Scarpinis," which was a direct reference to the detail-obsessed school of Carlo Scarpa. But he was also obviously referring to the fetishized details of Morphosis, Michael Rotondi, Eric Owen Moss, and others. At the time, he was right to point out a nascent school of thought, which grew out of a 1970s and 1980s reaction to macho urban gestures and histori-cist pastiche, but it never really gelled as a movement, and it sounds like you're saying Morphosis shifted itself eventually to less fussiness. Well, what happened was Rotondi and Mayne split. They were really a perfect couple in many ways, but I think Thom—to his credit— sensed there was an opportunity that existed outside that scale of operation. Rotondi and, in many ways, Moss are still operating at that level. Rotondi was doing things like spraying molten metal onto plywood structures on a house, similar to an early Richard Serra sculpture process. Moss's research followed a similar trajectory but with glass. But Thom realized that wasn't going to allow him to operate at the scale he wanted to develop.

I came away realizing that it wasn't like you had to go corporate if you chose a path outside of the avant-garde of architectural discourse. There was a way out of that dichotomy of being either avant-garde or corporate. **But where is the ground, if you're not doing either corporate work or academic work?** Well, I think that's where we've been trying to carve out a space. To begin with, we had a different starting place from our mentors—the generation of Mayne and Moss—at almost all levels. For example, we had the use of digital tools and CAD (computer-aided design) early on. The generation of Gehry and Mayne seems to have adopted them immediately as they became available, and in some ways they anticipated the need for those tools. But when I worked at Morphosis, we never had a computer. I only learned how to use a computer when I started my own practice and had no work, and had to figure out a way to use the time. In that way it was a more primitive process. You had to grope. There was opportunity and time to figure out what was useful about this thing.

At the same time, Morphosis was suddenly doing 40,000-square-foot buildings, and, over a 15-year period, they'd already worked out the need and urgency for those tools. **So what happened after four years at Morphosis? Why did you leave and where did you go?** Well, the economy collapsed in Tokyo. It was 1992, and the city became a ghost town. The ironic thing was that the construction documents were done. We were ready to break ground. My wife and I took a vacation to India and were incommunicado for six weeks while we were backpacking through the country. We came back and landed in Bangkok. I called the office, and Thom was almost in tears when he broke the news to me. "I fired everybody," he said. He went from forty-five people to two people within a month because all the jobs were gone. He said he was really sorry, but we lost all the Japan jobs and there was no need for me to return to Tokyo. I came back to LA and found him in the office basically alone, with perhaps one person on staff. That was another huge learning experience and not a lesson I want to learn again. Everything seems like it's in place, you've worked four years to get to the point where you're breaking ground, and then it's just gone. It puts everything in perspective.

But getting back to differences in terms of starting points, I think what we were trying to carve out in the beginning was almost not a choice, because we had to go commercial. It's funny because the typical starting point is residential—small practices do residential work, mom's house. We never got asked. The first 20 projects were retail and restaurant bars and cafes. I had this idea that someday, when I grow up, I'll do residential or a school project or something. But it just happened that in that gap between Thom's generation and mine, there was a shift away from doing that very customized, specialized work toward what was available in abundance, which was the huge build-out work of the commercial sector. **The idea of having a practice that does research is something that you probably also took away from Morphosis. When you do retail, how do you approach the project so that there's a research arm involved?** Again, it wasn't that we said, we're going to be a research practice. It came out of circumstance and necessity. Firstly, we had to learn a lot about what's called *branding*. We had to learn about our clients, their culture and customers, and in that way, we became pretty proficient at doing that kind of market research. Secondly, the kind of material practice that we got involved in—commercial work—was so different from the material practice that we'd learned at a boutique firm like Morphosis, where everything was one-off.

When you're doing a roll-out for 50 or a hundred stores it's a completely different dynamic. The parameters are completely different. You have to accept that these things are probably going to be made in Canada or China or some shop that you'll never visit. And you'll have to meet a 140-dollar-per-square-foot budget. So the Scarpini thing you mentioned earlier was impossible. Even though the architectural publications in front of us were totally about achieving those levels of resolution, we couldn't do it. **Did you hesitate to go into retail? There's a stigma attached to retail even now.** Really, only in hindsight. After a couple of years, it did strike us as an opportunity and a valuable lesson. For us, it had become about mass production and not the one-off. But our definition of mass production was different than our mentors' definition. It was no longer stigmatized. The challenge was how to give each of the modules or instances some differences or unique qualities. It was now possible with the new economy and with new tools and new material for practices to actually do that. This was in contrast to Thom's generation, where the attitude was about completely avoiding or resisting mass production. It's what led every-thing to be so… **Artisanal?** Yes. Crafted. Initially, we had to deal with mass produced objects and environments out of necessity, but we eventually found that you can make these things all different, given a control or mastery of the economies. And so that's what the MaxStudio stores allowed us to practice, as well as the multiple e-business centers for IBM. It's what Sony allowed us to practice, starting with the Sensorium competition, which was not only about the building, but also the space and all its accessories. Out of that came the Sony Design Center in Santa Monica, and another one in Shanghai.→74 **So for you there's a connection between spatial relationships and material research; it's not one or the other. Would it be fair to say it's**

a sort of holistic prototype? Yes. **It seems a lot of young firms are researching materials as a form of empowerment, because there are new modes of production and new ways of fabrication, which can afford experimentation. It's not a one-off, but you work through and within material constraints and push boundaries. It's a sort of return to the master builder idea. What role does material research play in your firm?** I think it's very much about empower-ment, or taking back responsibilities that at some point had drifted away from the scope of the architect. **At what level? Because you could take standardized parts and customize them, which is a different operation than working at the scale of the material itself.** We did start by taking off-the-shelf things and tricking them up. But we were also given the opportunity—where there were multiples—to do a much deeper analysis of each of the systems and work with people who were able to fabricate at a scale that was taking advantage of the latest technology to mass produce. For example, that piece over there is a fiberglass mold [gestures to model], which was the fourth →165 A:3 prototype produced for the MaxStudio project. Leon Max, the client, asked us to do kiosks so that people could use his website to access inventory that wasn't available in the store. That was a one-year-long process where we researched how to make fiberglass parts, found the right fabricators, and ended up finding a guy who had been making parts for the aerospace industry for 20 years. When we walked in to interview him, he had 20-odd pieces that were parts of F-18 ejection seats out on the floor. He came out of the military industrial complex. At the time—it was before the Iraq War—all the contracts for that kind of work were gone. He was open to anything, and even though he was used to working with the incredibly complex tolerances of things like F-18 parts, the process ended up being difficult. It took months just to work out how to make translucent parts. **How do you get clients who will give you the time to do material research? How do you fund the research?** In this case, the client was pretty savvy about what it would take to do the research. For his own business, he has to go to China or Mexico for production. He knows it takes research and development. He's not going to get the right pattern the first time around, and so on. It takes time to find the right manufacturer. So he was familiar with the process and gave us time. It took us a year to get to the first production parts. And then the IBM project came along…

Let's talk about IBM for a moment. I think it's inter-esting how you went after that project. Again, placing your practice in a nontraditional way, getting work in a nontraditional way, putting together a team in

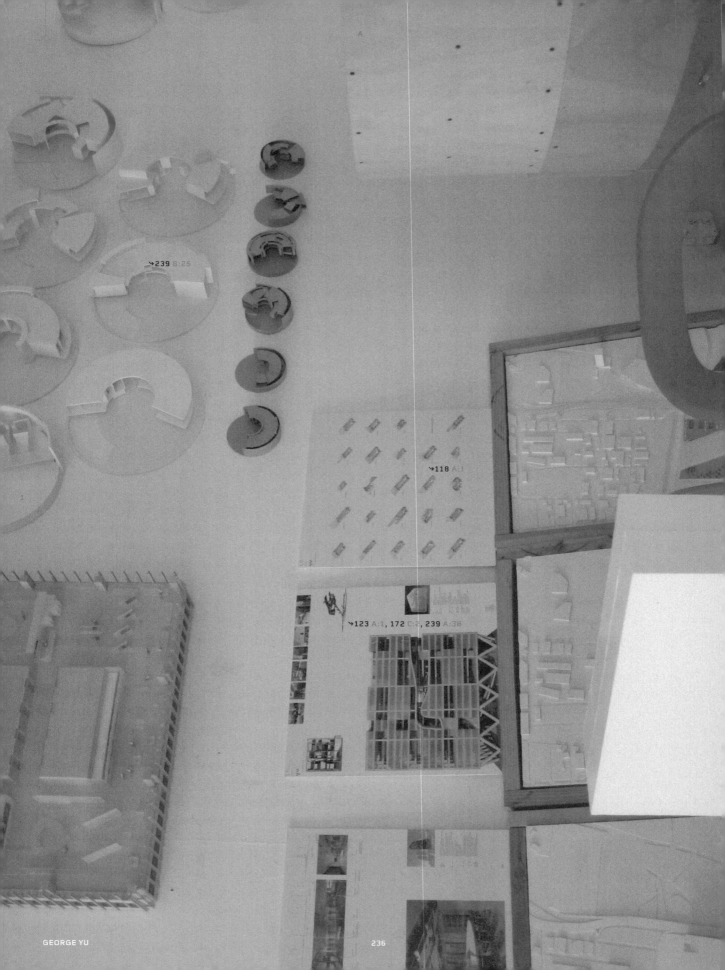

239 B:25

118 A:1

123 A:1, 172 C:2, 239 A:38

a new way. Yeah, that was 1999, and it's not like we planned to grow this way. There was no manifesto before we got this job, and in many ways it was totally by chance. We didn't have that much work then. Also, at the time I was teaching at SCI-Arc (Southern California Institute of Architecture), and one of the students in my studio had worked as a producer at Imaginary Forces (a multidisciplinary entertainment and design agency) and liked our work and introduced me to them. They were interested in spatial, environmental work; we were interested in new media. New media is a fuzzy term, but we thought it could be used to explore new ways of seeing space through different technological means.

Well, about six months later we heard through the grapevine that there was a potential project to be had with IBM e-business, and that they were looking for a team to take on the re-branding of their e-business division. At first, they didn't have a requirement for architecture or interior design; they were primarily looking for teams that were graphics- and branding-based. Imaginary Forces was doing a lot of advertising and branding work, so they found out about the opportunity and called us to put together a team with them. They cold-called IBM and begged, and we got our foot in the door. We were given a week to put together a pitch after they introduced the project to us. We understood it as a branding project, but we made the argument that they had to consider how architecture would be an integral component of this re-branding. Of course they had architects that were eventually going to be involved, but the process was set up first to figure out the branding and then let it trickle down to the architecture. The architecture was going to be handled by HOK (Hellmuth, Obata + Kassabaum) and SOM (Skidmore, Owings & Merrill) and different larger corporate firms who were already in long-term relationships with IBM. And our argument was that architectural, interior, and environmental design needed to be at the same table as your branding team. **How?** In our argument with Imaginary Forces, it was pretty specific. We said, here you have guys that can do interactive design video, media design, audio design—all those people can do all the advertising and branding—but we have the opportunity to make the space itself completely integral to all that look-and-feel stuff. And it seems really obvious now, but it wasn't to a company like IBM at the time. They were kind of shocked at first and thought, oh yeah, that makes total sense. **But now it's become integral to the way we experience retail, like the Apple Store.** And Koolhaas's work with Prada. It's the normal practice now, but this was 1999. At that time, it was normal practice to first do the look and feel, and then eventually work your way down to architecture, if at all. **So how did you approach that project? For instance,**

a practice like Sheila Kennedy's (Kennedy & Violich Architecture) would start with the infrastructure and technology, but that obviously was not your project. No, but it's interesting that you reference them, as they're pretty well-known material researchers who are also looking at ways of integrating technology into design. But our agenda was more sociological. It was a kind of probing of the relationships between the people in the space. **Do you think that comes from your planning background?** Possibly.

Could we go back for a moment and consider this abdication or retreat by architects in the 1980s from social analysis and social responsibility. I'm making some broad generalizations, but the retreat happened in many ways. The (Peter) Eisenmanian linguistic models are an example, as are the Scarpini detailings or the drawings that were considered complete works of architecture unto themselves. But you entered into practice saying you're not going to shy away from social programming and analysis. Well, in the mid-1980s—or probably beginning in the 1970s—something like programming was so marginalized and narrowly defined. It was one of those deadly boring courses you had to suffer through in your curriculum, along with professional practice. I found it really odd that something so important could be made so completely marginal and banal. When it came to the IBM project there was no manifesto or idea for re-socializing. What happened was, we pitched in New York after a one-week charrette. They gave us 50,000 dollars and challenged us to come back in a month and give them a report on what they should do. They didn't care if we were architects, interior designers, or whatever; they treated us as a consultant. So we flew around the country, visited their centers in New York, Atlanta, LA. We talked to their consulting staff and sat in on a number of presentations that their staff gave to clients; we sat in the back of the room and took notes. The team included myself and the creative director of Imaginary Forces. It became obvious to us that the problem didn't have anything to do with branding, as graphics or as media or as material. It didn't have anything to do with the product-design level. They were just really messed up in terms of how they sat together in a conference room. **But how do you translate or quantify that criticism? And then how do you convey that information visually?** Out of that month of research, we made comparisons, observations, and somewhat obvious statements about what they were doing or not doing, about how people were falling asleep and not paying attention during meetings. The biggest critique was that they were force-feeding information to clients in a typical American conference room at U-shaped or very long tables, with clients on one side, IBM on the other, using lecterns and screens with PowerPoint slide shows, or worse, overhead projectors. There was no dialogue, just a one-way force-feeding of data. Clients just had to accept it. There was no interaction, no collaborative process in which IBM was trying to understand what was going on from their client's side. The whole spatial dynamic was set up that way.

In our report to them we suggested that there were alternatives. That it was simply a case of putting people in different relationships spatially—like in a Chinese restaurant, you can sit around a round table—we can get together with equal access to the center and equal access to information with little or no hierarchies or leader. It also applied to the delivery of information. Make use of the technology to deliver information in a nonhierarchical way, don't present slides where the information is already digested and interpreted. That's what the interactive technology is great for anyway, to simulate the world and allow people to engage in that world. Whether you call it game-playing or whatever, we wanted to use it to present really complex information. IBM's e-business is doing consulting work for large Fortune 500 companies, and their customers are high-level executives coming in for a day of meetings. They're highly motivated, intelligent people who run large companies. They're discussing the futures of these companies. They're not buying hardware from IBM necessarily, but they're buying a mode of practice. IBM is collecting millions of dollars in fees and telling them how to run their business, and what they were doing was force-feeding regurgitated clichés spatially. We proposed to build a model right there at the table and use the technology to create something that was spontaneous and specific to the circumstances of these companies.

↳113 A:2

I'd call this scale of operation *medium space*. It's not product-design scale and it's not at the scale of building. It's hard to get your hands on what the limits of that are. Are the limits established by the extent of program, the use of the space? And how do you define the boundaries? Well, if you back up, what we were trying to do was create something spatial that would create community, a medium that would somehow encourage people to come together and interact and find—whether it's business models or whatever—a way of making music together for that day or for that particular culture. The question becomes about how to employ these different technologies to allow people to come together rather than hold them at bay, because technology can be as alienating as it is bridge-building. Part of this thing became a table, but really the definition of that space had to be very open. Openness became a key word for these series of projects.

That's interesting, because in doing that you're thinking about detail, not in a didactic way, but in terms of how two materials might join, for example. It requires that you think about what these details can do and how they perform. For example, how a table operates or how the ceiling relates to the table or how the edge of the floor surface can denote space as much as a wall can. It's performative detail rather than self-explanatory or reflective detail. I'm not saying that we've completely escaped the world of Charles Moore and icons and the importance of meaning in architecture. But the way the geometry of these rooms was determined had to do with the requirements of function, or performance. We really needed to open up to a gallery that needed to operate in a number of modes. For instance, the ceiling geometry was generated out of a way to escape using carpet material. Common convention would probably indicate that carpet makes for good acoustics, but we wanted to use terrazzo everywhere—a custom terrazzo that was translucent. It's a very hard surface with horrible acoustical properties for meetings. So the ceiling had to perform, to take up the role of the carpet. And at the same time we wanted to make certain the table wasn't seen as a piece of hardware. There was a clear directive from IBM not to make these spaces about ideas of hardware, because they said, "we're not a hardware company, we're about ideas." However ambiguously directed, it was clear we had to make it look good, make a beautiful product, but not make it be about hardware. So as a result everything—including all equipment—that usually loads up the table got sucked up into the ceiling, and the ceiling became this dense series of components. Normally the two-foot space above the ceiling isn't required to accommodate that much stuff, so we had to make a 3D model and trace every conduit, every piece of mechanical ductwork, every piece of equipment, and so on. **So rather than exposing infrastructure, you're hiding it. How is that different from the typical office space with the dropped ceiling?** Well, the dropped ceiling is usually only hiding lighting and mechanical systems. This scenario called for carrying projectors and other equipment such as speakers, microphones, special lighting, etc., so it's choreographing twice as many functions as the normal dropped ceiling. But getting back to why that was done, we never lost sight of meaning, or of the experience we were trying to create. As I said, the directive was to not make it look like they're selling hardware. At the same time, getting back to the discussion of social relationships, we tried to make a space in which people could come in and feel like they could communicate and collaborate. At the end of the day, there's still the look and feel, the physical experience, the surfaces, the finishes… They're still really important.

**How did this work get carried forth into the Sony
project? How did that project come to you? How did
you approach it?** I gave a lecture in Tokyo after we'd
finished IBM. In the audience were a number of people from
Sony Design Center who, after the lecture, invited us to
stay in touch. They said they had a very exciting project in
the works and seven months later contacted us and sent us
the brief. That was early 2001. They sent us one of the most
intelligent, thorough briefs for a competition that I'd ever
seen. It wasn't just an architectural brief; they really got
into the social and technological aspects of work space.
It was a kind of polemical statement: "This is the future of
work and Sony is going to own it." That kind of boldness.
**So how did you carry forth ideas from the IBM project
into Sony?** Well, on a number of levels. This was a totally
different scale. IBM was room-scale and suddenly we were
being asked to consider something practically at city scale.
At one point it was a 1.5-million-square-foot megastructure,
and at first this scared me and probably scared everybody
on the project, because it really was about ultimate control,
a totally controlled environment. In one way it was supposed to be a city, but in another way it wasn't, because
it's privately secured and there are definite thresholds and
you have to buy into it. But the intention in the brief was
to create something that, on my first impression, struck me
as a return to the idea of a mega-structural city, a return
to the Metabolists. The floor plate was 100,000 square feet,
while the IBM plate was 20,000 square feet, which was
the typical American office building floor plate. What we
were proposing was an area five times that size. The first
thought was that our biggest problem was going to be
creating porosity, so light can get into the center. And not
only that—how do you avoid having to have a journey of one
hundred meters walking from one edge to the other, while
creating enough variety or difference so that this thing would
really be a landscape or a city?

**The building is organized in a modular or cellular way,
but it seems that the module comes from a thinking
similar to the IBM project, where use and program
start to inform structure rather than structure
imposing itself on use?** Yeah, that's a good way to put it.
The Miesian model is really a unifying structural model. The
tectonic regularity allows for so-called universal flexibility,
but now 40 or 50 years later most spaces are driven by the
budget—leases especially—and not by spatial needs. What
we wanted to return to was something that was driven by
the quality of space, that module would multiply out and
then, yes, structure would serve to support an optimal
module. **Between the structure and the module—
these programmatic increments—there's a thread**

of landscape, weaving through, creating points of
variation or intense interaction. **Tell me more about
the thinking behind that landscape piece.** I'd say, the
way it's generated, the logic of it as a prototype idea, is the
most flexible. For instance, if the bays in the module are set
up to be repeated on any site at any proportion, that ribbon
is much more circumstantial and opportunistic, so that it
reconfigures to go from node to node. At street level, there's
one node, and at the second floor there's another node,
and then in the middle of the building there's another series
of nodes. These centers are distributed, so that everyone
has equal access to the amenities that are on a time-share
basis. The ribbon of circulation that infiltrates the structure
has to help everybody get to those nodes in the way that a
streetscape or geometry of streets in an urban sense allows
people to navigate a city. That's how we were thinking
about this ribbon, as a three dimensional connector. But
the problem is tectonic, because ultimately you completely
mess up your structural logic. If there's anything I would
try to do over in a different way, it would probably be that
system, because it ends up causing so much complexity,
geometrically and tectonically. **The exception becomes
the rule.** Yeah.

**It seems you're having a similar issue with the house
in Malibu. It foregrounds the overarching geometry
of a circle, but your tendency to impose decay on
that primary geometry creates tectonic complexity.
So there must be some pathology there. You like
to violate these primary forms and erode their order,
whether it's the gridded matrix of the Sony project
or a circle. Where do you think that predilection
comes from?** Well, that's probably a trace of my mentors'
generation, the influence of Morphosis. **What exactly is
that thinking? Is it a fear of symmetry, of perfection,
a fear of systems that are tautological, Miesian,
universal...?** Well, I think we're coming at it from a different starting point, from the tendencies of someone like
Eisenman. **You mean making a research out of
creating conflicts in the work?** Yes, and they were
mainly geometrical. Whereas, for better or worse, we were
arriving at repetitive, platonic geometries—at least in the
case of Sony—by looking at how you can economically
create a complex landscape within something like a
corporate box, without having to resort to an Eisenman
model. The ribbon idea was the violation. But there's
probably a different way to do it, systematically or through
other variables like site or program, where you could still
play within the modules and still get the same connection
through the building without the complete erasure of
that order.

We've talked about retail, landscape, social engineering… And those things, at least in our education, were kind of dismissed, but now you see it re-emerging in a lot of younger practices. We didn't start out planning to do this, but almost 20 years after graduate school that's where we've arrived—and with these stigmas maybe still intact in some parts of our culture. But it seems right that we could still take that stuff along and make it an interesting problem for our practices.

Where would you like to place your practice in the future? You know, previously there wasn't a lot of choice. You practice, you get an opportunity to do work, you don't get a chance to think about manifestos, and yet you can't really grow without theorizing. So many of us are now at a point where we're trying to make our research more intentional, to really hone them and direct them. **It's interesting that there's increasingly less of—or in some cases, no—divide between theory and practice for current firms. In other words, the development of a body of work through a theoretical position, followed by the translation of that position into built projects is not the way a lot of younger firms are operating.** For our generation practice is legitimized in a different way. The way we represent our work is different. We put a lot of emphasis on and really struggle with communicating what some people call performativity. A previous generation would have completely diagrammed that out and legitimized the project with a series of morphological logic, or used it as a sort of retroactive justification. In our firm's case, the legitimacy is not given in the form of a proof, arriving at an end product by rigorously, formulaically planning out your steps morphologically or otherwise. Rather, there is a real struggle with how to communicate performance. **So how is the performance legitimized?** That's the struggle. We still have to document it and describe it in some way, and I don't think anyone has really found that new way of describing performance, at least in two dimensions. You can go to the finished, built space and ask the user if the building *works*. You can use it and walk around it, and it can feel great. That's totally different from the images and diagrams we use to represent it.

Well, it's interesting you don't have people in these photographs of your work, or in renderings of unbuilt projects. Yet they're about the performative aspects of spaces or the programs that enable community. Yeah, that was the decision, right or wrong, in how to document these things. It was an ideological decision not to resort to good-looking models in the images.

It gets back to the problem of representation as a tool. I don't think we've theorized that issue properly yet…

Interview with George Yu was conducted in Los Angeles, California, in 2005 by Jon Dreyfous.

Camera Obscura
SHoP

↘102 A.1, 152 A.3, 199 A.8

↘142 B.16, 198 A.1

Avra Verde Residence
MARCH/Chris Hoxie consultant
Architect: Roy Joy Architects

�50, 83, 99 A:2, 147 A:3

Beijing National Stadium
Gehry Technologies consultant
Architect: Herzog & de Meuron

↘100 A:1, 150 A:1

Canopy
nARCHITECTS

↘104 A:1, 225 B:10, 202–203, 228 A:1

↘54, 201 A:1

225 A:15

200 B:2

China Central Television Headquarters (CCTV)
Front consultant
Architect: OMA

➜ 88 A:10, 105 A:1, 154 A:1

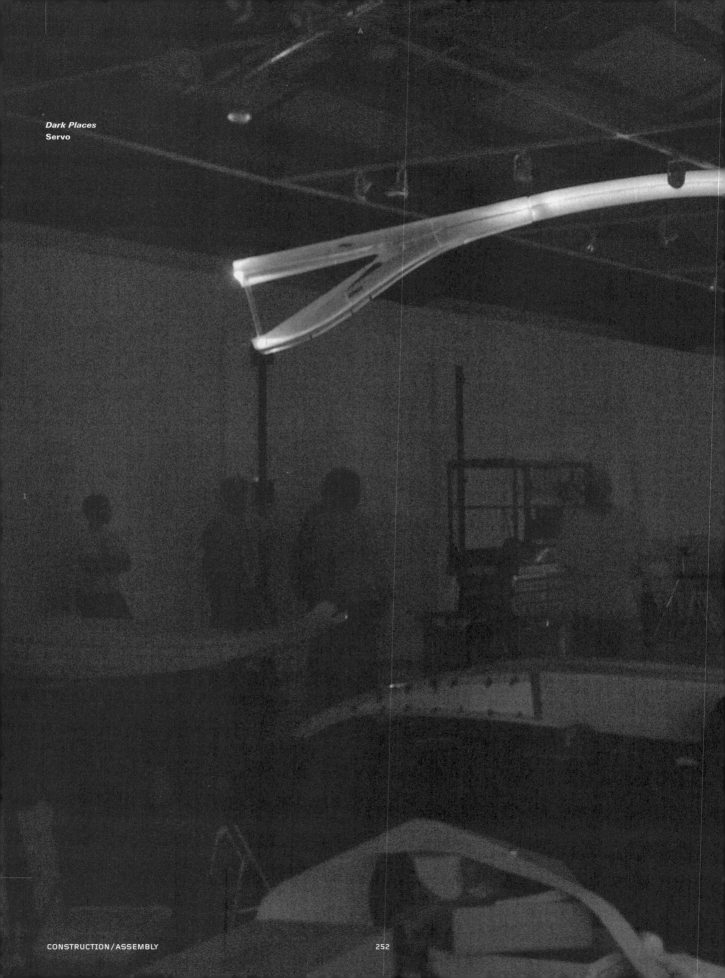

Dark Places
Servo

>12, 56–57, 108 A:1,
156 C:2, 190 A:1, 208 A:1
212 A:1

Fluff Bakery
Lewis.Tsurumaki.Lewis

KEEP
CLEAN

IBM Center for e-Business Innovation
George Yu Architects

Ini Ani Coffee Shop
Lewis.Tsurumaki.Lewis

LoRezHiFi
MY Studio/Meejin Yoon

↱164 C:3, 222 B:1-2, 223 B:1-2

↘115 A:1, 164 A:2

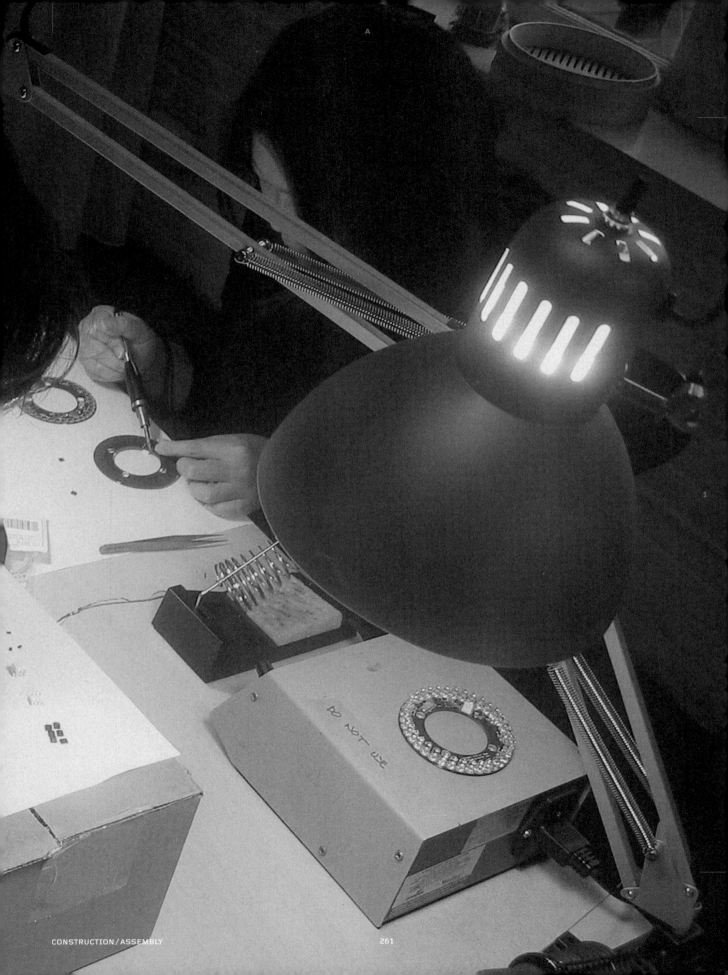

→66, 165 A:2, 180 B:14, 220–221, 222 B:1–2

Seattle Central Public Library
Front consultant
Architect: OMA/LMN joint venture

↳71, 88 ____, 122 ____, 174 ____

Shop Lift: Rethinking Retail, Transcending Type
George Yu Architects

A

1

→72–73, 124 and, 175

↗232 A:1, 273 A:1

1

White Noise/White Light
MY Studio/Meejin Yoon

↘126 A:2, 176 A:1, 224 A:1

Windshape
nARCHITECTS

↳127 , 226

↘78–79, 127 A:1, 226 A:43

Spread Out:
The Lateral Philosophies of George Yu

by Neil Denari

In his oddly shaped office on Washington Boulevard, a space
formed by an anomaly in Los Angeles' urban street grid,
George Yu enacted episodes of work and play with an equally
uncommon élan vital. Part DJ, part magus, part alchemist,
Yu conjured visions of a global landscape that deeply reflected
his commitment to a personal *lifedesign* strategy, one that
more or less resembled a blueprint for relaxed formalisms and
cool collaborations. If Andy Warhol's early Factories were to
be crossed with Q's deadly serious laboratory for secret-agent
gadgets, then one would begin to understand how Yu
could float across the cultural scene with the unmistakable
precision and attentiveness of a boffin inventor. Like the city
of Los Angeles, Yu's office physically and conceptually had
a tendency to spread out in the search for the next new
idea, the next new material, the next new event that could
shape his life and the lives of those around him.

Perhaps this LA mind-meld came from the fact that he actually lived there three different times. The first, a period of five years from 1986 to 1990 included his graduate training at UCLA. The next period, 1992 to 1996, began after two years of living and working in Tokyo. Finally, in 1999, after two years in Vancouver, Yu again returned to Los Angeles to re-establish his practice after circling the Pacific Rim for more than a decade. Like a New World explorer whose map went overboard, Yu discovered LA anew each time he came back. Indeed, while he found familiarity in the world-city connectivity of LA, Yu seemed to move through different circuitry with each passing phase, creating discrete environments that facilitated his expansive design ambitions.

Beginning in 1999 with a massive urban project for New York in collaboration with Morphosis, through to the end of 2002 with his brilliant submission for the new Sony headquarters in Tokyo, Yu's work reached a creative apex in the early years of his third tour of Los Angeles. In between these two major enterprises, Yu built his most impressive and most speculative work, the IBM Center for e-Business Innovation, located in Mies van der Rohe's slightly menacing black IBM building on the Chicago River. Here, Chicago was nothing more than a switching station for the continuous flow of techno-power, politics, money, and the possibility of a temporal yet deeply submersive (subversive?) environment, one capable of not only communicating information and

↳64, 113 A:1

ideas but also, like a fast-acting narcotic, capable of changing
one's perception. In multiplying this exercise in translucent
terrazzo, candy-colored resin, and the glaucous light of LCD
monitors by a factor of one hundred, Yu produced a work
of startling complexity for Sony. Perhaps through sheer
animus, he diagrammed the project in a matter of hours,
maybe even minute—this for a project of 1.5 million square
feet held within a one-hundred-meter cube. With the Sony
Sensorium, Yu attacked the concept of scale and proximity
↘123 A:1, 172 C:2, 239 A:38
with a rigorous conceptual and dimensional method that
dispensed with composition and instead promoted a
systematic modularity capable of nuanced flexibility and
spatial continuity. Based purely on the potential of initial
design conditions, the Sensorium became a cultivated
wilderness, a total freedomscape, subtly but operatively
undermined by the military structure of one of the world's
leaders in intelligent production. On each floor plate, Yu
turns Sony's landscapes of controlled ground into a more
open-ended, less predictable oceanic world, with each
moving body rippling the surface of corporate hierarchy.
To do this, one must be fully committed to the idea that
architecture works best when it causes psychic shifts or
that it performs only with people, not without. Like the
DJ, a maestro armed with tools and techniques, Yu
always preferred a scene, and this social imperative was
a considerably influential part of his lifedesign process.

As a group, these three projects embody Yu's smooth discourse of architectural urbanism, a premise based more on ambient conditions and a tai chi nonchalance than the forceful and collisive accumulations of his mentor Thom Mayne. Nonetheless, it would be a grave mistake to think that Yu's will to design was any less coercive, any less impulsive than Mayne's. Despite a method of working that engaged the trancelike and meditative qualities of certain Asian spiritual practices, Yu's pursuit of design was fired by a conventional motivation to constantly deliver product. After all, Yu's global citizenry required him to be active, not passive. However, this will to work never came at the expense of the freedom to spread out, to think laterally and loosely. Configured against the constricting rules of a specific medium, Yu's practice quite literally morphed, or possibly drifted, into an anything-goes multimedia world, limited only by time and money, never by rules. Only momentarily applied, rules became operative rather than limiting, a perfectly orchestrated world of (Brian) Enoesque intention: what comes out will be product of conceptual clarity and an emotional desire to see the unusual emerge.

Neil Denari is Principal of Neil M. Denari Architects based in Los Angeles, California. ↘111 A:2, 163 A:1

Postscript

What happened to the architects of the postmodern generation? And what did they teach us? In school, thinking outside the constraints of conventional practice was expected. It was a period of theory-based architectural practice, favoring postmodern positioning, embodied on paper, that has given way to a new generation of architects responding to the marketplace testing ground for real-world construction. We moved on. And so did many of our teachers.[1]

And yet ... If postmodernist probing taught us anything, it was *improvisation*. We learned, for instance, how to keep swimming—juggling inter-disciplinary methods, reading texts we could hardly understand—in some dangerously deep waters. We were taught a kind of productive diffusion that

has since enabled us to harness the transformative possibilities of previously unthinkable technological advancements. So, in a way, we've succeeded in doing what our professors taught us—to think outside the constraints of conventional practice. It's just beyond what we imagined. There's nothing essentially subversive or avant-garde about it. The point, after all, is to build. Our practices have been transformed, but in pursuit of new possibilities for shaping our environments.

And that's what we mean by *provisional*. It's a roll-up-your-sleeves kind of ethos, augmented by the newest technologies. It's an eschewal of aesthetic form for its own sake and a reorientation toward the practical, the opportunistic, and the sustainable. It's an approach of adaptation, and a relevant one within the context of multiple paradigm shifts in which we find ourselves. And it's a transformative process—a shift from grand visions to margins and technologies that reverberate and amplify across practice and culture.

What's different about this particular moment is the acceleration of change, as well as the attitude. Not burdened by crisis of meaning and explicit social/political agendas, innovative practices are transforming the field through negotiation and

synthesis of existing systems and emerging technologies. Admittedly, there is no clearly identifiable
"style" that one can attribute to this approach.
And much of the architecture is challenged and
advanced by seemingly contradictory motivations—
it's not uncommon for a single firm to produce
buildings addressing environmental strategies
at a local scale, as well as built-to-impress global
superstructures for powerful clients. Is it just
about technology and performance? What about
the ethics or aesthetics of this approach? Or some
deeper philosophical basis?

What if a unifying theory is not what's called for,
but rather the capacity to navigate a multivalent and
expanding network of approaches that generates
a relevant architecture now? Perhaps it's more about
the doing than the meaning, which will accumulate
and emerge over time, from the context, and from
the work itself. And perhaps, much more than being
a placeholder condition until the "next big thing"
comes along, provisional is a post-postmodern
state of being, the post-edge method for innovative
and meaningful practice.

1. This includes architects such as Rem Koolhaas and
Zaha Hadid—exalted as "avante-garde" while we were in
architecture school (from the mid-1980s to the mid-1990s)—
who emerged from academic precincts and manifested
big visions into big projects and mainstream practices
now adopted globally.

Credits & Acknowledgments

3 Degrees of Felt
Aztec Empire Exhibition
Guggenheim Museum
Location New York, New York
Completion 2004
Client Guggenheim Museum
Architect MY Studio/Meejin Yoon
in collaboration with Enrique
Norten/TEN Arquitectos
Computation Stylianos Dritsas
Images 49 Installation views from
The Aztec Empire, Solomon R.
Guggenheim Museum, New York,
October 15, 2004–February 13, 2005:
photographs by David Heald ©
The Solomon R. Guggenheim
Foundation, New York; **97–98**
(text and images), **145, 193**
(script by Stylianos Dritsas):
courtesy MY Studio/Meejin Yoon

Alice Tully Hall—Lincoln Center
Location New York, New York
Completion 2008
Architect Diller Scofidio + Renfro
in collaboration with FXFOWLE
Architects
Structural Engineer Arup NY
MEP Engineer Arup NY
Technology Consultant Gehry
Technologies
Construction Manager Turner
Construction
Images 145 Courtesy Susan
Constantine, Gehry Technologies

Arthouse at the Jones Center
Contemporary Art for Texas
Location Austin, Texas
Completion 2009
Client Arthouse at the Jones Center,
Contemporary Art for Texas

Architect Lewis.Tsurumaki.Lewis
Design Team Paul Lewis,
Marc Tsurumaki, David J. Lewis;
Michael Tyre, Matthew Roman,
Jason Dannenbring, Monica
Suberville, Hilary Zaic, Tamicka
Marcy, Mia Lorenzetti
Structural Engineer MJ Structures
Mechanical Engineers
Kent Consulting Engineers
Lighting Design Lightfield Inc.
Images 99 (text and image),
145–147: © LTL Architects, courtesy
Lewis.Tsurumaki.Lewis

Avra Verde Residence
Location Saguaro National Park
West; Tuscon, Arizona
Completion Digital construction
2007; built construction 2011
Client Tom Barton
Architect Rick Joy Architects
Design Team Rick Joy (Principal),
Philip Neher, Nicolas Norero
(Project Architects), Will Macivor,
Claudia Valent
Digital Consultant MARCH:
Kevin Cimini, Brandon Hicks
(Partners in Charge), Chris Hoxie
Structural Engineer Harris
Engineering
Civil Engineer Presidio Engineering
Electrical Engineer Matthews
Consulting & Design
Permitting Jim Portner
Pool Consultant Aquadesign
Solar Consultant Daniel Snyder
General Contractor
The Construction Zone
Images 50, 83, 99 (text and image),
147–149, 242–243: © MARCH
courtesy MARCH

Beijing National Stadium
Location Beijing, China
Completion 2008
Client China Olympic Committee
Architect Herzog & de Meuron,
with Arup Sport and the Beijing
CAG Design Institute
Structural Engineer Arup
Technology Services Consultant
Gehry Technologies
General Contractor Beijing
Urban Construction Group
Construction Manager Bouygues
France
Images 100 courtesy Cristiano
Ceccato, Gehry Technologies;
150–151: © Arup, courtesy Arup,
Herzog & de Meuron; **244–245**:
photo courtesy Martin Riese

Bornhuetter Hall
The College of Wooster
Location Wooster, Ohio
Completion 2004
Client The College of Wooster
Architect Lewis.Tsurumaki.Lewis
Design Team Paul Lewis,
Marc Tsurumaki, David J. Lewis;
David Takacs, Hye-Young Chung,
Carolynn Karp, Eric Samuels,
Clement Valla, Stephanie Tuerk,
Patri Vienravi
Construction Manager Bogner
Construction Management Company
Structural Engineer Robert
Silman Associates
Mechanical Engineer Point
One Design
Image 51 photo © Michael Moran;
100 (text and image), **150–152**,
194–195: © LTL Architects, courtesy
Lewis.Tsurumaki.Lewis

Brooklyn Arena—Atlantic Yards
Location New York, New York
Completion 2010
Client Forest City Ratner
Companies
Architect Gehry Partners LLP
Structural Engineer The
Thornton-Tomasetti Group Inc.
Services Engineer Flack + Kurtz
Inc.
Facade Engineering and Design
Consultancy Front Inc.
Contractor Turner Construction
Company
Images 152–153 © Gehry Partners
LLP

Camera Obscura
Mitchell Park, Phase 2
Location Greenport, New York
Completion 2005
Client Village of Greenport
Architects SHOP Architects, P.C.
Design Team Mark Ours,
Reese Campbell, Jason Anderson,
Keith Kaseman, Basil Lee
Images 52–53 photos © Seong
Kim, courtesy SHOP Architects;
101–103 (text and images),
152, 196–199, 241: courtesy
SHOP Architects

Canopy
MoMA/P.S.1 Young Architects
Program
Location P.S.1 Contemporary
Art Center; Queens, New York
Completion 2004
Client MoMA/P.S.1
Architect nARCHITECTS
Design Team Eric Bunge, Mimi
Hoang (Principals); Jorge Pereira

(Project Architect), Samuel Dufaux, Kayt Brumder, Phu Hoang, Claudia Martinho, Marica McKeel, Christopher Rountos, Dayoung Shin, Nik Vekic
Fabrication Eric Bunge, Nick Gelpi, Mimi Hoang, Matt Hutchinson, Ian Keough, Jonathan Kurtz, Jeannie Lee, Marica McKeel, Jorge Pereira, Aaron Tweedie, Anthony Acciavatti, Jenny Chou, Samuel Dufaux, Jennifer Fetner, Toru Hasegawa, Mark Hash, Hikaru Iwasaka, Sebastian Potz, Christopher Rountos, Kevin Sipe, Peter Thon, Nik Vekic
Material Dave Flanagan, President, Northeast Chapter American Bamboo Society, Boston
Engineering Markus Schulte, Ove Arup NY
Garden Marie Viljoen
Sound Environment José Ignacio Hinestrosa
Images 54 photo © Frank Oudeman; 55, 247 A:1 photo © Jorge Pereira; 153 A:3 photo by Elite Kedan; 104 (text and images); 153 A:3; 200–203; 228; 246, 247 A:2: courtesy nARCHITECTS

China Central Television Headquarters (CCTV)
Location Beijing, China
Completion 2008
Client China Central Television
Architect Office for Metropolitan
Project Team Architecture OMA: Ole Scheeren, Rem Koolhaas (Partners in Charge); Dongmei Yao (Project Manager); Charles Berman, David Chacon, Chris van Duijn, Erez Ella, Adrianne Fisher, Anu Leinonen, Andre Schmidt, Shohei Shigematsu, Hiromasa Shirai, Steven Smith (Project Architects)
Associate Architect and Engineer East China Architecture and Design Institute (ECADI), Shanghai
Structural Engineer Arup
Services Engineer Arup
Facade Engineering and Design Consultancy Front Inc.
Contractor China State Construction Engineering (Hong Kong) Limited
Facade Contractor Beijing Jianghe Richway Technology Development Co., Ltd.
Images 90, 154–155 (except for OMA images identified below): courtesy Front Inc.; 105–106 (text and images), 154 A:1, 154 B:2, 154 D:2, 248: CCTV/OMA Rem Koolhaas and Ole Sheeren image courtesy OMA, © OMA

D Gallery
Location Philadelphia, Pennsylvania
Completion 2007
Client Freedom Management
Architect Point B Design
Structural Engineer Keast & Hood Co.
Facade Engineering and Design Consultancy Front Inc.
Contractor W.S. Cumby & Son
Facade Contractor Via Glass LLC
Images 107 (text and images), 154–157 (except for Point B images identified below), 204–207, 249–251: courtesy Front Inc.; 156 D:1, 156 A:2, 157 A:1: © Point B Design

Dark Places
Exhibition at the Santa Monica Museum of Art
Location Santa Monica, California
Completion 2006
Architect Servo, in collaboration with Peter Cho and Elise Co
Curator Joshua Decter
Design Team David Erdman, Chris Perry, Marcelyn Gow; with Mike Hill, Jeremy Whitener, Ellie Abrons, Kim Watts
Installation Team Osinski Design, Mike Hill, Ellie Abrons, Kim Watts, Emmet Ashford-Trotter, Paul Locke, Jeff Sipprell, Celi Freeman, Fernando Olivera, Santa Monica Museum of Art Crew
Graphic User Interface and Interaction Design Elise Co, Peter Cho
Images 56–58: photo © Erdman Photography; 12, 108 (text and images), 156–158, 208–213, 252–253: courtesy Servo

Dee & Charles Wyly Theater Dallas Center for the Performing Arts
Location Dallas, Texas
Completion 2009
Client Dallas Center for the Performing Arts Foundation
Architect REX/OMA, Joshua Prince-Ramus (Partner in Charge) and Rem Koolhaas; with Kendall/Heaton Associates Inc Architects & Planners
Structural Engineer Magnusson Klemencic Associates
Services Engineer Cosentini Associates, TRANSSOLAR Energietechnik GmbH
Facade Engineering and Design Consultancy Front Inc.
Contractors McCarthy Construction Co.
Facade Contractor TISI Estructuras Metalicas

Images 109 (text); 158–159 (except for REX/OMA images identified below), 214–217 courtesy Front Inc.; 109 A:1: image courtesy Kendal/Heaton Associates and Office for Metropolitan Architecture; 158 A:2, 158 C:2, 158 C:3, 158 D:3, 159 A:1: images courtesy REX/OMA, Joshua Prince-Ramus (Partner in Charge) and Rem Koolhaas

East River Waterfront Master Plan
Location New York, New York
Completion Schematic Design, Master Plan May 2005
Client The City of New York
Architect SHOP Architects, Richard Rodgers Partnership, Ken Smith Landscape Architect
Project Team—SHOP Cathy Jones, Chad Burke, Vivian Lee, Matthew Liparulo, Angelica Trevino, Carrie Norman, Lisa Schwert
Images 109 (text and images), 139, 159–161: courtesy SHOP Architects; 140: screenshot image courtesy Economic Development Corporation, City of New York

Eavesdropping Exhibition/ Installation
Exit Art/The First World
Location New York, New York
Completion 1996
Client Exit Art/The First World
Architect Lewis.Tsurumaki.Lewis
Design Team Paul Lewis, Marc Tsurumaki, David J. Lewis (design); Chris Korsh, Mark Shephard, Bill Peterson, David Ruff, Jennifer Whitburn, Clarissa Richardson, Kim Yao (installation)
Images 160–161: © LTL Architects, courtesy Lewis.Tsurumaki.Lewis

Experience Music Project
Location Seattle, Washington
Completion 2000
Architect Gehry Partners LLP
Images 59: © Gehry Partners LLP

Fluff Bakery
Location New York, New York
Completion 2004
Client Chow Down Management Inc.
Architect Lewis.Tsurumaki.Lewis
Design Team Paul Lewis, Marc Tsurumaki, David J. Lewis; Eric Samuels, James Bennett, Lucas Cascardo, Alex Terzich, Alan Smart, Maya Galbis, Hilary Zaic, Michael Tyre, Matthew Roman, Ana Ivascu;
Contractor Real Time Inc.
Images 60: photo © Michael

Moran; 110 (text and image), 160–162; 254–255: © LTL Architects, courtesy Lewis.Tsurumaki.Lewis

FutureGen Power Plant United States Department of Energy
Location Prototype plant, multiple locations
Completion Digital construction 2007
Client United States Department of Energy
Architect MARCH: Kevin Cimini (Partner in Charge), Brandon Hicks, Chris Hoxie
Engineering Leonardo Technologies Inc.: Ron Engleman Jr. PE, Chris Munson
Cooling System Design Kinney Enterprises LLC: O. L. Kinney Jr., Jidong Yang
Images 61–63, 111: © MARCH, courtesy MARCH

High Line 23
Location New York, New York
Completion 2009
Architect Neil M. Denari Architects & Gruzen Sampton LLP with Marc I. Rosenbaum
Structural Engineer DeSimone Consulting Engineers, PLLC
Services Engineer Ambrosino, DePinto & Schmieder Consulting Engineers, PC
Facade Engineering Front Inc.
Contractor Bovis Lend Lease
Images 111 (text and image), 162–163: courtesy Front Inc.

Honda Advanced Design Center
Location Pasadena, California
Completion 2007
Client Honda
Architect George Yu Architects
Design Team – GYU George Yu, Sandra Levesque, Daniela Franz, Marius Eggli
Construction Pacific National Group
Images 112 (text and images), 163–165: courtesy George Yu Architects

IBM Center for e-Business Innovation
Location Chicago, Illinois
Completion 2001
Client IBM
Architect George Yu + Jason King: Design Office and Imaginary Forces
Executive Architect Hellmuth Obata & Kassabaum
Design Team George Yu, Jason King, Sandra Levesque, Davis

Marques, Kai Riedesser, Jonathan Garnett, Toshi Nagura, Hisako Ichiki, Samson Chua
Media Design Team Peter Frankfurt/Chip Houghton, Mikon Van Gastel, Matt Checkowski, Jed Alger, Matt Checkowski, Peter Cho, Chun-Chien Lien, Kirk Balden, Rob Trent, Jamie Houghton, Holly Kempner, Saffron Kenny
Music Musikvergnuegen
Engineering Tina Brookman, McGuire Engineers
Audio/Video Equipment Steve Villoria, Principal, Advanced Media Design
Interative Table Fabricator Chris Johanessen, Principal, KB Manufacturing
Construction Jeff Kennedy, Pepper Construction
Images 64: photo © Benny Chan/fotoworks; **65, 113** (text and images), **256:** courtesy George Yu Architects

Ini Ani Coffee Shop
Location New York, New York
Completion 2004
Client Kevin Mancini and Payam Yazdani
Architect Lewis.Tsurumaki.Lewis
Design Team Paul Lewis, Marc Tsurumaki, David J. Lewis; James Bennett, Lucas Cascardo, Alex Terzich
Contractor J. Z. Interior Renovations
Images 257–258: © LTL Architects, courtesy Lewis.Tsurumaki.Lewis

LoRezHiFi
Interactive Sidewalk and Lobby
Location Washington DC
Completion 2006
Architect Höweler + Yoon/MY Studio
Design Team J. Meejin Yoon, Eric Howeler, Carl Solander, Lisa Smith, Meredith Miller
Electronics Engineering Will Pickering, Parallel Development (for Low Rez)
Images 66, 114–117 (text and images), **164–165, 220–223, 259–263:** courtesy Höweler+Yoon/MY Studio

MaxStudio.com
Location various locations throughout the United States
Completion 1998–2007
Client Leon Max, Elias Abu Shanab
Architect George Yu Architects
Design Team George Yu, Jason King, Andrew Lindley, Sandra Levesque, Israel Kandarian, Barry

Jacob, Gavin Farley, Leslie Barrett, Pierre Gendron, Se Young Choi, Steve Slaughter, Jasmine Wu, Chris King, Toshi Nagura, Robert Fabianjiak
Graphic Design Alexei Tylevich
Engineering Thorson Baker & Associates
Electrical Engineer Hi-Tech Engineering
General Contractors JPM Construction, Retail Construction Services, Arnett Construction
Fixture Fabrication Orion Retail Services and Fixturing Incorporated, Builders Furniture
Images 67: photo © Benny Chan/fotoworks; **118–119** (text and images), **165:** courtesy George Yu Architects

Möbius Dress
Location N/A
Completion 2004
Architect MY Studio/Meejin Yoon
Images 68, 120 (text and image), **166–167:** courtesy MY Studio/Meejin Yoon

Museum Of Tolerance
Location Jerusalem, Israel
Completion N/A
Architect Gehry Partners LLP
Images 121: © Gehry Partners LLP

Olympic Sculpture Park
Seattle Art Museum
Location Seattle, Washington
Completion 2007
Client Seattle Art Museum
Architect Weiss/Manfredi
Structural and Civil Engineering Consultant Magnusson Klemencic Associates
Mechanical and Electrical Engineering Consultant ABACUS Engineered Systems
Digital Consultant MARCH: Chris Hoxie, Brandon Hicks (Partners in Charge), Kevin Cimini
Lighting Design Consultant Brandston Partnership Inc.
General Contractor Sellen Construction
Geotechnical Engineering Consultant Hart Crowser
Environmental Consultant Aspect Consulting
Aquatic Engineering Consultant Anchor Environmental
Graphics Consultant Pentagram
Security and AV/IT Consultant Arup
Catering and Food Service Consultant Bon Appetit
Kitchen Consultant JLR Design

Retail Consultant Doyle + Associates
Project Management Barrientos LLC
Images 69: photo © Paul Warchol; **166–169:** © BHCH LLC, courtesy MARCH

One Island East
Location Hong Kong, China
Completion 2008
Client Swire Properties Ltd.
Architect Wong & Ouyang (HK) Ltd.
Structural Engineer Ove Arup & Partners (HK) Ltd.
MEP Engineer Meinhardt (M&E) Ltd.
Technology Services Consultant Gehry Technologies
General Contractor Gammon Construction Ltd.
Cladding Subcontractor Josef Gartner & Co (HK) Ltd.
Images 70, 121 (text and image), **170:** courtesy Swire Properties

P.S.1: LOOP
Young Architects Program
Competition Entry
P.S.1 Museum Of Contemporary Art/MoMA.
Location unbuilt
Completion Finalist entry 2006
Architect Höweler + Yoon/MY Studio
Images 122 (text and image), **170–173:** courtesy Höweler + Yoon/MY Studio

Seattle Central Public Library
Location Seattle, Washington
Completion 2005
Architect Office for Metropolitan Architecture and LMN Architects (OMA/LMN) Joint Venture
Structural Engineers Magnusson Klemencic Associates, Arup
Services Engineer Arup
Facade Consultant Front Inc.
Contractor Hoffman Construction Company
Facade Contractor Seele GmbH
Images 71, 122 (text and image), **174–175, 264–265:** courtesy Front Inc.

Sensorium
Shibaura Office Development Project
Location Tokyo, Japan
Completion 2003 competition finalist, unbuilt
Architect George Yu Architects
Design Team George Yu, Jason King, Pierre Gendron, Sandra Levesque, Davis Marques,

Se Choi, Paul Anderson, Ralph Mueller
Images 123 (text and images), **172–173:** courtesy George Yu Architects

Shop Lift: Rethinking Retail, Transcending Type
Installation in the US Pavilion at the 2004 Venice Biennale
Location Venice, Italy
Completion 2004
Architect George Yu Architects
Design Team George Yu, Sandra Levesque, Jonathan Garnett, Konstantinos Chrysos, Marianthi Tatari
Images 72–73, 124–125 (text and images), **174–175, 266–267:** courtesy George Yu Architects

Sony Design Center
Location Santa Monica, California
Completion 2004
Client Sony
Architect George Yu Architects
Design Team George Yu, Sandra Levesque, Jonathan Garnett, Owen Gerst, Yosuke Sugiyama
Engineering Syska Hennessy Group
Research and Communications Linda Hart
Images 74: photo © Benny Chan/fotoworks

Weatherhead School Of Management
Peter B. Lewis Building
Case Western Reserve University
Location Cleveland, Ohio
Completion 2002
Architect Gehry Partners LLP
Images 75, 175: © Gehry Partners LLP

White Noise/White Light
Interactive Sound and Light Installation
Location Athens, Greece
Completion 2004
Client Athens 2004 Olympic Committee
Architect Höweler + Yoon/MY Studio
Design Team J. Meejin Yoon, Eric Howeler, Marlene Kuhn, Kyle Steinfeld, Lisa Smith, Naomi Munro
Electronics Engineering Matt Reynolds
Images 76–77: photo © Andy Ryan; **126** (text and images), **176, 224, 268:** courtesy Höweler + Yoon/MY Studio

Windshape

Location Lacoste, France
Completion 2006
Client Savannah College of
Art & Design (SCAD)
Architect nARCHITECTS
Design Team Eric Bunge,
Mimi Hoang (Partners);
Daniela Zimmer (Project Architect),
Kazuya Katagiri, Takuya Shinoda,
Shuji Suzumori
Fabrication nARCHITECTS and
SCAD (Jim Bischoff, Michael Gunter,
Cindy Hartness, Michael Porten,
Ryan Townsend, Troy Wandzel,
Natalie Bray, Sarah Walko).
All components were fabricated
by nARCHITECTS + SCAD, with the
exception of the aluminum collars,
which were fabricated by Monsieur
J. F. Mathieu, of Apt, France.
Images 78–79: photos courtesy
Daniela Zimmer; 269: photos
courtesy Natalie Bray; 127–128
(text and images), 270–272:
courtesy nARCHITECTS

Xing Restaurant

Location New York, New York
Completion 2005
Client Michael Lagudis and Chow
Down Management Inc.
Architect Lewis.Tsurumaki.Lewis
Design Team Paul Lewis,
Marc Tsurumaki, David J. Lewis;
Eric Samuels, (project architect);
Lucas Cascardo, Alex Terzich,
Matthew Roman, Katherine Hearey,
Adam Frampton
Mechanical Engineer Jack Green
Associates
Contractor Gateway Design Group
Images 80: photo © Michael Moran

Additional Image Credits

Chris Hoxie
30: diagram courtesy Chris Hoxie;
285: photo by Elite Kedan

Front
10–11, 16: photos by Elite Kedan

Gehry Technologies
4–5: photo by Elite Kedan;
183, 187: images courtesy Gehry
Technologies

George Yu Architects
8–9, 233, 236: photos by Elite
Kedan

Lewis.Tsurumaki.Lewis
1, 133, 135: photos by Elite Kedan
2–3, 26: photos courtesy Lewis.
Tsurumaki.Lewis; 218–219:
lighting layout for new office on
West 29th Street, courtesy Lewis.
Tsurumaki.Lewis

MY Studio/Meejin Yoon
6–7: photo courtesy MY Studio/
Meejin Yoon

nARCHITECTS
227, 231, 286–287 (Chris Hoxie
visiting Mimi Hoang at office of
nARCHITECTS): photos by Elite
Kedan

SHoP
284: photo by Elite Kedan

SOM
43: diagrams featured in Paul
Seletsky's essay, "The Digital Design
Ecosystem: Toward a Prerational
Architecture" © 2008 SOM, courtesy
Skidmore, Owings & Merrill

Acknowledgments

In this, our "prototype" publication,
we would above all like to thank
the participating practitioners who
shared their insights with us and
contributed their time and efforts
during a dynamic period in their
practices.

In addition, we were fortunate
to work with individuals pivotal
in lending us their expertise and in
facilitating dialogue with the
featured practitioners: Paul Seletsky
graciously assisted us in navigating
the evolving landscape of emergent
architectural and digital practices,
and Warren Techentin, himself
a talented practitioner, generously
fostered communication with and
introduced us to the innovative
architectural groups of Los Angeles.
We would also like to thank LA
architects Peter Zellner and Sharon
Johnston for their relevant input.

We are deeply indebted to the
friends and colleagues who provided
invaluable guidance and encouragement during the making of this
book: Cynthia Ottchen, Chad
Evans and colleagues at Florida
International University in Miami,
including Nathaniel Belcher,
Adam Drisin (Chair of the School
of Architecture), David Rifkind,
and John Stuart. Special thanks in
particular go to Paul Soulellis
of Soulellis Studio for his critical
insight and counsel.

We are grateful to Carole Yu and
Sandra Levesque for their gracious
support and assistance in collecting
and featuring the work of George
Yu; as well as to Neil Denari for
his personal and poetic story of the
resonance of Yu's work.

We extend our appreciation to
copyeditors David Giles and Tim
Mennel for helping us refine the
content and tone of the text portions
of the book. We would also like
to thank Drew Freeman and Emma
Goldsmith for their valuable assistance at the outset of the project.
Thanks also to the photographers
who graciously permitted use of
their work: Iwan Baan, Benny Chan,
Michael Moran, Andy Ryan, and
Paul Warchol.

Design was a core priority from
the outset for this project. During
the making of this book, we had the
privilege of working with the
very talented designers at Project
Projects: enormous thanks to Prem
Krishnamurthy, Adam Michaels,
Mary Voorhees, and Molly Sherman

for their intelligence, skill, creativity,
and patience in transforming our
vision and content into a beautiful
and provocative book, and for
making this process an engaging
and stimulating one.

We extend our appreciation to
the expert forces at Princeton
Architectural Press: Special thanks
to Jennifer Thompson and Becca
Casbon for their hard work, support,
and know-how in bringing this
book to fruition; as well as to Nettie
Aljian, Russell Fernandez, and
Katharine Smalley Myers for their
valuable advice and guidance.

Finally, the editors of this
book gratefully acknowledge the
encouragement and patience
of our families, throughout this
process, and always.

→202-203

Colophon

Published by
Princeton Architectural Press
37 East Seventh Street
New York, New York 10003

For a free catalog of books, call 1.800.722.6657.
Visit our website at www.papress.com.

Direction
Elite Kedan

Editors
Elite Kedan, Jon Dreyfous, Craig Mutter
Princeton Architectural Press Project Editor:
Becca Casbon

Design
Project Projects
Prem Krishnamurthy, Adam Michaels,
Mary Voorhees, Molly Sherman

Copyeditors
David Giles, Tim Mennel

Special thanks to: Nettie Aljian, Bree Anne Apperley,
Sara Bader, Nicola Bednarek, Janet Behning, Carina
Cha, Penny (Yuen Pik) Chu, Carolyn Deuschle, Russell
Fernandez, Pete Fitzpatrick, Wendy Fuller, Jan Haux,
Clare Jacobson, Aileen Kwun, Nancy Eklund Later, Linda
Lee, Laurie Manfra, John Myers, Katharine Myers, Lauren
Nelson Packard, Dan Simon, Andrew Stepanian, Jennifer
Thompson, Paul Wagner, Joseph Weston, and Deb Wood of
Princeton Architectural Press
—Kevin C. Lippert, publisher

Library of Congress Cataloging-in-Publication Data

Provisional : emerging modes of architectural practice USA /
edited by Elite Kedan, Jon Dreyfous, and Craig Mutter.
    p. cm.
 Includes index.
 ISBN 978-1-56898-878-8 (alk. paper)
 1. Architectural practice—United States. I. Kedan, Elite.
 II. Dreyfous, Jon (F. Jonathan) III. Mutter, Craig. IV. Title:
 Emerging modes of architectural practice USA.
 NA1995.P76 2009
 720.23—dc22

                                    2009011559